Advances in Computer Vision and Pattern Recognition

The field of computer vision and pattern recognition has a rich history of nearly 50 years. In the past decade, however, the field has experienced remarkable advances in scene understanding and image generation. This advancement is driven by three key factors: (a) the availability of large, diverse datasets, (b) the accessibility of cloud and personal computing, and (c) the open release of advanced neural network architectures and models. These breakthroughs have led to significant successes across numerous application domains, including intelligent transportation, augmented reality, healthcare, agriculture, oceanography, and more. The ACVPR book series aims to introduce, analyze, and synthesize recent and foundational research, offering valuable references to both beginners and expert practitioners. The series covers timely topics such as:

- Deep Learning for Vision
- Large-scale Foundational Models
- Generative Methods
- Multimodal Learning (vision, audio, language, action, etc.)
- Neural Fields for Vision
- 3D Computer Vision
- Computational Photography, Display and Illumination
- Video Understanding and Synthesis
- Virtual, Mixed and Augmented Reality
- Biological and Human Vision
- Physics-based Vision
- Vision for Graphics
- Ethics in Computer Vision
- Applications (Robotics, Agriculture, Health, Intelligent Transportation, Oceanography, Safety/Security, etc.)

This series includes monographs, introductory and advanced textbooks, and state-of-the-art collections. Furthermore, it supports Open Access publication mode.

Wei Qi Yan

Robotic Vision

From Deep Learning to Autonomous Systems

Springer

Wei Qi Yan
Department of Computer and Information
Sciences
Auckland University of Technology
Auckland, New Zealand

ISSN 2191-6586 ISSN 2191-6594 (electronic)
Advances in Computer Vision and Pattern Recognition
ISBN 978-981-95-4359-5 ISBN 978-981-95-4360-1 (eBook)
https://doi.org/10.1007/978-981-95-4360-1

This Springer imprint is published by the registered company Springer Nature Singapore Pte Ltd.
The registered company address is: 152 Beach Road, #21-01/04 Gateway East, Singapore 189721, Singapore

Preface

This book has been drafted based on my lectures and seminars in recent years for postgraduate students at Auckland University of Technology (AUT), New Zealand. We have integrated and synthesized materials on robotics, machine vision, machine intelligence, and deep learning. Compared with conventional books, this book leads authors to use the knowledge from digital image processing and computer vision to control robots with autonomous systems. Our aim is to provide a resource that benefits postgraduate students, particularly those who are working on their theses, by sharing our research outputs and teaching work to augment their projects.

In this book, we have structured the content with a focus on knowledge obtained from our seminars. We begin by explaining fundamental concepts in robotics from computational point of view. We delve into robotic vision with deep learning methods. We add new content from what we have known and applied robotic vision to robotic control. At the end of each chapter, we emphasize on the practical implementation of algorithms by using Python-based platforms and MATLAB toolboxes. Additionally, we provide a lab session for each chapter with demonstrations and experiment reporting as well as a list of questions for the purpose of discussion and reflection.

In this book, our focus is on robotic vision. The book is to follow our research methodology of computer science with mathematical background, modeling, algorithms, experimental implementation, result analysis, and comparisons.

Before reading this book, we strongly encourage our readers to have a solid foundation in postgraduate mathematics. Developing computational knowledge will not only aid readers to quickly understand this book but also enable them to engage with relevant journal articles and conference papers.

This book was written for research students, computer engineers, computer scientists, and anyone interested in robotic vision for both theoretical research and practical applications. Additionally, it is relevant for researchers in the fields such as machine intelligence, pattern analysis, and control theory.

Auckland, New Zealand
June 2025

Wei Qi Yan

Acknowledgements In the past years, we have endowed in all aspects of robotics to make the book full and perfect. Following the instructions from our Springer editors, students, and audiences, the author has detailed the vocal descriptions, flowchart, data structures, pipelines, deployments, equations, and algorithms, as well as updated each chapter with the latest references and citings. Compared to others, this book emphasizes on fundamentals of robotics, mobile robots and arm-type robots, robotic vision, digital image processing, stereo vision, 3D object reconstructions, deep learning, robotic intelligence and control, reinforcement learning, and supercomputing as well as MATLAB Toolboxes and examples.

Thanks to Springer editors who had iterative discussion for this book to be published. Thanks to our peer colleagues and students whose materials were referenced and who have given invaluable comments on this book, especial thanks to my supervised students, B. Ma, X. Gao, Z. Chen, G. Yang, R. Tantiya, D. Peng, Y. Huan, Dr. S Mehtab, Dr. J. Qi, Dr. K. Gedara, and Dr. F. Younus, and my colleagues, Dr. W. Zhu, Prof. X. Wang, Prof. X. Li, and Prof. M. Nguyen.

Competing Interests The author has no competing interests to declare that are relevant to the content of this manuscript.

Contents

About the Author

Wei Qi Yan is with the Department of Computer and Information Sciences at the Auckland University of Technology (AUT), New Zealand. His expertise covers robotics, deep learning, machine intelligence, computer vision, and multimedia computing.

He is an Associate Editor of *ACM Transactions on Multimedia Computing, Communications and Applications*, a Senior Area Editor of *IEEE Signal Processing Letters*, a Section Editor of Springer journal *Discover Artificial Intelligence (AI)*.

He has worked as an exchange computer scientist between the Royal Society Te Apārangi (RSNZ) and the Chinese Academy of Sciences (CAS) in China. He is the director of joint research laboratory with the Shandong Academy of Sciences (SDAS) Shandong China, and the director of the joint laboratory with China Jiliang University (CJLU), Zhejiang China. He is recognized as one of the "Top Two Percent of Scientists in the World," currently holds the position of Chair of ACM Multimedia Chapter of New Zealand, and is a Fellow of Engineering New Zealand (FEngNZ).

List of Symbols

$\arg\max(\cdot)$	Argument of the maxima
$\arg\min(\cdot)$	Argument of the minima
$p(\cdot\vert\cdot)$	Conditional probability
$J(\cdot)$	Cost function
$\triangleq$	Definition
$\frac{df(x)}{dx}$ or $f'(x)$	Derivative
$det(\cdot)$	Determinant
$(b_i)_{n\times 1}$	Element b_i of vector $\mathbf{b}_{n\times 1}$
$(w_{ij})_{m\times n}$	Element w_{ij} of $m \times n$ matrix $\mathbf{W}_{m\times n}$
$\mathscr{E}$	Euclidean space
$\exists$	Exist
$\mathbf{E}(\cdot)$	Expected value function
$\exp(\cdot)$	Exponential function
$\mathbf{C}^1$	First-order parametric continuity
$\forall$	For all
$\overline{1, n}$	From 1 to n, i.e., $1, 2, \cdots, n$
$\mathbf{C}$	Function continuity
$\mathbf{N}(\cdot)$	Gaussian or normal distribution
$\tanh(\cdot)$	Hyperbolic tangent function
$\mathbf{C}^\infty$	Infinite continuity
∞	Infinity
$< \cdot >$	Inner or dot product
$\int$	Integral
$\cap$	Intersection of sets
$\Vert \cdot \Vert_0$	$\mathbf{L}^0$ Norm
$\Vert \cdot \Vert_1$	$\mathbf{L}^1$ Norm
$\Vert \cdot \Vert_2$	$\mathbf{L}^2$ Norm
$\Vert \cdot \Vert_p$	$\mathbf{L}^p$ Norm
$\Vert \cdot \Vert_\infty$	$\mathbf{L}^\infty$ Norm
$\log(\cdot)$	Logarithm base 10

$\mathscr{L}$	Loss function
$\mapsto$	Mapping
$\mathbf{W}^\top$	Matrix **W** transpose
$\max(\cdot)$	Max function
μ	Mean
$\in$	Member
$\ln(\cdot)$	Natural logarithm
$\mathscr{N}$	Set of natural numbers
$\|\cdot\|$	Norm
$\frac{\partial f}{\partial x}$	Partial derivative
$\perp$	Perpendicular
$\pm$	Plus or minus
$\mathbf{P}$	Point
$\prod$	Product
$\subset$	Proper subset
$\mathbf{C}^2$	Second-order parametric continuity
$\mathbf{S}$	Set
$\mathscr{Z}$	Set of integer numbers
$\mathscr{Z}^+$	Set of positive integer numbers
$\mathscr{R}$	Set of real numbers
$\mathbf{b}$	Shift vector
$sgn(\cdot)$	Sign function
$\subseteq$	Subset equal
$\sum$	Sum
$\mathscr{T}$	Tensor space
$\cup$	Union of sets
σ	Variance
$\mathbf{b}^\top$	Vector transpose
$\mathbf{W}$	Weight matrix

Acronyms

ACCV	Asian Conference on Computer Vision
ACM	Association for Computing Machinery
ADAS	Advanced Driver Assistance Systems
AI	Artificial Intelligence
ANN	Artificial Neural Networks
ASCII	American Standard Code for Information Interchange
BERT	Bidirectional Encoder Representations
CapsNet	Capsule Neural Network
CNN	Convolutional Neural Network
ConvNet	Convolutional Neural Network
CoT	Chain-of-Thought
CPU	Central Processing Unit
CVPR	International Conference on Computer Vision and Pattern Recognition
DBM	Deep Boltzmann Machine
DDPG	Deep Deterministic Policy Gradient
DDS	Data Distribution Service
DETR	Detection Transformer
DiT	Diffusion Transformer
DL	Deep Learning
DNN	Deep Neural Network
DoF	Degree of Freedom
DQN	Deep Q-Network
ECCV	European Conference on Computer Vision
EQ	Emotional Quotient
EI	Emotional Intelligence
KF	Kalman Filtering
FCNN	Fully Connected Neural Network
FFNN	Feedforward Neural Network
FK	Forward Kinematics
FN	False Negative
FoV	Field of View

FP	False Positive
FSD	Full Self Driving
FSM	Finite State Machine
FRU	Fully Gated Unit
GA	Genetic Algorithm
GAN	Generative Adversarial Network
GPT	Generative Pre-trained Transformer
GPU	Graphics Processing Unit
GRU	Gated Recurrent Unit
HVS	Human Vision System
IBVS	Image-Based Visual Servoing
ICCV	International Conference on Computer Vision
IoU	Intersection over Union
IQ	Intelligence Quotient
IK	Inverse Kinematics
IRL	Inverse Reinforcement Learning
LLM	Large Language Models
LMS	Least Mean Squares
LSTM	Long Short-Term Memory
MDP	Markov Decision Process
MGU	Minimal Gated Unit
ML	Machine Learning
MLP	Multilayer Perceptron
MNIST	Modified NIST Database
MPC	Model Predictive Controller
MRP	Markov Random Process
NLP	Natural Language Processing
NPU	Neural Processing Unit
NURBS	Non-Uniform Rational B-Splines
PBVS	Pose-Based Visual Servo
PRM	Probabilistic Roadmap
RBM	Restricted Boltzmann Machine
R-CNN	Region-Based CNN
ReLU	Rectified Linear Unit
ResNet	Residual Neural Network
RNN	Recurrent Neural Network
ROI	Region of Interest
ROS	Robot Operating System
RPN	Region Proposal Network
RRT	Rapid-Exploring Random Tree
SAD	Sum of Absolute Differences
SGD	Stochastic Gradient Descent
SSD	Sum of Squared Differences

TN	True Negative
TP	True Positive
TPU	Tensor Processing Unit
ViT	Vision Transformer
VS	Visual Servoing
YOLO	You Only Look Once

Chapter 1
Introduction to Robotic Vision

Abstract In this chapter, robotic vision is delineated along with robotic control, deep learning, and autonomous systems. Robotic vision is a crucial subject of robotics and the application of deep learning. This chapter explores robotic vision using video and image data from diverse robots (arm-type, mobile, aerial, etc.). The goal is to build foundational knowledge for vision-based control systems. The significance of this chapter is to convey the holistic view of robotic vision.

1.1 Overview of Robotic Vision

Robotic vision—computer vision applied to robotics—enables machines to perceive environments, interpret, and interact with the designated environment. By using digital cameras, sensors, and AI-based algorithms, robotic vision aids robots to recognize visual objects, navigate spaces, and make intelligent decisions. In this book, the solutions are derived for robotic vision and visual control characterized by using specifics of image data and deep learning algorithms [7, 87]. This chapter encapsulates the fundamentals of robotic vision [37]. With respect to this book, there are two concepts, one is robotic vision, and the other is robot vision. Robotic vision is academic and formal. Robot vision is informal or casual.

The performance of robotic vision will be critically assessed with deep learning algorithms, benchmark data, performance measures, and the ways to define ground truth. The opportunities of using robotic vision as a way of information acquisition through complex robotic systems and applications in artificial intelligence (AI) [14, 61, 71] will be examined.

In this book, the key concepts, methods, and algorithms are introduced. The content is based on pixel-level digital images, with a focus on robotic vision, including camera properties and calibration [93]. The methods are further explored to extract edges, blobs, motif, silhouette, contour, or shape of visual objects [38]. Thus, the focus of this chapter is on object segmentation, object detection and recognition, and object tracking in robotic vision.

Typically, mobile cameras are considered. Modern mobile phones allow effortless image capture; unlike analog-era media requiring digital conversion with a

W. Q. Yan, *Robotic Vision*, Advances in Computer Vision and Pattern Recognition,
https://doi.org/10.1007/978-981-95-4360-1_1

simple tap on the screen, an image or video can be taken. But previously we have many photos on newspapers or images from analog videos, and the images and videos were analogy-based in cassette. Thus, a digital-to-analog converter (DA converter) is needed for the purpose of conversion for these images and videos.

Unlike mobile cameras, surveillance cameras are usually fixed in place [58, 86]. Usually, object detection and recognition, as well as object tracking [2, 3, 49], in surveillance are implemented through camera panning, tilting, and zooming (PTZ). However, mobile cameras can be moved to anywhere, operating with translation and rotation, etc.

While early digital cameras were costly, modern ubiquitous sensors enable everyone to take pictures. Nowadays, everyone has very small cameras mounted on mobile phones. The camera specifications are beyond 20 years ago, which are available through metadata such as EXIF. Given an image from mobile camera, what we would like is to understand that how good this camera is and what function could be applied to which purpose.

Recently, Tesla conducted FSD (Full Self-Driving) testing. In the testing, the entire system is completely camera-based. This is an innovation for robotic vision and control without any LiDAR support. We should take the step and follow up this change with our knowledge in deep learning and computer vision [37, 87].

In camera calibration, the distance based on grid board is calculated with black and white grid patterns. Regarding the cameras with mega pixels, camera calibration or sensor calibration is always needed in scene understanding of this real world so as to correct the distortion and measure the distance from sensors to the targeted objects [93]. Camera calibration is called geometric camera calibration, and the term also refers to photometric camera calibration or is restricted for the estimation of intrinsic parameters only. Exterior orientation and interior orientation mean the determination of the extrinsic and intrinsic parameters, respectively. Through digital images with pixels for camera calibration, we are able to reconstruct 3D objects. Cameras can reconstruct the 3D space, including the origin and spatial dimensions.

The cameras reflect the positions located in 3D space. The locations are offered by using two cameras so that they quickly convert the pixel space to the corresponding real 3D space, bridging the gap between them. Due to various conditions and scenarios, we may get an image with visual artifacts that may be too dark, too bright, or too blurry. In image processing, if the image is too blurry, that means the camera is moving too fast or zooming operation is very rapid. Hence, how to remove blurs is challenging work in image processing [88, 89].

If a car is being driven in motorway with the speed of 100 kilometers per hour, the car is a fast-moving robot. For example, when a traffic sign appears beside the road, a key challenge is whether the robot can recognize it clearly [85, 96]. It means a camera is needed to be mounted on the moving vehicle to capture images [43]. How to capture the image of this traffic sign [65] timely and visibly with the cameras on high-speed car is a real problem. The task is relevant to the speed of our algorithms for image processing and object detection and recognition. Another example is that, after landed on the Mars, robots need to facilitate with an unmanned vehicle, and the car is required to be controlled remotely. The photographs will be taken by using

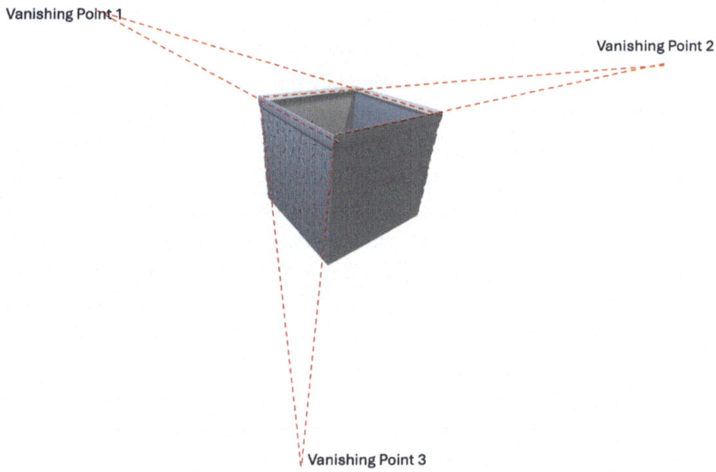

Fig. 1.1 Three vanishing points in 3D space

digital cameras on the vehicle to explore the lands from the Earth. The outcomes of image processing and analysis are employed for further exploration.

Stereo vision is built on 3D reconstruction. Computer vision is related to the 3D information from digital images. By comparing visual information related to a scene from two vanishing points as shown in Fig. 1.1, the 3D information can be reconstructed by examining the relative positions of visual objects. This is similar to the biological process of stereopsis.

Stereo vision uses two cameras at least to estimate depth. By comparing horizontal offsets (disparity), it generates a depth map where larger disparities indicate closer objects. The values in this disparity map are inversely proportional to the scene depth at the corresponding pixel locations. For example, in cinema, 3D trains can be seen on screen. All of these are based on 3D vision. When we watch the movie through a pair of special glasses, 3D scene will be generated in our mind. That is applied to movie industry. In 3D object reconstruction, for example, if we take a slew of photographs, the 3D objects will be rebuilt.

Stereo vision is highly significant in fields such as robotics to locate the relative position of 3D objects in the vicinity of autonomous systems [53]. Other applications for robotics include visual object recognition, where depth information allows for the system to separate occluding image components.

1.2 Importance and Applications of Robotic Vision

Having established camera basics, we now discuss robotic vision. Robotic vision plays a crucial role in enabling robots to perceive, interpret, and respond to our surrounding environment [94]. With multiple images from a group of cameras working together, the robot is able to understand scenes deeply. Robots with full intelligence, namely agents, have the ability to make decision independently after observed the 3D world. Robots equipped with computer vision systems can understand the surroundings and make smart decisions without human intervention.

Digital cameras have been designed with very high resolutions. Assisted with GPS information, vision-based systems improve the accuracy of robotic operations and manipulations, such as pick and place, assembly, inspection, and navigation. Vision-based robots enhance the safety in industries by detecting hazards and avoiding collisions. With the well-trained deep learning models, vision-based robots can be operated within the given work envelop, understand the scene depth, and predict what will happen from the past disasters [72]. Robots with vision systems are adaptive to dynamic environments. Vision-equipped robots are adaptive to any changing conditions in real time based on scene understanding from the acquired visual information. We thus have the special feature to showcase that robot perception directly determines the operational decisions.

Vision systems reduce the needs for complex guides and sensors, thus lower operational costs. Multiple sensors equipped on robots will fuse the information and avoid to generate misunderstandings due to errors [86, 87]. The images and videos from digital cameras will provide accurate blobs, edges, silhouette, skeleton, and textures. However, the point cloud systems acquired from a LiDAR (Light Detection and Ranging) system could not [54] provide the relevant information. LiDAR systems use a laser to measure distance and object depth.

1.3 Key Challenges in Robotic Vision

Robotic vision faces the key challenges that impact the effectiveness and reliability of robots in real-world applications. Visual object detection and recognition are the predominant tasks of robotic vision. Accurately identifying and classifying objects from a camera in diverse environments are tough due to variations in lighting, view angles, object occlusions, object appearance, etc. Vision models to handle these variations robustly remain a significant challenge.

Another challenge is real-time image processing in robotic vision. Robotics, especially in mobile or autonomous systems, is waiting for real-time results of vision processing to take the next step. This places high demands on computing power and lower complexity of algorithms to accelerate the process of visual object classification and make decisions instantly. Compared to audio and images, video processing is much slower and needs GPU assistance, as well as parallel computing facilities to support the process based on pixel arrays.

Robots are operating with a real-time system. The changes of lighting in indoor and weather conditions in outdoor environments significantly affect the robots to perceive the scenes. Developing vision systems in real world requests the robustness of algorithms to observe the environmental variability. This makes sure that robots can get correct information.

In dynamic environments, keeping correct track of moving objects while maintaining an accurate map of the environment is a must. Tracking moving objects across video frames without losing the identity is computationally expensive and error-prone. Visual objects may be partially obscured by other objects, making it exigent for the system to deeply understand holistic scene. Designing the vision algorithms that can handle partial occlusions [78, 79], accurately identify objects, and friendly interact with robots is important for the tasks like grasping and manipulation.

Pertaining to depth perception, understanding 3D environment from 2D images remains a significant gap, especially for the tasks like manipulation and navigation. Depth sensors, stereo vision, and structure-from-motion (SfM) techniques are often adopted, but they all have limitations such as accuracy or robustness on specific hardware. Regarding sensor fusion, integrating data from multiple sensors (e.g., cameras, LiDAR, etc.) to create a coherent understanding of 3D scene is complicated. The fusion process is accurate and efficient for the tasks like navigation and autonomous decision-making.

Robots are controlled from human and machine interactions (HMIs) through robot operating system (ROS). As robotic vision is increasingly harnessed to real-world applications, we need to ensure the safety of both robots and humans interactions and guarantee the requirements of ethics in decision-making. Implementing robotic vision systems that perform well in outdoor conditions as opposed to controlled indoor environments involves dealing with noise in sensor data, unpredictable object movements, and unexpected environmental changes.

Chatbots using Large Language Models (LLMs) integrated with Open WebUI, Dify, CompfyUI, and Ollama models have been successfully deployed to robotic control [63, 92]. The input and output of LLMs are challenges of modern computing. The prompts for inputs and outputs of LLM models should be filtered, especially visual information from generative models such as Generative Adversarial Networks (GANs), autoencoders, and diffusion models [87]. The hallucination outputs generated from the LLMs due to unexpected changes should be treated seriously in case of violation of ethics regulations. Retrieval-Augmented Generation (RAG) and Model Context Protocol (MCP) are thought as the solutions to resolve these problems, accompanying with Agent-to-Agent (A2A) technology [40, 61, 81, 92].

1.4 Foundational in Machine Learning and Deep Learning

In deep learning (DL), because of new development, all computer vision textbooks have to be updated at present. For example, conventional algorithms in face detection and recognition are based on Viola-Jones object detection framework and Principal Component Analysis (PCA) algorithms, and the algorithms based on CNN and RNN models are popular at present. In computer vision, we have developed a plethora of algorithms from deep learning for object segmentation, object detection and recognition, object tracking [2, 3, 49, 71], etc.

Deep learning algorithms are relevant to datasets and ground truth. The ground truth refers to labels of visual data. Given the data as samples, we have the labeling process, and also we have annotations, labels, or tags. After trained our models by taking advantage of the datasets, the algorithms can output results [20, 21]. We evaluate the performance, and this evaluation should be quantitative and reflected in computational way.

Why deep learning algorithms are better than those general machine learning methods? Because deep learning is end to end-based which can bring various results for us that are able to give better measurements and comparisons. The previous algorithms may only conduct face detection and recognition from the front view; now the new methods can conduct human face detection and recognition from side views [1, 22, 78, 79].

Deep learning (DL) uses multilayered artificial neural networks (ANNs). Inspired by biological neurons, these networks process data hierarchically—extracting features from raw pixels to high-level semantics [13, 52]. Artificial neural networks (ANNs) works like our human brain [61, 80]. The neurons in human brain can be connected together [35, 56]. We assume a full connection is that any neurons can establish connections mutually [56]. But the situation is not true. A few old neurons will be died, and a large number of new neurons will be grown up. The neurons will be enlarged or shrunken during its life.

If neurons are connected with each other [56], they will be deployed with layers. The layer-based structure has been employed for deep learning algorithms. Hence, multiple layers of neurons are connected together. Deep learning refers to the depth of what neural networks were constructed [35]. The deep learning is a simple change; however, it is powerful, based on the work of Professor Geoffrey Hinton from Canada, who created the realm of deep learning, especially for his great contributions in Restricted Boltzmann Machine, Capsule Neural Networks (CapsNets), and Deep Belief Nets [29, 33, 45, 70]. Professor Hinton received ACM Turing Award 2018 in 2019 and Nobel Prize in physics in 2024.

In 2024, OpenAI created the Sora, a text-to-video model. The model generates short video clips based on user prompts, which can extend the existing short videos [62]. The model is a diffusion transformer: a denoising latent diffusion model with one transformer as the denoiser. A video is generated in latent space by denoising 3D patches. A video-to-text model was applied to create detailed captions on videos. This is a great advance. Furthermore, OpenAI ChatGPT and DeepSeek are red-hot currently. How to embed the deep learning algorithms into chatbots to develop our own interface and applications is an interesting topic.

If we look at the history of modern computers, it is easy to find how this technology was developed. In 1945, the first electronic computer ENIAC (i.e., Electronic Numerical Integrator and Computer) was developed. ENIAC was the first programmable, electronic, general-purpose digital computer, completed in 1945. In 1957, this world saw a perceptual IBM computer. We saw the chain rule in 1974 as shown in the Appendix of this chapter. Later, we have the multilayer perceptron.

From 1995 to 2015, Support Vector Machine (SVM) was taken into dominant consideration. The SVM algorithm was the primarily part of machine learning. In machine learning, SVMs are supervised max-margin models that analyze data for pattern classification [1, 14, 24, 64].

Pertaining to deep learning, the state-of-the-art (SOTA) model is transformer [12, 29]. Transformer models have the advantage without recurrent units and require less training time than earlier recurrent neural architectures (RNNs) such as long short-term memory (LSTM). Later variations have been widely adopted for training Large Language Models (LLMs) on large datasets [4, 6].

While CNNs and RNNs dominated early deep learning, newer architectures like transformers now offer advantages in speed and scalability. Reinforcement learning [9, 57], transfer learning [60], etc. further expand capabilities. With these algorithms, robots now can clean floors, charge batteries, etc. When the robots start working, they will avoid obstacles [74]. Figure 1.2 shows a mobile robot is working.

Reinforcement learning is based on agent interactions with an environment [9, 57]. Given ample data for the algorithms to be trained, the reinforcement learning models are spirally becoming better through iterative interactions, namely updating states, actions, and rewards; these elements follow the episode sequence of reinforcement learning [73].

In deep learning, the existing models are harnessed to conduct classification with unknown classes of samples. The accuracy is not so high at very beginning, but if more samples are fed up, the accuracy rate of this model will be beefed, and this is called transfer learning [60].

We have a deep learning playground prototype which was developed by Google based on TensorFlow. On the interface, we add layers and neurons of neural networks and operate the neuron connections [56, 87]. Most of beginners started studying deep learning from this software. While increasing the number of layers and the number of neurons on each layer, the classification accuracy will be increased.

Fig. 1.2 A mobile robot is working

A second part of deep learning models is called RNN (recurrent neural network). In RNNs, we have the input layer, hidden layers or invisible layers, and output layer. The input layer and output layer are called visible layers, and the invisible layers are named as latent layers. Through using LSTM, we are able to predict the state changes, like weather changes, changes of exchange rates, changes of housing markets, stock markets, or share markets. RNNs are seen as very deep feedforward networks (DFNs) in which all the layers share the same weights [35]. RNNs process an input sequence maintaining in the hidden units that implicitly contains information about the history of all the past elements of sequence [13]. Most Natural Language Processing (NLP) systems rely on gated RNNs [6], such as LSTMs and gated recurrent units (GRUs), with added attention mechanisms [34, 75, 95]. RNNs (LSTM, GRU, etc.) have been firmly established in sequence modeling and transduction problems such as language modeling [44, 50] and machine translation [6].

RNNs follow the mechanism of Turing machine. Turing machine is an idealized model of a central processing unit (CPU) that controls all data manipulation throughout a computer. Turing machines (e.g., FSM) and memory networks are being employed for the tasks that would normally require reasoning [24, 61] and symbol manipulations [5, 61].

Transformer is based solely on attention mechanisms [34, 75, 95], dispensing on recurrence and convolutions entirely [44, 50]. Transformers are the state-of-the-art (SOTA) deep learning model for dealing with sequences [48], e.g., in text processing [6], machine translation [36], etc. Transformers were invented in 2017 by Google Brain for NLP problems, replacing RNN models (e.g., LSTM) [83].

Transformer models are trained with large datasets. Transformer is a deep learning model that adopts the mechanism of self-attention [75, 95], deferentially weighting the significance of each part of the input data. Like RNNs, transformers were designed to handle sequential input data. Unlike RNNs, transformers do not necessarily process the data in order [48]. The attention mechanism [34, 75, 95] provides context for any position in the input sequence.

Transformers were previously employed for English and French translation. English has its grammar, and correspondingly, French has the relevant grammar. While speaking English, the speech can automatically be translated to French by using machine translation [41, 42]. Now, this has been implemented in Microsoft Office software like Microsoft PowerPoint and Microsoft Teams. If we play a PowerPoint file, the captions between two languages could be toggled in real time [6]. In transformer models, token pairs are taken into consideration. If we translate English to other languages [44, 50], another corresponding set of tokens should be already there. For example, there is a set in Chinese around 10,000 tokens. Hence, the transformers will search for a high probability matching between the two languages for translating.

Supercomputing can serve us in computing acceleration; the typical one is NVIDIA GPU. GPUs are thought as the computing power. We need these chips because transformer is parallel computation-based. In parallel algebra, if two vectors are added together, GPU computing is much faster than that of CPUs. With GPUs,

Fig. 1.3 A GPU laptop is working

all the results will be popped up at the same time, and we take advantage of parallel computing. Currently, the multicore programming and multi-thread computing are adopted to carry out these tasks. Figure 1.3 shows a GPU laptop is working for object detection and recognition.

As well known, Tesla has developed and adopted the ASD system, which is completely computer vision-based. This new solution for robotic vision and visual control tasks is characterized by using the strengths and specifics of image data and deep learning algorithms, as well as scene understanding for vehicle control. Visual control means we make use of digital cameras to understand the scene and control the mobile robot. Previously, we made use of sensors and computers to control robots. Nowadays, a high-resolution and high-speed camera is mounted on an unmanned vehicle to control the car. Consequently, visual servoing and ROS through wireless communications in robotics play the decisive role in operating unmanned vehicles. Hence, this is the reason why we make use of robotic vision as the key part of autonomous systems.

Robots assist human in waste classification and fruit pick and place [18, 19, 55, 82–84], serving the industry like moving bags with milk power, beef and lamb, or other agricultural products. Especially for the countries that have not so much population, robots are an effective tool to save human labor and resolve the lack of professionals, such as for cleaning high buildings and painting on the surface of cars. The toxic work is very hazardous, which is not beneficial for human health and safe. But robots have not these constraints and limitations. While cleaning our floor, if we have a robot to vacuum and mop the ground, it works for us without stopping. Even if it runs out of battery, it can go back to the charging station and charge itself. After charged, the robot continues the cleaning work. This is a typical kind of applications.

Robotics is a typical application of deep learning [7, 51]. For example, while walking, if we close our eyes, we cannot walk too far. Compared with human hearing system, human vision system (HVS) is much crucial, which occupied 75% information intake [8, 10]. From this point of view, lost vision is a real troublesome issue. Robots are facilitated with sensors and digital cameras. Boston Dynamics is good at computer vision. All of vision systems are relevant to computable methods or algorithms, no matter whether our computers are fast or slow, because a computer is robot's brain, we thus process information in multiple ways [52, 80].

Generally, CPU is a bottleneck in modern computers, and we cannot take breakthrough for a few of years. The limited space could hold too many adders in a CPU; it is called bottleneck for computing power. Fundamentally, this problem could be resolved by using advanced algorithms like DeepSeek, from software point of view the GPU (Graphics Processing Unit), TPU (Tensor Processing Unit), and NPU (Neuron Processing Unit) can resolve the problems from hardware point of view. Under GPU support, the moving speed of a robot will be much faster than our human body. In these cases, the urgent issue is computing power. Computing power is the essence of supercomputing. After read this book, our readers are expected to create the fastest robots by using GPU chips at hand, which will accelerate resolving these problems in the real world.

MATLAB software was designed for numerical analysis and simulation which is applied to scientific research, like robot navigation and control because MATLAB software is robust, reliable, and stable [76]. The arm-type robots could be controlled by using MATLAB software collaborating with Robot Operating System (ROS). ROS is a set of middle software (Middleware) with multiple libraries and tools that assists us to explore and exploit robotic applications. If a robot is required to be operated, it will be started or halted immediately under the control, independent of other hardware. MATLAB ROS is excellent in robotic control, which provides the standard interface, which is the reason why industry sector likes using MATLAB software.

1.5 Mathematics Background

A Bézier curve [16] is presented as a parametric curve in computer graphics [17]. The curve is defined by a set of control points $\mathbf{P}_0$ through $\mathbf{P}_n$, where n is the order of curve ($n = 1$ for linear, $n = 2$ for quadratic, $n = 3$ for cubic, etc.). The first and last control points are always the end points of the curve. This set of discrete points defines a smooth and continuous curve [66, 91] as shown in Fig. 1.4.

Typically, a Bézier curve with a control polygon was developed for designing curves in car industry. The algorithm is based on *De Casteljau's* algorithm. The pseudocode is shown in Algorithm 1. In numerical analysis [59], De Casteljau's algorithm is a recursive method to implement polynomials in Bernstein form or Bézier curves [15, 16]. De Casteljau's algorithm is employed by splitting a single Bézier curve into two with an arbitrary parameter. The algorithm is numerically stable compared to direct evaluation of polynomials. Figure 1.4 shows a Bézier curve

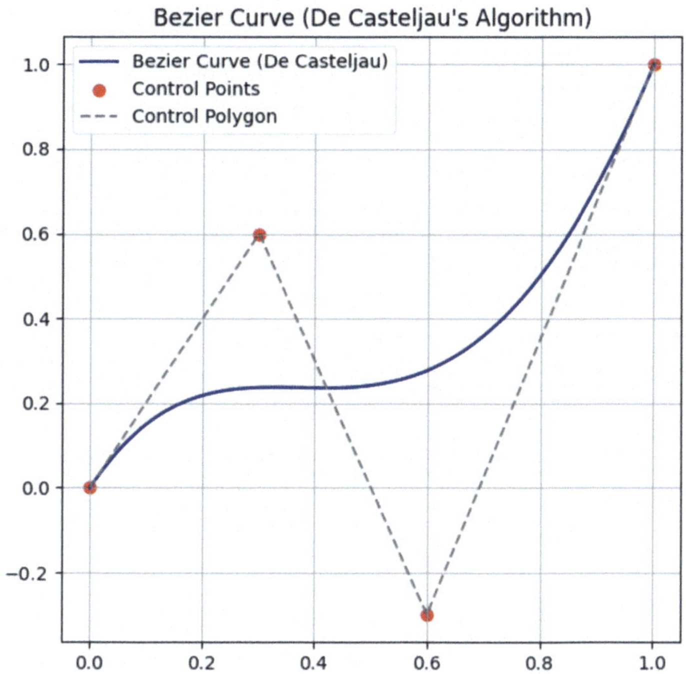

Fig. 1.4 The control polygon and Bézier curve

which was implemented by using De Casteljau's algorithm [17]. The corresponding source code in Python is shown in Fig. 1.5.

Algorithm 1: The algorithm for Bézier curve implementation

Input: List of control points $\mathbf{P}_0, \mathbf{P}_1, \ldots, \mathbf{P}_n \in \mathscr{R}^2$; parameter $t \in [0, 1]$
Output: Point $B(t)$ on the Bézier curve

Let $\mathbf{B}_i^{(0)} \leftarrow \mathbf{P}_i$, for $i = 0$ to n;
for $r \leftarrow 1$ **to** n **do**
  for $i \leftarrow 0$ **to** $n - r$ **do**
    $\mathbf{B}_i^{(r)} \leftarrow (1 - t) \cdot \mathbf{B}_i^{(r-1)} + t \cdot \mathbf{B}_{i+1}^{(r-1)}$;
return $\mathbf{B}_0^{(n)}$

The polygon formed by connecting the control points with straight lines is called control polygon. The convex hull of control polygon contains the Bézier curve. A quadratic Bézier curve is the path traced by the function $\mathbf{B}(t)$, given points $\mathbf{P}_0$, $\mathbf{P}_1$, and $\mathbf{P}_2$.

$$\mathbf{B}(t) = (1 - t)^2\mathbf{P}_0 + t(1 - t)\mathbf{P}_1 + t^2\mathbf{P}_2, t \in [0, 1] \tag{1.1}$$

```
import numpy as np
import matplotlib.pyplot as plt

# De Casteljau's algorithm to calculate a point on the Bezier curve at parameter t
def de_casteljau(control_points, t):
    """Recursively calculates a point on the Bezier curve at parameter t using De Casteljau's algorithm."""
    control_points = np.array(control_points)
    while len(control_points) > 1:
        control_points = (1 - t) * control_points[:-1] + t * control_points[1:]
    return control_points[0]

# Function to generate the Bezier curve using De Casteljau's algorithm
def bezier_curve_de_casteljau(control_points, num_points=100):
    t_values = np.linspace(0, 1, num_points)
    curve = np.array([de_casteljau(control_points, t) for t in t_values])
    return curve

# Control points for the Bezier curve
control_points = np.array([[0, 0], [0.3, 0.6], [0.6, -0.3], [1, 1]])

# Generate the Bezier curve using De Casteljau's algorithm
bezier_casteljau = bezier_curve_de_casteljau(control_points)

# Plotting the Bezier curve
plt.figure(figsize=(6, 6))
plt.plot(bezier_casteljau[:, 0], bezier_casteljau[:, 1], label="Bezier Curve (De Casteljau)", color="blue")
plt.scatter(control_points[:, 0], control_points[:, 1], color="red", label="Control Points")
plt.plot(control_points[:, 0], control_points[:, 1], linestyle="--", color="gray", label="Control Polygon")
plt.title("Bezier Curve (De Casteljau's Algorithm)")
plt.legend()
plt.grid(True)
plt.show()
```

Fig. 1.5 The source code for implementing a Bézier curve in Python

The first derivative of Bézier curve with respect to t is

$$\mathbf{B}'(t) = 2(1-t)(\mathbf{P}_1 - \mathbf{P}_0) + +2t(\mathbf{P}_2 - \mathbf{P}_1), t \in [0, 1] \tag{1.2}$$

The second derivative of Bézier curve with respect to t is

$$\mathbf{B}''(t) = 2(\mathbf{P}_2 - 2\mathbf{P}_1 + \mathbf{P}_0), t \in [0, 1] \tag{1.3}$$

A quadratic Bézier curve is a segment of a parabola. The cubic curve is defined as a linear combination of two quadratic Bézier curves

$$\mathbf{B}(t) = t\mathbf{B}_{\mathbf{P}_0,\mathbf{P}_1,\mathbf{P}_2}(t) + (1-t)\mathbf{B}_{\mathbf{P}_1,\mathbf{P}_2,\mathbf{P}_3}(t), t \in [0, 1] \tag{1.4}$$

Hence, the Bézier curve of degree n is recursively implemented by using a linear interpolation of a pair of corresponding points in two Bézier curves. Hence, we have

$$\mathbf{B}(t) = \sum_{i=0}^{n} b_n^i(t)\mathbf{P}_i(t), t \in [0, 1] \tag{1.5}$$

where the points $\mathbf{P}_i, i = \overline{0, n}, n \in \mathscr{N}$, are called control points. The polynomial $b_n^i(t)$ is the Bernstein basis of degree n.

$$b_n^i(t) = C_n^i (1-t)^i t^{(n-i)}, t \in [0, 1] \tag{1.6}$$

where $i = \overline{0, n}, n \in \mathscr{Z}^+$.

$$C_n^i = \frac{n!}{i!(n-i)!}, n \geq i, i, n \in \mathscr{Z}^+ \tag{1.7}$$

The derivative for a curve is

$$\mathbf{B}'(t) = n \sum_{i=0}^{n-1} b_{n-1}^i(t)(\mathbf{P}_{i+1} - \mathbf{P}_i), t \in [0, 1] \tag{1.8}$$

Given $n + 1$ control points $\mathbf{P}_0, \mathbf{P}_1, \ldots, \mathbf{P}_n$, the rational Bézier curve is given by

$$\mathbf{C}(t) = \frac{\sum_{i=0}^n b_n^i(t) w_i \mathbf{P}_i}{\sum_{i=0}^n b_n^i(t) w_i} = \sum_{i=0}^n R_n^i(t)\mathbf{P}_i, t \in [0, 1], 0 \leq w_i \in \mathscr{R}^+ \tag{1.9}$$

where

$$R_n^i(t) = \frac{b_n^i(t) w_i}{\sum_{i=0}^n b_n^i(t) w_i}, t \in [0, 1], 0 \leq w_i \in \mathscr{R}^+ \tag{1.10}$$

More generally, we have nonuniform rational B-spline curves (NURBS) [11, 90, 91]

$$\mathbf{C}(t) = \frac{\sum_{i=0}^n N_n^i(t) w_i \mathbf{P}_i}{\sum_{i=0}^n N_n^i(t) w_i} = \sum_{i=0}^n R_n^i(t)\mathbf{P}_i, t \in [0, 1], 0 \leq w_i \in \mathscr{R}^+ \tag{1.11}$$

where $N_n^i(t)$ is the basis function of a B-spline curve.

This algorithm is applied to the smooth trajectories in robotics [51]. Because the control polygon allows to show whether or not the path collides with any obstacles [74], Bézier curves are harnessed in producing robot trajectories [91]. The derivatives are utilized in calculation of dynamics and control effort (torque profiles) of the robotic manipulator.

1.6 Prerequisite Mathematics for Robotic Vision

1.6.1 Linear Algebra

In image processing, as well known, images are stored as an array of pixel values. Correspondingly, linear algebra is needed, especially vectors and matrices like what we have developed in MATLAB. Vectors and matrices in linear algebra combine separate scalar data into a single, multidimensional group, which are to form finite sequences of numbers with a fixed length, such as vector **V** and matrix **M**.

$$\mathbf{V} = (v_1, v_2, \ldots, v_n)^\top \tag{1.12}$$

where the dimension of vectors is n, v_i, $i = 1, 2, \ldots, n$, and $n \in \mathscr{N}$ is the element of vector **V**. Similarly, we have matrix **M** with dimension $n \times n$

$$\mathbf{M}_{n\times n} = \begin{bmatrix} m_{11} & m_{12} & \cdots & m_{n1} \\ m_{21} & m_{22} & \cdots & m_{n2} \\ \vdots & \vdots & \ddots & \vdots \\ m_{n1} & m_{n2} & \cdots & m_{nn} \end{bmatrix} \tag{1.13}$$

where $m_{i,j} \in \mathscr{R}$, $i = 1, \ldots, n$ and $j = 1, \ldots, n$, is the element of matrix $\mathbf{M}_{n\times n}$. In linear algebra, matrix **M** has its determinant $det(\mathbf{M})$, eigenvalues, and eigenvectors which has been applied to resolve various mathematical problems such as solving linear systems. MATLAB can assist us to resolve these problems quickly.

In image processing, image manipulations (e.g., rotation, scaling, and translation) and image analysis in frequency domain need the transformation matrices $\mathbf{T}_{3\times 3}$.

$$\begin{pmatrix} x' \\ y' \end{pmatrix} = \mathbf{T}_{2\times 2} \cdot \begin{pmatrix} x \\ y \end{pmatrix} \tag{1.14}$$

where (x, y) and (x', y') are the locations of a pixel on the image before and after the transformation.

$$\mathbf{T}_{3\times 3} = \begin{bmatrix} \beta \cdot \cos(\alpha) & \sin(\alpha) & \Delta x \\ -\sin(\alpha) & \gamma \cdot \cos(\alpha) & \Delta y \\ 0 & 0 & 1 \end{bmatrix} \tag{1.15}$$

where α is the angle of rotation along z-axis, and β and γ are scaling factors along x and y directions, respectively. Δx and Δy are the shifts along x, y, directions, respectively. Hence, $det(\mathbf{T}) \neq 0$. More broadly, the matrix **T** is employed to represent geometric transformations in 3D space. The matrix could be generalized for Affine transformation and projective transformations. An affine transformation is

$$\mathbf{T}_{3\times 3} = \begin{bmatrix} t_{11} & t_{12} & t_{13} \\ t_{21} & t_{22} & t_{23} \\ t_{31} & t_{32} & t_{33} \end{bmatrix} \tag{1.16}$$

where $t_{i,j}$ is the element (i, j) of matrix $\mathbf{T}_{3\times 3}$, $\det(\mathbf{T}) \neq 0$. Regarding rotation, given two angles $\alpha \in \mathscr{R}$ and $\beta \in \mathscr{R}$, we have

$$\cos(\alpha + \beta) = \cos(\alpha)\cos(\beta) - \sin(\alpha)\sin(\beta) \tag{1.17}$$

$$\sin(\alpha + \beta) = \sin(\alpha)\cos(\beta) + \cos(\alpha)\sin(\beta) \tag{1.18}$$

By using rotation matrices (orthogonal matrices), the determinant equals 1.

$$\mathbf{R}_{2\times 2} = \begin{bmatrix} \cos(\alpha) & \sin(\alpha) \\ -\sin(\alpha) & \cos(\alpha) \end{bmatrix} \tag{1.19}$$

where α is the angle of clockwise rotation. Regarding counterclockwise rotation,

$$\mathbf{R}_{2\times 2} = \begin{bmatrix} \cos(\alpha) & -\sin(\alpha) \\ \sin(\alpha) & \cos(\alpha) \end{bmatrix} \tag{1.20}$$

Regarding translation using a shift matrix for translation,

$$\mathbf{S}_{2\times 3} = \begin{bmatrix} 1 & 0 & \Delta x \\ 0 & 1 & \Delta y \end{bmatrix} \tag{1.21}$$

where Δx and Δy are the shifts along x and y directions, respectively. If rotation and translation are combined in a homogeneous transformation matrix, then

$$\mathbf{H}_{2\times 3} = \begin{bmatrix} \cos(\alpha) & \sin(\alpha) & \Delta x \\ -\sin(\alpha) & \cos(\alpha) & \Delta y \end{bmatrix} \tag{1.22}$$

The homogeneous transformation $\mathbf{H}$ is operated in this way

$$\begin{pmatrix} x' \\ y' \\ 1 \end{pmatrix} = \begin{bmatrix} \cos(\alpha) & \sin(\alpha) & \Delta x \\ -\sin(\alpha) & \cos(\alpha) & \Delta y \\ 0 & 0 & 1 \end{bmatrix} \cdot \begin{pmatrix} x \\ y \\ 1 \end{pmatrix} \tag{1.23}$$

A perspective transformation is a linear transformation that changes the appearance of lines and objects. The perspective transformation is

$$\begin{pmatrix} x' \\ y' \end{pmatrix} = \frac{f}{z} \begin{bmatrix} 1 & 0 \\ 0 & 1 \end{bmatrix} \cdot \begin{pmatrix} x \\ y \end{pmatrix} \tag{1.24}$$

where $(x, y, z) \in \mathscr{R}^3$ is a point in 3D space, and f is the focal length of the camera.

1.6.2 Geometry

In geometry, a straight line is

$$Ax + By + C = 0 \tag{1.25}$$

where $A, B, C \in \mathscr{R}$ are constants, and $(x, y) \in \mathscr{R}^2$. Typically, this equation is applied to pattern classification. We denote the straight line in parametric form

$$\begin{cases} x = x_0 + t \cdot (x_1 - x_0) \\ y = y_0 + t \cdot (y_1 - y_0) \end{cases} \tag{1.26}$$

where (x_0, y_0) and (x_1, y_1) are starting point and end points of a straight line, respectively, and $t \in \mathscr{R}$ is the parameter. If the slop is denoted as k,

$$k = \frac{y_1 - y_0}{x_1 - x_0}, x_1 \neq x_0 \tag{1.27}$$

We have

$$y = y_0 + k \cdot (x - x_0) \tag{1.28}$$

where k is the slope rate. The slope of a straight line is a measure of its steepness. Mathematically, the slope is calculated as the change in y divided by change in x. Hence,

$$y = k \cdot x + b \tag{1.29}$$

where b and k are constants. Furthermore, we denote conic curves or quadratic curve as

$$F(x, y) = Ax^2 + Bxy + Cy^2 + Dx + Ey + F \tag{1.30}$$

where $A \neq 0, A, B, C, D, E, F \in \mathscr{R}$ are the constants. (x, y) is the point in 2D space. Hence, the quadratic curve is

$$F(x, y) = (x, y)\mathbf{M} \begin{pmatrix} x \\ y \end{pmatrix} \tag{1.31}$$

where $\mathbf{M}_{2,2} = \{m_{i,j}\}_{2\times 2}$ is a matrix

$$\mathbf{M} = \begin{bmatrix} m_{11} & m_{12} \\ m_{21} & m_{22} \end{bmatrix} \tag{1.32}$$

Hence, any quadratic curves are possible to be converted to its standard form after a series of transformations

$$\begin{bmatrix} \lambda_1 & 0 \\ 0 & \lambda_2 \end{bmatrix} = \mathbf{X}^{-1}\mathbf{M}\mathbf{X} \tag{1.33}$$

where $\mathbf{X}$ is the matrix consisting of eigenvectors, $det(\mathbf{X}) \neq 0$. $\lambda_1 \neq 0$ and $\lambda_2 \neq 0$ are eigenvalues.

$$\mathbf{I} = \begin{bmatrix} 1 & 0 \\ 0 & 1 \end{bmatrix} = \begin{bmatrix} \lambda_1 & 0 \\ 0 & \lambda_2 \end{bmatrix} \begin{bmatrix} \frac{1}{\lambda_1} & 0 \\ 0 & \frac{1}{\lambda_2} \end{bmatrix} \tag{1.34}$$

Thus, we obtain function $F'(x, y)$ after a series of transformations from function $F(x, y)$

$$F'(x, y) = x^2 + y^2 \tag{1.35}$$

Given a polynomial,

$$f(x) = x^2 + 2x + 1 \tag{1.36}$$

where $x \in \mathscr{R}$. We denote it in the way of matrix

$$f(x) = (x, 1) \begin{bmatrix} 1 & 1 \\ 1 & 1 \end{bmatrix} \begin{pmatrix} x \\ 1 \end{pmatrix} \tag{1.37}$$

Generally, if we have a general polynomial,

$$f(x) = a_0 + \sum_{i=1} a_i x^i \tag{1.38}$$

where $a_n \neq 0, a_i \in \mathscr{R}, i = 0, 1, \ldots, n, n \in \mathscr{N}$. We denote it as

$$f(x) = (x^s, x^{s-1}, \ldots, 1) \begin{bmatrix} p_{11} & p_{12} & \cdots & p_{1t} \\ p_{21} & p_{22} & \cdots & p_{2t} \\ \cdots & \cdots & \cdots & \cdots \\ p_{s1} & p_{s2} & \cdots & s_{2t} \end{bmatrix} \begin{pmatrix} x^t \\ x^{t-1} \\ \cdots \\ 1 \end{pmatrix} \tag{1.39}$$

where $s + t = n$, $n, s, t \in \mathscr{N}$. If a curve is smooth, the derivatives exist $f(x) \in \mathbf{C}^n[a, b], n \in \mathscr{N}$. If $n = 0$, the function $f(x)$ is continuous.

A curvature is the reciprocal of radius of curvature, that is,

$$k = \frac{1}{R} \tag{1.40}$$

where R is the radius of the osculating circle. A parametrically defined curve in three dimensions is given in Cartesian coordinates by using $\gamma(t) = (x(t), y(t), z(t))^\top$, and the curvature is

$$k = \frac{\|\gamma' \times \gamma''\|}{\|\gamma'\|^3} \tag{1.41}$$

where $\times$ denotes the vector cross product.

In geometry, a geodesic is a curve that is the locally shortest path (arc) between two points in a surface or more generally in a Riemannian manifold [39]. The international nautical mile is defined as exactly 1,852 meters. The derived unit of speed is knot, namely one nautical mile per hour.

In this section, we denote all elements of linear algebra in the matrix way. The reason is that we expect to easily compute the values on computers for various programming.

1.6.3 Probability

Starting from Bayes' theorem, Bayes' law or Bayes' rule is

$$p(x|y) = \frac{p(y|x)p(x)}{p(y)} \tag{1.42}$$

where $p(x|y) \in [0, 1]$ is the conditional probability of $p(x) \in [0, 1]$, given $p(y) \in [0, 1]$. $p(x, y) \in [0, 1]$ is the joint probability.

$$p(x, y) = p(x|y)p(y) = p(y|x)p(x) \tag{1.43}$$

If $p(x, y)$ is independent, we have

$$p(x, y) = p(x|y)p(y) = p(y)p(x) \tag{1.44}$$

Entropy is the measure of missing information before reception. The definition of information entropy is expressed in terms of a discrete set of probabilities

$$H(X) = -\sum_{x_i \in X} p(x_i) \ln p(x_i) \tag{1.45}$$

where $X = \{x_i, i = 1, \ldots, n, n \in \mathcal{N}\}$. Mutual entropy is based on Bayes' theorem.

$$H(X, Y) = H(X|Y) + H(Y) = H(Y|X) + H(X) \tag{1.46}$$

where $Y = \{y_i, i = 1, \ldots, n, n \in \mathcal{N}\}$.

Hence,

$$H(Y) = H(X, Y) - H(X|Y) \tag{1.47}$$

$$H(X) = H(X, Y) - H(Y|X) \tag{1.48}$$

Relative entropy is called Kullback-Leibler (KL) divergence or I-divergence, which is a type of statistical distances, a measure of how much a model probability distribution Q is different from a true probability distribution P.

$$H_{KL}(P\|Q) = \sum_{x_i \in X} P(x_i) \frac{P(x_i)}{Q(x_i)} \tag{1.49}$$

where $H_{KL}(P\|Q) \neq H_{KL}(Q\|P)$.

1.7 Structure of the Book

This book is organized in a natural order that aligns with our understanding of robotics. We first explore what robots are and how they function. Then, we delve into image processing and computer vision for robotic scene understanding, with a particular focus on stereo vision and 3D surface reconstruction.

Rather than relying on traditional machine learning methods, we directly utilize deep learning for object detection and recognition in robotic vision. We investigate how deep learning can be applied to robot control and navigation. Additionally, we introduce Robot Operating System (ROS), parallel computing (e.g., GPU, FPGA, etc.), and mobile computing for human and robot interactions (HRIs). Through our design and analysis of robotic systems, we aim to expand the application of robots into broader research areas, including manufacturing, industrial automation, autonomous vehicles, and various applications. Finally, we discuss the emerging trends and urgent applications in the field.

1.8 Lab Session: Introduction to Tools and Platforms

At the end of this chapter, all readers are recommended to complete the lab report. Please fill in the form shown in Table 1.1 after each lab session (2 hours).

Table 1.1 Lab report for robotic vision

Name	<First Name Last Name >
Email	<firstname.lastname@mailbox >
Lab date	<dd-mm-yy >
Submitted date	<dd-mm-yy >
Project title	<A clear and concise title that accurately reflects the content of the experiment or project >
Lab objectives	<The goal, aim, or purpose, hypotheses, etc. >
Configurations and settings	<The preferences, software, hardware, platforms, tools, etc. >
Methods	<The relevant scientific theories or concepts >
Workflow	<The step-by-step procedure for the experiment >
Datasets	<The data and materials for your experiments >
Input	<image filename, size, resolution >
Output	<image filename, size, resolution >
Testing steps	<Functional and non-functional testing methods step by step >
Bugs or problems	<The system error code, lines of the code >
Result analysis	<The tables, graphs, and figures, etc. >
Conclusion/reflection	<The strengths and weaknesses, or learned from this project >
References	<MATLAB website >

Appendix: <Source codes with comments and line numbers >

1.9 Exercises

Question 1.1 In robotics, why the position and orientation of robots are so important?

Question 1.2 In robotics, how to understand the trajectory of a moving object?

Question 1.3 Why De Casteljau's algorithm for implementing Bézier curves is independent on device resolution?

Question 1.4 What are the challenges of robotic vision?

Question 1.5 What are the differences between machine learning and deep learning?

Question 1.6 In deep learning, what is the relationship between RNNs and Transformers?

Question 1.7 What is NURBS curve in Computer-Aided Geometry Design (CAGD)?

Appendix: History of Computing

- 2025: ACM Turing Award 2024 (Andrew Barto and Richard Sutton)
- 2025: Qwen3, YOLOv13
- 2024: Nobel Prize in Physics (J. Hopfield and G. Hinton) and Chemistry (D. Hassabis)
- 2024: OpenAI Sora, YOLOv9, YOLOv10, YOLO11
- 2023: YOLOv8, Diffusion Transformer(DiT), DALL·E
- 2022: ChatGPT, YOLOv7 [23, 46] and YOLOv6
- 2021: Vision Transformer (ViT)
- 2020: YOLOv4 and YOLOv5, GPT-3
- 2019: ACM Turing Award 2018
- 2018: YOLOv3 and Mask R-CNN [32]
- 2017: CapsNets and YOLO9000 [47, 49]
- 2016: You Only Look Once (YOLO) [67]
- 2015: ResNet [30, 31, 77], GoogLeNet, and Fast/Faster R-CNN [25, 68]
- 2014: GAN and VGG [28], AlphaGo (DeepMind)
- 2013: Region-Based CNN(R-CNN) [26, 27]
- 2012: AlexNet (ImageNet) [69]
- 1997: Long Short-Term Memory [4] (LSTM)
- 1990: Convolutional Neural Networks (CNNs or ConvNets)
- 1986: Restricted Boltzmann Machine (RBM)
- 1986: Iterative Dichotomiser 3 (ID3)
- 1974: Multilayer Perceptron (MLP)
- 1970: Automatic Differentiation (AD, e.g., Chain rule)
- 1969: XOR Logic Function
- 1960: Least Mean Squares (LMS)
- 1957: Perceptron (IBM 704)
- 1945: ENIAC (Electronic Numerical Integrator and Computer)

References

1. Alpaydin E (2009) Introduction to machine learning. MIT Press, Cambridge
2. An N (2020) Anomalies detection and tracking using siamese neural networks. Master's thesis, Auckland University of Technology, New Zealand
3. An N, Yan W (2021) Multitarget tracking using Siamese neural networks. ACM Trans Multimedia Comput Commun Appl 17:1–16
4. Bengio Y, Simard P, Frasconi P (1994) Learning long-term dependencies with gradient descent is difficult. IEEE Trans Neural Netw 5(2):157–166
5. Caruana R, Lawrence S, Giles CL (2001) Overfitting in neural nets: backpropagation, conjugate gradient, and early stopping. In: Advances in neural information processing systems, pp 402–408
6. Collobert R, Weston J (2008) A unified architecture for natural language processing: deep neural networks with multitask learning. In: International conference on machine learning, pp 160–167
7. Corke P (2017) Robotics, vision and control, 2nd edn. Springer Nature, Berlin

8. Cover T, Thomas J (1991) Elements of information theory. Wiley, Hoboken
9. Dabney W et al (2020) A distributional code for value in dopamine-based reinforcement learning. Nature 577:671–675
10. De Boer PT, Kroese DP, Mannor S, Rubinstein RY (2005) A tutorial on the cross-entropy method. Ann Oper Res 134(1):19–67
11. de Boor C (1978) A practical guide to splines. Springer, Berlin. ISBN 978-35-40903-56-7
12. Dosovitskiy A et al (2021) An image is worth 16×16 words: transformers for image recognition at scale. In: International conference on learning representations
13. Dunne RA, Campbell NA (1997) On the pairing of the softmax activation and cross-entropy penalty functions and the derivation of the softmax activation function. In: Australia conference on the neural networks, vol 181, p 185
14. Ertel W (2019) Introduction to artificial intelligence. Springer International Publishing, Berlin
15. Farin G (1997) Curves and surfaces for computer-aided geometric design. Elsevier, Amsterdam. ISBN 978-01-22490-54-5
16. Farin G (2002) Curves and surfaces for CAGD: a practical guide, 5th edn. Morgan Kaufmann, Burlington
17. Foley van D (1996) Computer graphics: principles and practice, 2nd edn. Addison-Wesley, Boston
18. Fu Y (2020) Fruit freshness grading using deep learning. Master's Thesis, Auckland University, New Zealand
19. Fu Y (2020) Fruit freshness grading using deep learning. Springer Nature Computer Science, Berlin
20. Gao X (2021) A method for face image inpainting based on generative adversarial networks. Master's Thesis. Auckland University of Technology, New Zealand
21. Gao X , Nguyen M, Yan W (2021) Face image inpainting based on generative adversarial network. In: IEEE IVCNZ
22. Gao X, Nguyen M, Yan W (2023) A high-accuracy deformable model for human face mask detection. In: PSIVT
23. Gao X, Nguyen M, Yan W (2024) Human face mask detection based on deep learning using YOLOv7+CBAM. In: Handbook of research on AI and ML for intelligent machines and systems, pp 94–106
24. Gashler M, Giraud-Carrier C, Martinez T (2008) Decision tree ensemble: small heterogeneous is better than large homogeneous. In: International conference on machine learning and applications, pp 900–905
25. Girshick R (2015) Fast R-CNN. In: IEEE international conference on computer vision, pp 1440–1448
26. Girshick R, Donahue J, Darrell T, Malik J (2016) Region-based convolutional networks for accurate object detection and segmentation. IEEE Trans Pattern Analy Mach Intell 38(1):142–158
27. Gkioxari G, Girshick R, Malik J (2015) Contextual action recognition with R-CNN. In: IEEE ICCV, pp 1080–1088
28. Goodfellow I, Pouget-Abadie J, Mirza M, Xu B, Warde-Farley D, Ozair S, Courville A, Bengio Y (2014) Generative adversarial networks. In: International conference on neural information processing systems, pp 2672–2680
29. Goodfellow I, Bengio Y, Courville A (2016) Deep learning, MIT Press, Cambridge
30. He K, Zhang X, Ren S, Sun J (2016) Deep residual learning for image recognition. In: IEEE CVPR, pp 770–778
31. He K, Zhang X, Ren S, Sun J (2016) Identity mappings in deep residual networks. In: European conference on computer vision, pp 630–645
32. He K, Gkioxari G, Dollar P, Girshick R (2017) Mask R-CNN. In: IEEE ICCV, pp 2980–2988
33. Hinton G, Osindero S, Teh YW (2006) A fast learning algorithm for deep belief nets. Neural Comput 18(7):1527–1554
34. Ji H, Liu Z, Yan, W, Klette R (2019) Early diagnosis of Alzheimer's disease based on selective kernel network with spatial attention. In: IAPR ACPR, pp 503–515

35. Kasabov N (1996) Foundations of neural networks, fuzzy systems, and knowledge engineering. The MIT Press, Cambridge
36. Kim Y (2014) Convolutional neural networks for sentence classification. In: Conference on empirical methods in natural language processing, pp 1746–1751
37. Klette R (2014) Concise computer vision: an introduction into theory and algorithms. Springer-Verlag London, London
38. LeCun Y, Bengio Y, Hinton G (2015) Deep learning. Nature 521:436–444
39. Lee JM (2018) Introduction to riemannian manifolds. Springer, Berlin
40. Lewis P et al (2020) Retrieval-augmented generation for knowledge-intensive NLP tasks. In: Advances in neural information processing systems, 33
41. Liang S (2021) Multi-language datasets for speech recognition based on the end-to-end framework. Master's Thesis, Auckland University, New Zealand
42. Liang S, Yan W (2022) A hybrid CTC+Attention model based on end-to-end framework for multilingual speech recognition. Multimedia Tools Appl 81:41295–41308
43. Liu X (2019) Vehicle-related scene understanding using deep learning. Master's Thesis, Auckland University of Technology, New Zealand
44. Liu Y (2022) Sign language recognition from digital videos using feature pyramid network with detection transformer. Master's Thesis, Auckland University of Technology
45. Liu X, Yan W (2021) Traffic-light sign recognition using capsule network. Multimedia Tools Appl 80(10):15161–15171
46. Liu X, Yan W (2023) Vehicle detection and distance estimation using improved YOLOv7 model. In: Deep learning, reinforcement learning and the rise of intelligent systems. IGI Global Scientific Publishing, Hershey
47. Liu X, Yan W, Kasabov N (2020) Vehicle-related scene segmentation using CapsNets. In: IEEE IVCNZ, pp 1–6
48. Liu Z et al (2021) Swin transformer: hierarchical vision transformer using shifted windows. In: IEEE ICCV
49. Liu X, Yan W, Kasabov N (2023) Moving vehicle tracking and scene understanding: a hybrid approach. Multimedia Tools Appl 83:1–18
50. Liu Y, Nand P, Hossain M, Nguyen M, Yan W (2023) Sign language recognition from digital videos using feature pyramid network with Detection Transformer. Multimedia Tools Appl 82:21673–21685
51. Lynch K, Park (2017) F modern robotics: mechanics, planning, and control. Cambridge University Press, Cambridge, MA
52. Manning C, Raghavan P, Schutze H (2008) Introduction to information retrieval. Cambridge University Press, Cambridge
53. Mehtab S (2022) Deep neural networks for road scene perception in autonomous vehicles using LiDARs and vision sensors. PhD Thesis, Auckland University of Technology, New Zealand
54. Mehtab S, Yan W, Narayanan A (2022) 3D vehicle detection using cheap LiDAR and camera sensors. In: International conference on image and vision computing New Zealand
55. Mi Z, Yan W (2024) Strawberry ripeness detection using deep learning models. Big Data Cogn Comput 8(8):92
56. Mignan A, Broccardo M (2019) One neuron versus deep learning in aftershock prediction. Nature 574(7776):E1–E3
57. MnihV et al (2015) Human-level control through deep reinforcement learning. Nature 518:529–533
58. Molchanov VV, Vishnyakov BV, Vizilter YV, Vishnyakova OV, Knyaz VA (2017) Pedestrian detection in video surveillance using fully convolutional YOLO neural network. In: Automated visual inspection and machine vision II, vol 10334
59. Muscat J (2014) Functional analysis, Springer, Berlin
60. Niculescu-Mizil A, Caruana R (2007), Inductive transfer for Bayesian network structure learning. In: International conference on artificial intelligence and statistics

61. Norvig P, Russell S (2016) Artificial intelligence: a modern approach, 3rd edn. Prentice Hall, Upper Saddle River
62. Peebles W, Xie S (2023) Scalable diffusion models with transformers. In: IEEE/CVF international conference on computer vision (ICCV), pp 4172–4182
63. Peng D (2025) Vision perception optimization and adaptive control for resource-constrained platform: a ping-pong ball pick & place system. Master's Thesis, Auckland University of Technology, New Zealand
64. Qi J, Nguyen M, Yan W (2023) CISO: Co-iteration semi-supervised learning for visual object detection. Multimedia Tools Appl 83:1–17
65. Qin Z, Yan W (2020) Traffic-sign recognition using deep learning. In: ISGV
66. Ravankar A, Ravankar AA, Kobayashi Y, Hoshino Y, Peng C-C (2018) Path smoothing techniques in robot navigation: state-of-the-art, current and future challenges. Sensors 18(9):3170
67. Redmon J, Divvala S, Girshick R, Farhadi A (2016) You only look once: unified, real-time object detection. In: IEEE CVPR, pp 779–788
68. Ren S, He K, Girshick R, Sun J (2015) Faster R-CNN: towards real-time object detection with region proposal networks. In: Advances in neural information processing systems, pp 91–99
69. Russakovsky O, Deng J, Su H, Krause J, Satheesh S, Ma S, Berg AC (2015) ImageNet large scale visual recognition challenge. Int J Comput Vision 115(3):211–252
70. Sarikaya R, Hinton GE, Deoras A (2014) Application of deep belief networks for natural language understanding. IEEE/ACM Trans Audio Speech Language Process 22(4):778–784
71. Schmidhuber J (2015) Deep learning in neural networks: an overview. Neural Netw 61:85–117
72. Singh CD, He B, Fermüller C, Metzler C, Aloimonos Y (2024) Minimal perception: enabling autonomy in resource-constrained robots. Front Rob AI 11:1431826
73. Sutton R, Barto A (2018) Reinforcement learning: an introduction, 2nd edn. MIT Press, Cambridge
74. Tokunaga S, Premachandra C, Premachandra HWH, Kawanaka H, Sumathipala S, Sudantha BS (2021) Autonomous spiral motion by a small-type robot on an obstacle-available surface. Micromachines 12(4):375
75. Vaswani A et al (2017) Attention is all you need. In: The conference on neural information processing systems (NIPS)
76. Vedaldi A, Lenc K (2015) MatConvNet: convolutional neural networks for MATLAB. In: ACM international conference on multimedia, pp 689–692
77. Veit A, Wilber MJ, Belongie S (2016) Residual networks behave like ensembles of relatively shallow networks. In: Advances in neural information processing systems, pp 550–558
78. Wang H (2018) Real-time face detection and recognition based on deep learning. Master's Thesis, Auckland University of Technology
79. Wang H, Yan W (2022) Face detection and recognition from distance based on deep learning. In: Aiding forensic investigation through deep learning and machine learning. IGI Global, Hershey
80. Webb S (2018) Deep learning for biology. Nature 554:555–557
81. Weiss G (2013) Multiagent systems, 2nd edn. MIT Press, Cambridge, MA
82. Xia Y, Nguyen M, Yan W (2023) Kiwifruit counting using KiwiDetector and KiwiTracker. In: Intelligent systems, pp 629–640
83. Xiao B, Nguyen M, Yan W (2023) Apple ripeness identification from digital images using transformer. Multimedia Tools Appl 83:7811–7825
84. Xiao B, Nguyen M, Yan W (2023) Fruit ripeness identification using transformers. Appl Intell 53:22488–22499
85. Xing J, Yan W (2021) Traffic sign recognition using guided image filtering. In: Springer ISGV. Springer, Cham, pp 85–99
86. Yan W (2019) Introduction to intelligent surveillance: surveillance data capture, transmission, and analytics, 3rd edn. Springer, Berlin

87. Yan W (2023) Computational methods for deep learning: theory, algorithms, and implementations, 2nd edn. Springer, Berlin
88. Yan W, Kankanhalli M (2002) Detection and removal of lighting & shaking artifacts in home videos. In: ACM international conference on multimedia, pp 107–116
89. Yan W, Kankanhalli M (2009) Cross-modal approach for Karaoke artefacts correction. In: Handbook of multimedia for digital entertainment and arts, pp 197–218
90. Yan W, Qi D (1999) Many-knot spline interpolating curves and their applications in font design. Comput Aided Draft Design Manuf 9(1):1–8
91. Yan W, Ding W, Qi D (2001) Rational many-knot spline interpolating curves and surfaces. J Image Graph 6(6):568–572
92. Yin S, Fu C, Zhao S, Li K, Sun X, Xu T, Chen E (2024) A survey on multimodal large language models. Natl Sci Rev 11:nwae403
93. Zhang Z (2000) A flexible new technique for camera calibration. IEEE Trans Pattern Analy Mach Intell 21(11):1330–1334
94. Zhao H, Xu S, Yan W, Xu D (2025) Design and optimization of target detection and 3D localization models for intelligent muskmelon pollination robots. Horticulturae 11(8):905
95. Zheng A, Yan W (2024) Attention-based multimodal fusion model for breast cancer prediction. In: ICONIP
96. Zhu Y, Yan W (2022) Traffic sign recognition based on deep learning. Multimedia Tools Appl 81:17779–17791

Chapter 2
Robotics

Abstract In this chapter, a variety of robots and their operations will be detailed. This includes mobile robots and humanoid robots as well as robotic navigation and localization. Correspondingly, MATLAB automatic driving toolbox will be illustrated. Our goal is to equip cameras on mobile robots and acquire the dynamic images reflecting the scene. In this chapter, a variety of robots such as arm-type robots, robotic kinetics, robotic dynamics, and robotic control are taken into account. The significance of this chapter is that the problems of robotic control are resolved by using the available visual information and knowledge. The manipulator and the end-effector(s) of robots are controlled within 3D space.

2.1 Mobile Vehicles

Mobile robots are a class of automobile machines, and they are able to move through the designated space [20]. The robots will select the best path [26, 28] to reach its destination, and it may encounter challenges such as obstacles that might block its way or having an incomplete map or no map at all [68]. The necessary maps will be dynamically created or updated when the environment changes. The generated maps will be applied to direct the robots where to go. One straightforward strategy is to have simplified perception of the world and react to what is sensed.

Sensing means we make active use of sensors. Once the robots with sensors move from side to side, it quickly acquires information about its surroundings. That is the way how robots acquire the environmental information. An alternative way is to create a map of its environment and plan a path from the starting point to the destination. This space will be scanned with SLAM algorithm (i.e., Simultaneous Localization and Mapping [52, 58]). Based on the map with scene understanding, a path is needed to be planned. Thus, we choose which path is the best and the shortest one for the robot to reach the destination.

The free-range mobile robots and wheeled robots typically make use of the fixed infrastructure for guidance, such as bicycle. Bicycles have pedal and handlebar basically as shown in Fig. 2.1. Generally, the robot's velocity is controlled like a

W. Q. Yan, *Robotic Vision*, Advances in Computer Vision and Pattern Recognition,
https://doi.org/10.1007/978-981-95-4360-1_2

Fig. 2.1 A bike and the forces to the ground in red arrows

bicycle to be proportional to the distance from the point $(x, y) \in \mathscr{R}^2$ to the goal $(x^*, y^*) \in \mathscr{R}^2$,

$$v^* = K_v\sqrt{(x^* - x)^2 + (y^* - y)^2}, K_v \in \mathscr{R}, v^* \in \mathscr{R} \tag{2.1}$$

With the relative angle,

$$\theta^* = \tan^{-1}\left(\frac{y^* - y}{x^* - x}\right), \theta^* \in \mathscr{R} \tag{2.2}$$

By using a proportional controller as shown in Fig. 2.2,

$$\gamma = K_h(\theta^* - \theta), 0 < K_h \in \mathscr{R}, \gamma \in \mathscr{R} \tag{2.3}$$

where K_v and K_h are the constants.

Most people have the experience of riding a bicycle or know how it operates. The pedals of a bike are the source where the power is from. The handlebar is adapted to control where the direction will be. While moving slowly, the handlebar of bike should have an angle to support the moving. Especially, the direction is altered. At this time, the handlebar and the pedals should keep the angle. Given a fixed angle, the bicycle will remain the balance and keep going further. Hence, the unmanned bicycle was designed and implemented, and the bicycle can be run automatically. The gyroscope is installed on the robot to keep the balance and direction. If the bicycle is working in the proper direction, it can be driven smoothly and stably. Thus, the bike is possible to be controlled remotely, and batteries will provide energy and power. A simple proportional controller turns the steering wheel so as to drive the robot toward the destination. The proportional controller adjusts the steering angle, which drives the robot following the straight line:

$$\alpha_d = -K_d \cdot d, 0 < K_d \in \mathscr{R} \tag{2.4}$$

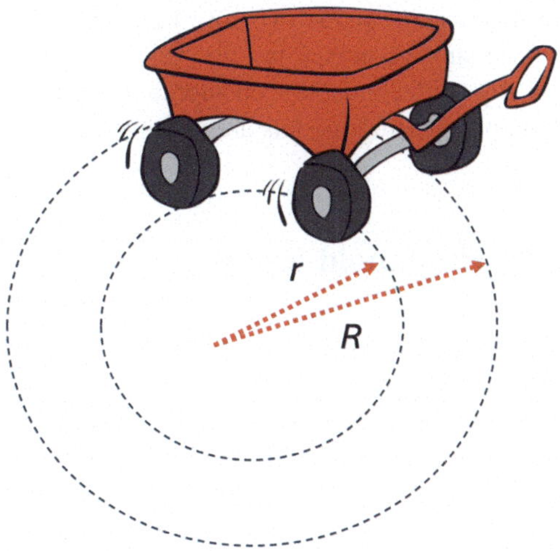

Fig. 2.2 A proportional controller and its radii

where K_d is a constant.

$$d = \frac{(a, b, c) \cdot (x, y, 1)^\top}{\sqrt{a^2 + b^2}}, a^2 + b^2 \neq 0, d \in \mathscr{R} \tag{2.5}$$

This proportional controller is distinct from the mechanical system of bicycle. Basically, a bicycle has two wheels: one is in front, and the other is at the back. But for this pair of controllers, which has four wheels, if the direction is changed, the four wheels will be turned in various directions. Hence, mobile robots follow the two radii. Following a straight line, two controllers are required to adjust the steering. One controller steers the robot to minimize the robot's normal distance from the straight line. Two controllers are required to adjust steering. One controller steered the robots to keep the balance and distance from the straight line. This trailer will be operated and run along the straight line [42]. The second controller adjusts the heading angle or orientation and controls the vehicle to be parallel to the straight line. The two controllers must jointly work together and control the robots to move forward. But the problem is how to make use of computers to guide robots from the starting point to the end point.

$$ax + by + c = 0 \tag{2.6}$$

where $a, b, c \in \mathscr{R}$ are constants.

$$\theta^* = \tan^{-1}\left(-\frac{b}{a}\right), a \neq 0, \theta^* \in \mathscr{R} \tag{2.7}$$

The Ackermann steering geometry [34] is a geometric arrangement of linkages in the steering of a car or other vehicles designed to solve the problem of wheels on inside and outside of a turn needing to trace out circles of different radii. Exact Ackermann geometry is only valid at low speeds or tight turns. At high speeds, tire slip angles must be considered; therefore, approximate Ackermann geometry or dynamic steering models are employed.

2.2 Humanoid Robots

A humanoid robot as shown in Fig. 2.3 is a robot resembling human body in shape. In general, humanoid robots have a torso as shown in Fig. 2.4, including a head, two arms, and two legs, though a few humanoid robots may replicate only a part of human body. Androids are humanoid robots to aesthetically resemble humans. A few robots have wheels, and the feet are wheeled [80]. A logo of Android mobile system is a robot. The android, the original name or original meaning refers to a robot.

Sensors sense the position, orientation, and speed of humanoid's body and joints, along with internal values. Actuators are the motors responsible for motion in robots. In robots, most of the joints are equipped with motors. The motors take advantage of torque to control arms, allowing them to raise or lower, so do the legs. For example, if we hold a weighty object on air, a group of motors is working together to keep pose of the object. By using motors, the controller gives a force

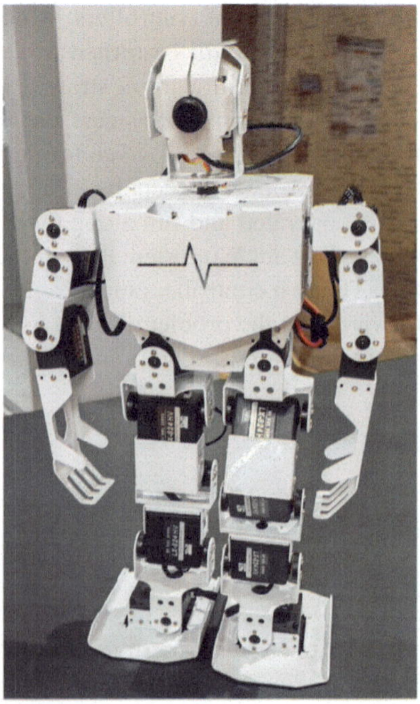

Fig. 2.3 A humanoid robot

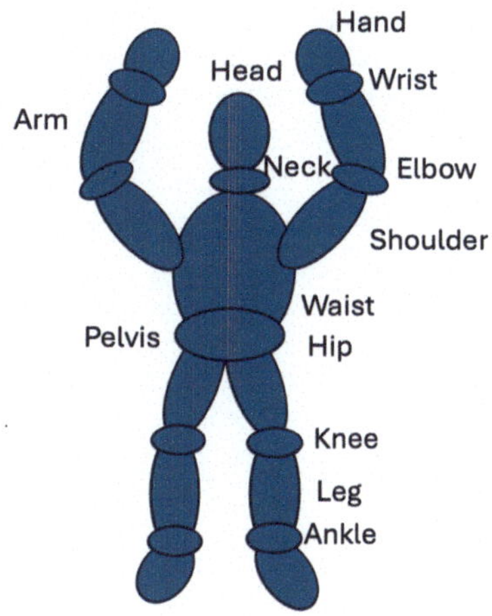

Fig. 2.4 A torso of human body and its joints

to control the pose, which is called payload. In robots, the motors control the position and orientation of an arm. In total, a torso has 24 degrees of freedom (DoF) after added all dimensions of axes together. Pertaining to the number of axes, a torso has multiple rotational axes and translational axes. If a computer is employed for controlling robots, the motors in each joint should be exactly controlled for rotational and translational operations.

Google MediaPipe is a computer vision software that is able to capture 33 key points of human body as shown in Fig. 2.5. Our human body includes head, arms, legs, and feet before a camera, and the 33 points could be detected in real time [16, 23, 74, 76]. Correspondingly, the angles between any two links could be utilized to control the torso of robots. Hence, we take use of these features for robotic control via human pose detection and recognition. Therefore, the key issue is how to automatically map these points to a humanoid robot so as to save our operating time. The robotic vision should have the ability to resolve this mapping problem through robot operating system (ROS) and visual servoing.

2.3 Navigation

2.3.1 Automata

A robot is a goal-oriented machine that is able to sense, plan, and act, like insects [46]. Insects, such as moth, butterfly, and bird, follow Charles Darwin's theory of evolution. Particularly in winter time, birds usually fly to the north because the north in the southern hemisphere is warm [29] and vice versa. This movement is triggered by factors like changing day length, temperature, and food availability. Birds fully take advantage of a plethora of cues to navigate, including the Sun, the

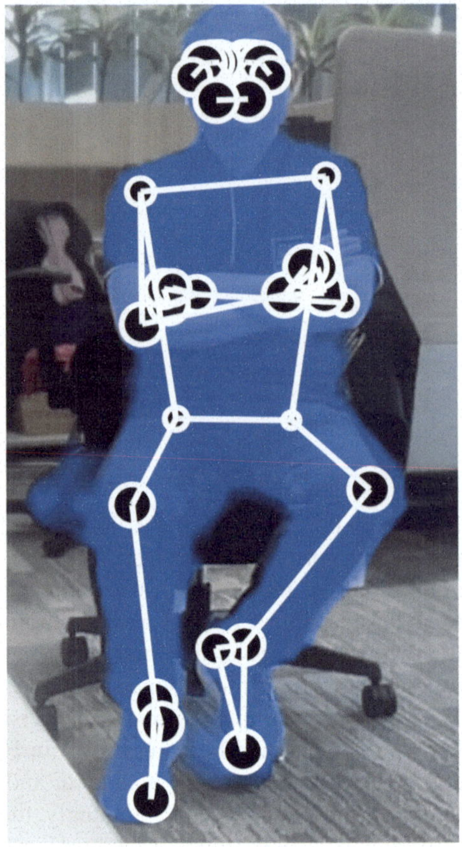

Fig. 2.5 An example of Google MediaPipe software for capturing human pose

Moon, stars, the Earth's magnetic field, and landmarks. Robots are inspired and learned from this bird migration or seasonal movements. The simple class of robots is known as Brandenburg robots. That is a class of goal-oriented robots, and they are characterized by using direct connections between sensors and motors.

When light rays are emitted from the Sun or the Moon and when human moves from one place to another at night, the location of the Moon or stars in sky is utilized for positioning. Most of insects also need position of the Moon in night. While the insects are moving toward the destination, they always retain and withhold the angle toward the direction of light rays like moths. Hence, the path is called moth curve [73] (Fig. 2.6).

Because robots need take actions, they have their own behaviors. The behavioral robots essentially are automata [12]. In computer science, automaton is called Finite State Machine (FSM). The automata [32] is a system which serves us well. For example, the simple automaton is a computer operating system, like Microsoft Windows, Linux, or MacOS. In computer control or machine intelligence, the automata are always needed. The reason why the robot is much intelligent is that

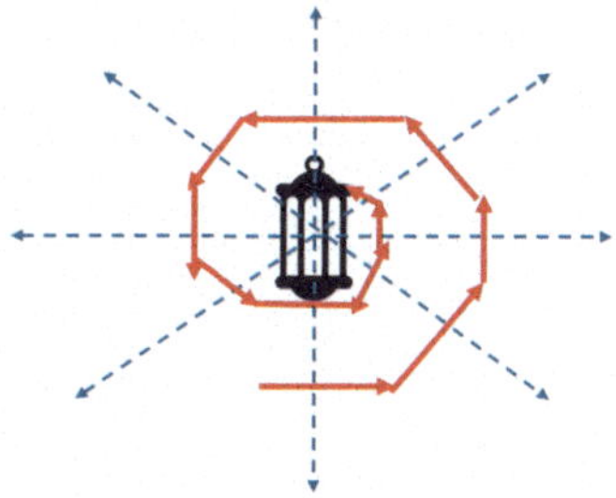

Fig. 2.6 A moth would like to fly along a curve that is perpendicular to ray direction; thus, it is called moth curve. A Braitenberg robot is to move along the moth curve

automaton is smart, and it simply reacts to the actions within the environment. A simple automaton shares the ability to sense when they are in proximity to an obstacle. The automaton [32] includes an FSM and other logic between sensors and motors. The simple robot performs goal seeking in the presence of non-drivable areas or obstacles [68].

Initially, robots do not know the environment well, but after iterative interactions, they acquire the lore from environment and understand the surroundings; they gradually become familiar with the scene. If robots deeply understand logical relationships in the scene, the robots cannot move from one place to another due to the existing obstacles. Hence, robots have the ability to avoid obstacles [11]. If robots understand the updated maps well, they move toward the correct direction. Automata have memory, and a robot is able to be operated in correct way like the automata.

The central issue of robot navigation is path planning [44]. If such a map is available, robots need to make a reasonable plan of how to leave current place or how to return starting place. The key to achieve the best path is to explore this map. The Google map for navigation needs the starting point in a plan to get the destination. The best way is to have a Google map, which instructs us the orientation of roads, traffic congestion, bridges, obstacles, etc.

A simple and computer-friendly representation is the occupancy grid [24]; the memory is required to hold the occupancy. We segment a map into regions. The memory is required, which stores the grids. The robot is operated in a grid world which occupies one grid cell. The robot does not have any non-holonomic constraints that can move to any neighboring grid cells each time. It is able to determine the position of a robot on the plane. The robot is able to compute the path it will take. The holonomic way of robots is based on global view. A sophisticated planner might consider kinematics and dynamics of a robot and avoid paths that involve turns. In a map, the derivable regions or obstacles are presented as polygons, comprising a list of vertices or edges. This is potentially a compact format, but determining potential collisions between robots and obstacles [68]. This navigation algorithm has exploited its global view of the world, through exhaustive computations so as to find the shortest path. Like riding bus or train, we need to pay the fare within one zone as shown in Fig. 2.7. The robot does not have any holistic

Fig. 2.7 A bus and train fare zone

constraints to arrive any neighboring grid cells. That is the reason why robots need to understand the scene so that the robots can travel from one cell to another.

In a plan, if a robot already occupies one place or cell, the robot is able to follow the map and compute the path it will follow. This is called holistic plan. A robot can proceed moving from any places to where it decides to go by following instructions, and the navigation algorithm has explored global view of this world. If a robot would like to seek the shortest path by using a map, the map keeps offering optimal solutions for the robot. The traffic on the dynamic map is being updated in real time. Robots have the ability to quickly find the states of the planned roads [51]. The best part of this algorithm is the computational cost from the starting point to the destination. The cost is the crucial factor for making holistic decision for a robot.

A fairly complex planning problem has been converted into one that can be handled by using a Braitenberg-class robot. This makes local decisions based on the distance to the goal [44]. Brandenburg robot is an elemental one; a local decision is needed to make. A robot thus needs to think of the neighbors and reach to the next grid cell. The penalty for achieving the optimal path is the computational cost. The roadmap methods provide an effective means to find the paths in large maps that greatly reduce computational costs. Suppose a robot has a slew of ways to leave, firstly it needs to make local decision. The mobile robots have equipped with feet or wheels. Along with the well-designed direction, the robot can quickly attain the destination [15].

2.3.2 D Algorithm*

D* algorithm (pronounced "D star") was designed for resolving path planning problems [31, 66], where a robot will be navigated to the given destination in unknown terrain [62]. D* algorithm and its variants have been widely employed for mobile robot and autonomous vehicle navigation [42]. The algorithm supports computationally cheap and incremental replanning ways for small changes in a map [63]. It generalizes the occupancy grid to a cost map, and the map represents the cost of traversing each cell in the horizontal or vertical direction [24].

Algorithm 2: D* path planning algorithm

```
Input: Start node s_start, Goal node s_goal, Grid map with initial cost
       estimates
Output: Path from s_start to s_goal
Initialize open list with s_goal;
Set g(s_goal) ← 0, rhs(s_goal) ← 0;
foreach state s ≠ s_goal do
    g(s) ← ∞, rhs(s) ← ∞;
ComputeKey(s_goal);
while open list is not empty and (key(s_start) > key(top) or
  rhs(s_start) ≠ g(s_start)) do
    s ← state with smallest key in open list;
    if g(s) > rhs(s) then
        g(s) ← rhs(s);
        remove s from open list;
        foreach predecessor s' of s do
            UpdateVertex(s');
    else
        g(s) ← ∞;
        foreach predecessor s' of s and s itself do
            UpdateVertex(s');
Function UpdateVertex(s):
    if s ≠ s_goal then
        rhs(s) ← min_{s'∈Succ(s)}(g(s') + c(s, s'));
    remove s from open list;
    if g(s) ≠ rhs(s) then
        insert s into open list with key ComputeKey(s);
Function ComputeKey(s):
    return [min(g(s), rhs(s)) + h(s_start, s), min(g(s), rhs(s))];
```

D* algorithm was designed for planning with a minor change [44]. If the given map has a puny change, the robot can quickly react to the change. This is a responsible way to minimize the total cost of a travel. The algorithm supports incremental replanning. That means it is possible to have a new plan because of environmental changes. D* algorithm allows updates to the map at any time, while a robot is moving. After replanning, the robot simply positions to an adjacent cell with the lowest cost which ensures the continuity of motions. The pseudocode is shown in Algorithm 2. While a robot is shifting, the map will be dynamically updated as we are driving a car using Google road map.

Google road map will automatically present the dynamic routine path for a driver. Similarly, if a robot deviates to a wrong way, the navigation map could quickly check the routine; if the robot averts somewhere nearby, the map can quickly guide the bot to go back. After replanning, the bot simply adjusts the cell with the lowest cost, which ensures that the continuity holds even if the plan has been changed. The plan change will not impact the final destination. Thus, the cost should be reduced as much as possible.

2.3.3 Voronoi Diagram

In mathematics, a Voronoi diagram is a partition of a plane into regions close to each of a given set of objects [10]. The map is segmented into multiple regions. Subsequently, a robot needs to decide where the best direction is and how the bot will move to the next region in the created Voronoi roadmap. In MATLAB, a Voronoi diagram is based on distance to a specific set of points. An example of Voronoi diagram is shown in Fig. 2.8.

The skeleton of this free space is a network of adjacent cells, no more than one cell thick. The skeleton is a free space, indicated by using white cells. The white markers show that the skeleton of free space is networked. The skeleton with obstacles is overlaid in red, and the junction points are marked in blue. Regarding

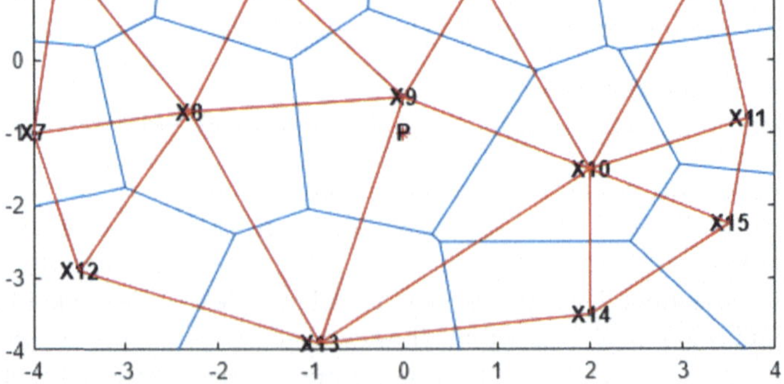

Fig. 2.8 An example of Voronoi diagram and Delaunay triangulation

the distance of obstacles, pixel values correspond to the distance of the nearest obstacle. Usually, the Voronoi diagram is triangle-based. Because the triangle is basic, once all of them are obtained, the centers are connected together. Thus, a graph is created. The graph basically shows the information of links. The roadmap with junctions will be marked in blue. If a region has an obstacle, it is marked in red. If there is a junction between two regions, it is marked in blue. Regarding the distance between the two regions, the Voronoi diagram can save calculations. For calculating the distance, norms $\mathbf{L}_0$, $\mathbf{L}_1$, $\mathbf{L}_2$, $\mathbf{L}_p$, and $\mathbf{L}_\infty$ are employed for a vector $\mathbf{V}$. More generally, we have p-norm in functional analysis

$$\|\mathbf{V}\|_p = \left(\sum_{i=1}^{n} x_i^p\right)^{\frac{1}{p}} \tag{2.8}$$

where $x_i \in \mathscr{R}, i = 1, 2, \ldots, n \in \mathscr{R}$ is the component of an n-dimensional vector $\mathbf{V}$, $p = 0, 1, 2, 3, \ldots, \infty$. Most of the time, we make use of norms $\mathbf{L}_2$ (Euclidean distance), which indicate the distance from one place to another as shown in Eq. (2.9).

$$\|\mathbf{V}\|_2 = \left(\sum_{i=1}^{n} x_i^2\right)^{\frac{1}{2}} \tag{2.9}$$

An interesting distance is Manhattan distance which is block-based. Manhattan distance, Taxicab distance, or block distance is an ($\mathbf{L}_1$) metric applied to determine the distance between two points in a grid-like path [47] as shown in Eq. (2.10).

$$\|\mathbf{V}\|_1 = \sum_{i=1}^{n} |x|_i \tag{2.10}$$

An example of Voronoi-based robot path planning [21] is shown in Algorithm (3), the corresponding result is shown in Fig. 2.9.

Algorithm 3: Voronoi-based robot path planning

Input: Set of obstacle points $O = \{o_1, o_2, \ldots, o_n\}$, start point s, goal point g

Output: Path from s to g avoiding obstacles

Compute Voronoi diagram V from obstacle points O
Extract finite Voronoi edges E from V
Add s and g to the diagram as additional nodes
Connect s and g to nearest Voronoi vertices or edges
Construct a graph $G = (V, E)$ from Voronoi edges and added connections
Use Dijkstra's or A* algorithm to find shortest path from s to g in G
return Safe path from s to g along Voronoi edges

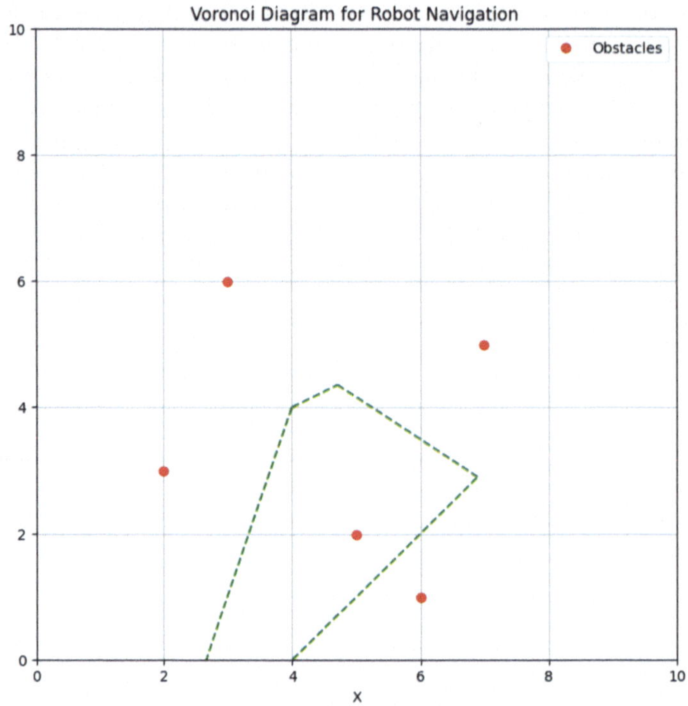

Fig. 2.9 An example of Voronoi-based path planning in Python. The dash line in green shows the path for robot navigation

2.3.4 PRM: Probability-Based Method

A probabilistic roadmap (PRM) [36] is a network of possible paths in a given roadmap based on free and occupied spaces. This probability-based method reduces computational costs by using probability sampling. Sampling means only a portion of samples are selected randomly.

The PRM algorithm takes advantage of a network of connected nodes to find an obstacle-free path from a starting point to the end. Increasing the nodes allows for more direct and correct path but adds more computational time or execution time. Because of the random placement of points, the path is not always direct or efficient. Using a small number of nodes can make paths worse and restricts the ability to find a complete path. The advantage of PRM is that a few of relative points need to be tested to affirm that the points and the paths between them are obstacle free. Each edge of the graph has an associated cost which is the distance between the two nodes. The color of a node indicates which component it belongs to and which component is assigned a unique color. The pseudocode of PRM algorithm is shown in Algorithm 4.

Algorithm 4: Probabilistic roadmap (PRM) for robot navigation

Input: Start state q_{start}, goal state q_{goal}, number of samples N
Output: Path from q_{start} to q_{goal}

Learning Phase (Roadmap Construction):
Initialize empty graph $G = (V, E)$;
for $i = 1$ *to* N **do**
    Sample a random collision-free configuration q_{rand};
    $V \leftarrow V \cup \{q_{\text{rand}}\}$;
    foreach *neighbor* q_{near} *in k nearest neighbors of* q_{rand} *in* V **do**
        if *Path(*q_{rand}, q_{near}*) is collision-free* **then**
            $E \leftarrow E \cup \{(q_{\text{rand}}, q_{\text{near}})\}$;
Query Phase:
Add q_{start} and q_{goal} to V;
Connect q_{start} and q_{goal} to nearest neighbors using same method as above;
Use Dijkstra's or A* to find a path from q_{start} to q_{goal} in G;
if *a valid path is found* **then**
    return path;
else
    return failure (no path found);

Traversal across the roadmap involves searching toward the neighboring node which has the lowest cost, which is the closest to the goal. The process is repeated till the node in a graph closest to the goal is reached. The important trade-off in achieving computational efficiency is to use random sampling. Each graph has an associated cost. The color node indicates which component it belongs to. If the distance from two different places is calculated, the planner can select samples and create a network consisting of disjoints.

The underlying random sampling of free space means that a distinct graph is created each time, while the planner is being started up, resulting in various paths and lengths. The planner can fail by creating a network consisting of disjoint components. The long narrow gaps between the obstacles are unlikely to be exploited because the probability of randomly chosen points that lie along the gaps is extremely low. We need multiple samples along these long narrow gaps.

MATLAB provides an example for PRM algorithm as shown in Fig. 2.10. In MATLAB, a probabilistic roadmap (PRM) is a network graph of possible paths in a given map based on free and occupied spaces. The algorithm takes advantage of the network with the connected nodes to find an obstacle-free path from the start to an end location. In this MATLAB example, a small number of nodes are created

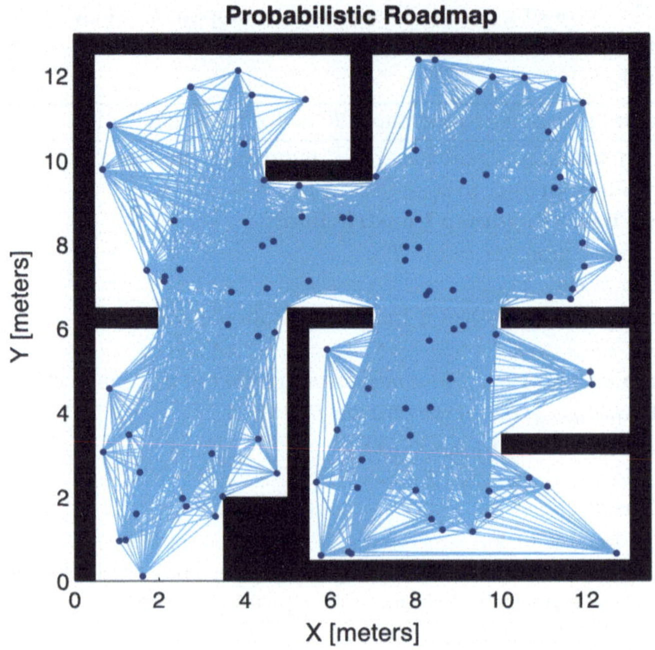

Fig. 2.10 An example of PRM algorithm

in roadmap. Increasing the number of nodes will enhance the efficiency of path by giving more feasible paths. The PRM algorithm recalculates the node placement and generates a new network of nodes.

2.3.5 RRT: Rapid-Exploring Random Tree

Another algorithm for this map planning is to rapid-exploring random tree (RRT) [1]. The RRT algorithm easily deals with various obstacles and differential constraints. Compared with other algorithms, RRT method works fast, which has less cost. This is feasible to control orientation of a robot, where it is positioned [35]. The pseudocode is shown in Algorithm 5. If we start seeking the initial parameters, this is computed with the inputs that move the robot from the existing points to others. Given a starting point, robots quickly walk along the map to get another point. This is a repeated process with multiple attempts, and the inputs with the best performance are chosen.

Algorithm 5: Rapidly exploring random tree (RRT)

Input: Start state x_{start}, Goal region $\mathscr{X}_{goal}$, Obstacle space $\mathscr{X}_{obs}$, Maximum iterations N
Output: Path from x_{start} to goal, if found

Initialize tree T with root node x_{start}
for $i \leftarrow 1$ **to** N **do**
    Sample random state x_{rand} from $\mathscr{X}$
    $x_{nearest} \leftarrow$ Nearest neighbor to x_{rand} in T
    $x_{new} \leftarrow$ Steer($x_{nearest}, x_{rand}$)
    if *ObstacleFree*($x_{nearest}, x_{new}$) **then**
        Add x_{new} to T with an edge from $x_{nearest}$
        if $x_{new} \in \mathscr{X}_{goal}$ **then**
            return Path from x_{start} to x_{new}

return Failure: No path found within N iterations

The RRT algorithm is computed for the model with a velocity, steering angle, integration period, and initial configuration. The algorithm is to compute the control input that moves the robot from an existing point in the graph. The RRT algorithm makes use of a kinematic model to create paths that are feasible to move. The algorithm takes into account of the orientation of the robot and its position. An example is shown in Fig. 2.11. The random number generator is reset to ensure reproducible results. The path is planned from the starting point to the destination.

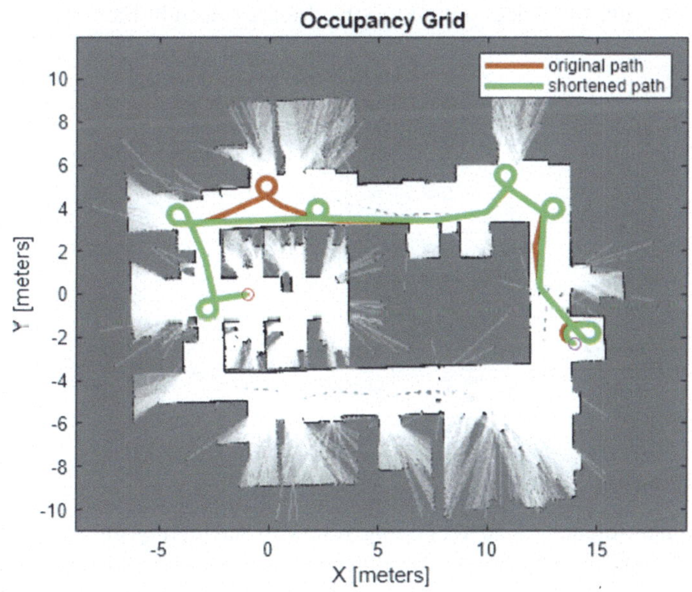

Fig. 2.11 An example of RRT algorithm

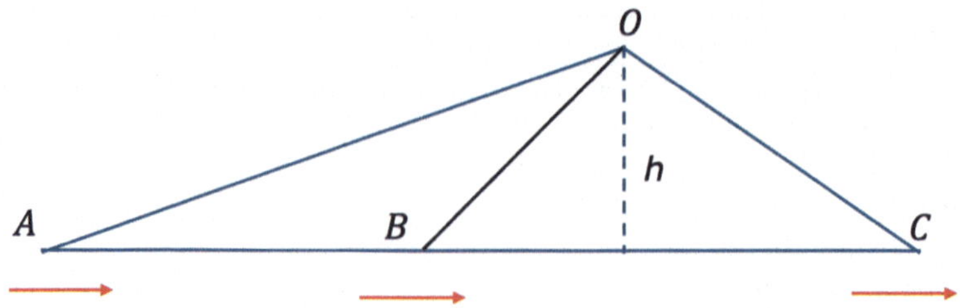

Fig. 2.12 A triangulation for surveying

2.3.6 Dead Reckoning

In navigation, dead reckoning is the process of calculating the current position of a moving object by using a previously determined position and incorporating estimates of speed, heading angles (or direction or course), and elapsed time. The estimation of current ship location is based on previous speed, direction, and time of travel, in case a ship misses its direction during voyage on sea [56].

Location estimation by using dead reckoning is based on robot position and the estimated distance traveled. Sectioning is the way of estimation of position by measuring the bearing angles of known landmarks. Triangulation (surveying) is the estimation of position by measuring the bearing angles to the unknown point from each of the landmarks [19]. Figure 2.12 shows triangulation for surveying calculation. When a ship passed location points **A**, **B**, and **C**, we are able to calculate the distance h from the object point **O** to the directed straight line $\overrightarrow{AC}$.

$$l = 1_1 + l_2 \tag{2.11}$$

where $l, l_1, l_2 \in \mathscr{R}$

$$\tan(\alpha) = \frac{h}{l_1}, l_1 \neq 0 \tag{2.12}$$

$$\tan(\beta) = \frac{h}{l_2}, l_2 \neq 0 \tag{2.13}$$

$$l = h\left(\frac{\cos(\alpha)}{\sin(\alpha)} + \frac{\cos(\beta)}{\sin(\beta)}\right) = h\frac{\sin(\alpha+\beta)}{\sin(\alpha)\sin(\beta)}, \alpha \neq 0, \beta \neq 0. \tag{2.14}$$

$$h = l\frac{\sin(\alpha)\sin(\beta)}{\sin(\alpha+\beta)} \tag{2.15}$$

In computer science, dead reckoning refers to navigating an array of data by using indexes based on location. Computer vision is employed to visual odometry with observations of the world. Most platforms have proprietary motion control systems that accept motion commands from users (speed and direction) and report odometry information. An odometer is a sensor that is able to measure the distance traveled, typically by measuring the angular rotation of robot wheels. The direction of traveling can be measured by using an electronic compass, and the change in heading angles can be calculated by using a gyroscope or differential odometry.

Originally, dead reckoning is a method to estimate location that is for the ship voyage. The dead reckoning is an estimation based on a coastline to speed up the action at time. From a voyage perspective, previously estimated GPS signals are not reliable. GPS signals are extremely weak sometimes which can lead to jam. Suppose a ship is traveling along seashore, the ship captain needs to calculate the distance from the reckon. Given a fixed distance, the captain should keep the bearing angle. Thus, the ship will make an excursion and cannot loss its way.

The dead reckoning calculates the new position $(x', y') \in \mathscr{R}^2$ by using the current position $(x, y) \in \mathscr{R}^2$, velocity v, heading angle θ, and time step Δt. This assumes the robot moves in a straight line with a constant speed and direction. The pseudoscope for dead reckoning algorithm is shown in Algorithm 6. The code in Python and the corresponding results are shown in Figs. 2.13 and 2.14.

$$\begin{cases} x' = x + v \cdot \cos(\theta)\Delta t \\ y' = y + v \cdot \cos(\theta)\Delta t \end{cases} \tag{2.16}$$

where $x, y, x', y', \theta, \Delta t \in \mathscr{R}$.

```python
# Example usage
if __name__ == "__main__":
    initial_pose = (0.0, 0.0, 0.0)  # Start at origin, facing right (0 radians)
    delta_t = 0.1  # 100 ms time step
    steps = 100

    # Simulate constant forward motion with slight right turn
    velocities = [(1.0, 0.1) for _ in range(steps)]

    trajectory = dead_reckoning(initial_pose, velocities, delta_t)

    # Plotting the trajectory
    x_vals = [pose[0] for pose in trajectory]
    y_vals = [pose[1] for pose in trajectory]

    plt.figure()
    plt.plot(x_vals, y_vals, label="Dead Reckoning Path")
    plt.scatter(x_vals[0], y_vals[0], color='green', label="Start")
    plt.scatter(x_vals[-1], y_vals[-1], color='red', label="End")
    plt.title("Dead Reckoning Trajectory")
    plt.xlabel("X Position")
    plt.ylabel("Y Position")
    plt.axis('equal')
    plt.legend()
    plt.grid(True)
    plt.show()
```

Fig. 2.13 The code in Python for dead reckoning algorithm

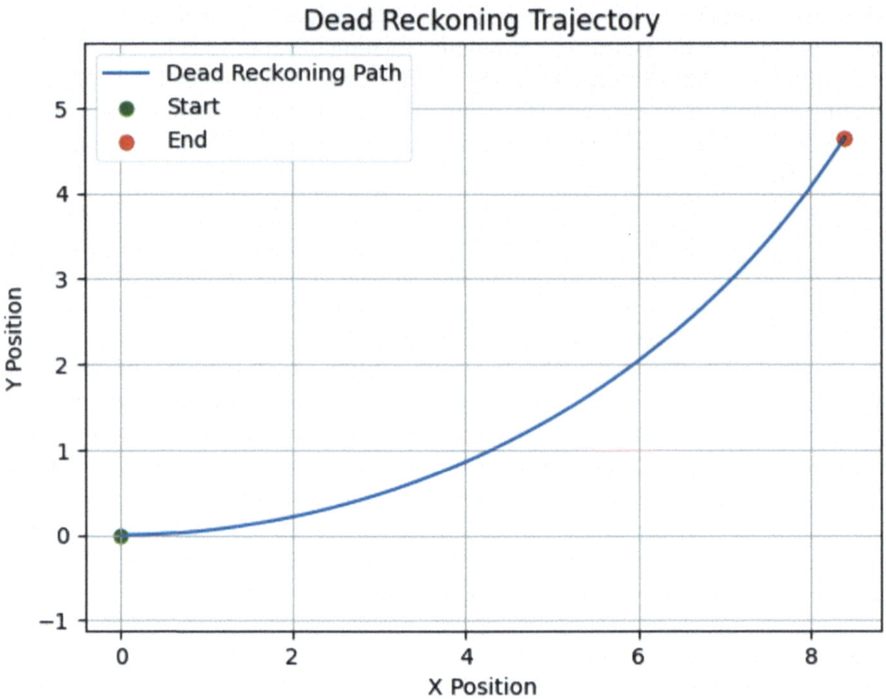

Fig. 2.14 The results of dead reckoning algorithm in Python

Algorithm 6: Dead reckoning for robot localization

Input: Initial position (x_0, y_0), initial orientation θ_0, velocity v, angular velocity ω, time step Δt, number of steps N

Output: Estimated trajectory $\{(x_t, y_t, \theta_t)\}_{t=0}^{N}$

Initialize: $x \leftarrow x_0$, $y \leftarrow y_0$, $\theta \leftarrow \theta_0$

Store initial state (x, y, θ)

for $t \leftarrow 1$ **to** N **do**

  $x \leftarrow x + v \cdot \cos(\theta) \cdot \Delta t$

  $y \leftarrow y + v \cdot \sin(\theta) \cdot \Delta t$

  $\theta \leftarrow \theta + \omega \cdot \Delta t$

  Store state (x, y, θ)

return trajectory $\{(x_t, y_t, \theta_t)\}$

2.4 Mathematics Background

Kalman filtering [77] is an iterative algorithm that updates, at each time step, the optimal estimate of the unknown true configuration and the uncertainty associated with that estimate based on the previous estimate and noisy measurement. Pertaining to Kalman filtering [33, 41], the signals follow zero mean. That means the optimality of Kalman filter algorithm regards that errors have a normal (Gaussian) distribution.

Kalman filtering is an iterative algorithm, which keeps updating and what each step estimate is known. The state is associated with previous states and noise measurements. The next is that how it can be implemented based on previous steps [41]. Kalman filtering allows data from various sensors to update the state [82]. Kalman filtering provides the best estimate of where robots are. A map of locations is created, while the robot is in its expedition with landmarks. A state vector comprises estimated coordinates of the landmarks that have been observed as $\hat{\mathbf{x}}$. The corresponding estimated covariance is $\mathbf{P}$

$$\mathbf{P}(k|k) = cov[\mathbf{x}(k) - \hat{\mathbf{x}}(k|k)] \tag{2.17}$$

and

$$\mathbf{P}(k|k-1) = cov[\mathbf{x}(k) - \hat{\mathbf{x}}(k|k-1)] \tag{2.18}$$

The prediction equation is

$$\hat{\mathbf{x}}(k+1|k) \leftarrow \hat{\mathbf{x}}(k|k) \tag{2.19}$$

While the covariance matrix is

$$\mathbf{P}(k+1|k) \leftarrow \mathbf{P}(k|k) \tag{2.20}$$

the updated state estimate is

$$\hat{\mathbf{x}}(k+1|k+1) \leftarrow \hat{\mathbf{x}}(k+1|k) \tag{2.21}$$

and

$$\mathbf{P}(k+1|k+1) \leftarrow \mathbf{P}(k+1|k) \tag{2.22}$$

The invariant of expectation is

$$\mathbf{E}[\mathbf{x}(k) - \hat{\mathbf{x}}(k|k)] = \mathbf{E}[\mathbf{x}(k) - \hat{\mathbf{x}}(k|k-1)] = 0 \tag{2.23}$$

That means all estimates have a mean error of zero. This process is called prediction. Given $k-1$ step, the state vector is expressed as what it was estimated, the coordinates of landmarks have been observed. The corresponding estimates are called covariance. The covariance is square root sum. The prediction equation is like this; one gets $\mathbf{x}_{k|k}$. We predict $\mathbf{x}_{k+1|k}$. The coherence matrix will be calculated correspondingly. We update the states by using $x_{k+1|k+1}$, given $x_{k|k+1}$ to get this $X_{k+1|k+1}$. Meanwhile, this prediction is the covariance matrix which has been updated. The means of the expectation of $x_{k|k}$ and expectation of $x_{k|k-1}$ are all zero. This expectation is the sum that all the variables are

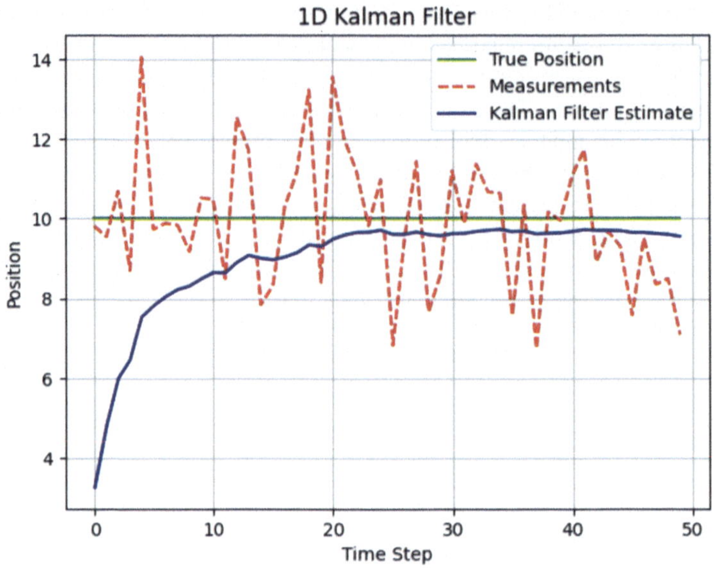

Fig. 2.15 The implementation of Kalman filtering algorithm

added together and divided by using number k, namely the average. Given the signals with noise, after Kalman filtering, the signals usually have not so many changes. Figure 2.15 is an example of Kalman filtering in 1D by using Python coding. The Python code is shown in Fig. 2.16. If the algorithm is simplified, the algorithm is able to be written by using pseudocode as shown in Algorithm 7.

Algorithm 7: Kalman filtering algorithm (pseudocode)

Input: Initial state estimate $\hat{x}_0$, initial covariance P_0
State transition model F, control model B, control input u
Observation model H, process noise covariance Q, measurement noise covariance R
Measurements $\{z_t\}$ for $t = 1 \ldots N$
Output: State estimates $\{\hat{x}_t\}$ and covariances $\{P_t\}$

Initialize: $\hat{x} \leftarrow \hat{x}_0$, $P \leftarrow P_0$
for $t \leftarrow 1$ **to** N **do**
  Prediction Step:
    $\hat{x}^- \leftarrow F \cdot \hat{x} + B \cdot u$
    $P^- \leftarrow F \cdot P \cdot F^T + Q$
  Update Step:
    $K \leftarrow P^- \cdot H^T \cdot (H \cdot P^- \cdot H^T + R)^{-1}$ // Kalman Gain
    $\hat{x} \leftarrow \hat{x}^- + K \cdot (z_t - H \cdot \hat{x}^-)$
    $P \leftarrow (I - K \cdot H) \cdot P^-$
  Store $(\hat{x}, P)$
return $\{\hat{x}_t, P_t\}$

```
# Parameters
true_position = 10
initial_state = 0
initial_covariance = 1
process_variance = 1e-5
measurement_variance = 2
num_steps = 50

# Run the Kalman filter simulation
true_positions, measurements, estimates = simulate_kalman_filter(
    true_position, initial_state, initial_covariance, process_variance, measurement_variance, num_steps)

# Plot the results
plt.plot(true_positions, label='True Position', color='g')
plt.plot(measurements, label='Measurements', linestyle='--', color='r')
plt.plot(estimates, label='Kalman Filter Estimate', color='b')
plt.xlabel('Time Step')
plt.ylabel('Position')
plt.legend()
plt.grid(True)
plt.title('1D Kalman Filter')
plt.show()


# Example: 1D Kalman filter for tracking a constant position with noise
def simulate_kalman_filter(true_position, initial_state, initial_covariance, process_variance, measurement_variance, num_steps):
    kalman_filter = KalmanFilter(initial_state, initial_covariance, process_variance, measurement_variance)

    # Simulate noisy measurements and apply the Kalman Filter
    estimates = []
    measurements = []
    true_positions = []

    for step in range(num_steps):
        # Simulate the true position (constant)
        true_pos = true_position
        true_positions.append(true_pos)

        # Simulate a noisy measurement
        measurement = true_pos + np.random.normal(0, np.sqrt(measurement_variance))
        measurements.append(measurement)

        # Kalman filter predict and update
        kalman_filter.predict()
        kalman_filter.update(measurement)

        # Record the state estimate
        estimates.append(kalman_filter.get_state())

    return true_positions, measurements, estimates

[3] import numpy as np
    import matplotlib.pyplot as plt

    class KalmanFilter:
        def __init__(self, initial_state, initial_covariance, process_variance, measurement_variance):
            self.x = initial_state  # initial state estimate
            self.P = initial_covariance  # initial covariance estimate
            self.Q = process_variance  # process variance
            self.R = measurement_variance  # measurement variance

        def predict(self):
            # Prediction step (state prediction and covariance prediction)
            self.P = self.P + self.Q  # Increase uncertainty with process variance

        def update(self, measurement):
            # Kalman Gain
            K = self.P / (self.P + self.R)

            # Update step (state update and covariance update)
            self.x = self.x + K * (measurement - self.x)  # Correct the prediction with measurement
            self.P = (1 - K) * self.P  # Update the covariance

        def get_state(self):
            return self.x
```

Fig. 2.16 The code in Python for implementing Kalman filtering algorithm

2.5 Robot Arm Kinematics

Given a robot, the robot is navigated to the destination with a well-planned path [26, 62]. The joints of a robot inherently stand on its body [46]. If there is a bottle on table, the camera installed on the arm needs to find where the bottle is. The end-effector will grasp this bottle and pick up the bottle and then place to another location. Hence, the robot can pick and place the bottle from one place to another. This operation is within robot's payload. A small robot showcases the effects for cooking and cleaning in 3D space. Because the given space is limited, the robot is able to use its end-effector for food security and safety [3–8]. The arm-type robots or robot manipulators have a static base and therefore are possible to be operated

Fig. 2.17 A wheeled robot is within the "envelop"

within the workspace. Usually, the robot will be enclosed within a forbidden fence. As we know, the premise is called work envelop (Fig. 2.17).

A robot manipulates objects by using its end-effector. We make use of end-effector to find visual object and move objects [37, 72]. A serial-link manipulator comprises a chain of mechanical links and joints. Our human arm is working as a joint chain. Each joint can move its outward neighboring link with respect to its inward neighbor. One end of the chain, the base, is generally fixed, and the other is free to move in the space and holds a tool as the end-effector. A serial-link manipulator comprises a set of bodies, called links, in a chain and connected by joints [20]. Each joint has one degree of freedom (DoF) [53], either translational joint (a sliding joint or prismatic joint) or rotational joint (a revolute joint). The motion of a joint alters the relative angle or position of its neighboring links [19]. The joints of most robots are revolute because we have motors inside to take effects. Meanwhile, the prismatic joint is moving along the straight line.

Between two joints, there is a link. A link is considered as a rigid body that defines the spatial relationship between two neighboring joints. The link can be specified by two parameters: length and twist. The link offset is the distance from one link coordinate frame to the next along an axis of the joint. The joint angle is the rotation of one link with respect to the next joint. The truly useful robots have a task space enabling arbitrary position and attitude of the end-effector. Hereinafter, the attitude refers to orientation. The task space has six spatial degrees of freedom (DoF): three translational and three rotational. At present, this 3+3 DoF is the standard configuration.

In robotics, robotic kinematics applies geometry to the movement of multi-DoF kinematic chains that form the structure of robotic systems. Robotic kinematics offers force to kinematic chains. The force is governed by Newton's second law of motion. The relationship between the dimensions, connectivity of kinematic chains, the position, velocity, and acceleration of each link in the robotic system. Robotic kinematics is explored and exploded (EE), in order to plan and control movement and to compute actuator forces and torques. The actuator is the "muscle" of robots. There are two broad classes of robots: serial manipulators and parallel manipulators. The time derivative of the kinematics yields Jacobian matrix of robots, which relates to linear velocity and angular velocity of the end-effector [20].

$$\mathbf{J_F} = \begin{bmatrix} \frac{\partial f_1}{\partial x_1} & \frac{\partial f_1}{\partial x_2} & \cdots & \frac{\partial f_1}{\partial x_n} \\ \frac{\partial f_2}{\partial x_1} & \frac{\partial f_2}{\partial x_2} & \cdots & \frac{\partial f_2}{\partial x_n} \\ \cdots & \cdots & \cdots & \cdots \\ \frac{\partial f_m}{\partial x_1} & \frac{\partial f_m}{\partial x_2} & \cdots & \frac{\partial f_m}{\partial x_n} \end{bmatrix} \tag{2.24}$$

where $\mathbf{J_F}$ is the Jacobian matrix, and $\frac{\partial f_i}{\partial x_j}$ is the gradient of function $f_i, i = 1, 2, \ldots, m$, with j-th gradient x_j, $j = 1, 2, \ldots, n$.

The forward kinematics (FK) is often expressed in functional form with the end-effector pose as a function of joint coordinates. The kinematics can be computed for any serial-link manipulator irrespective of the number of joints or the types of joints. The simple two-link robot is limited in the poses that it can achieve.

Forward kinematics makes use of joint parameters to compute the configuration of chain. Pertaining to human body, for example, if we touch an object [72], to determine the links starting from our feet to fingers, it is called FK. Inverse kinematics reverses this calculation to determine the joint parameters that achieve a desired configuration [64, 79]. The comparison between IK and FK is shown in Fig. 2.18.

A pose may be unachievable due to singularity where the alignment of axes reduces the effective degrees of freedom [53]. Hence, a trajectory is chosen, which moves through a robot singularity. The singularity point could not be reached.

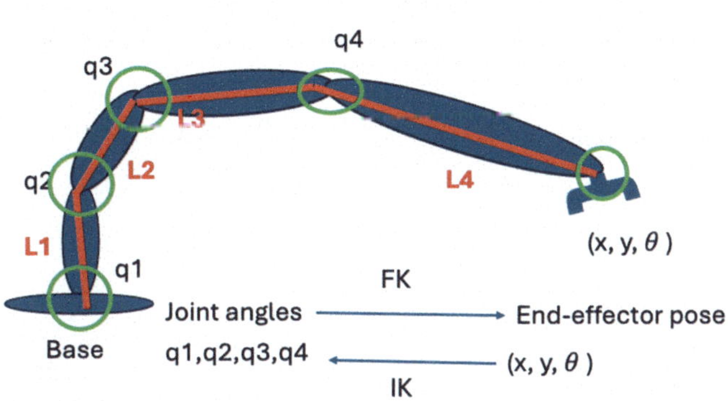

Fig. 2.18 The comparison between FK and IK

Thus, simulation can assist us to resolve the singularity problem. In robotics, the singularity point problem refers to configurations of a robotic system where its mathematical models, particularly the kinematic or dynamic equations, become undefined or degenerate [20]. These points trigger problems such as loss of control or infinite joint velocities, which severely limit the robot's ability to move or perform tasks. Singularity problems are especially important in robotic manipulators and robotic arms in precision tasks, as they disrupt the robot's ability to perform tasks accurately and safely.

Kinematics [13] is the study of motion without considering the cause of motion. Inverse kinematics (IK) is an example of the kinematic analysis of a constrained system of rigid bodies or kinematic chain. IK makes use of kinematics to determine the motion of a robot to reach a desired position [64, 79].

The grasping end of a robot arm is designated as the end-effector. The robot configuration is a list of joint positions within the position limits of the robot model that do not violate any constraints. Given the desired end-effector positions, inverse kinematics (IK) is able to determine an appropriate joint configuration for which the end-effectors move to the target pose [64, 79].

Algorithm 8: Closed-form IK for a two-link planar arm

Input: Target coordinates (x, y), link lengths l_1, l_2
Output: Joint angles θ_1, θ_2
Compute $d \leftarrow \sqrt{x^2 + y^2}$ `// Distance to target`
if $d > l_1 + l_2$ ***or*** $d < |l_1 - l_2|$ **then**
  return Error: Target unreachable
Compute $\cos(\theta_2) \leftarrow \frac{x^2+y^2-l_1^2-l_2^2}{2l_1l_2}$
Compute $\theta_2 \leftarrow \arccos(\cos(\theta_2))$
Compute $k_1 \leftarrow l_1 + l_2 \cos(\theta_2)$
Compute $k_2 \leftarrow l_2 \sin(\theta_2)$
Compute $\theta_1 \leftarrow \arctan 2(y, x) - \arctan 2(k_2, k_1)$
return (θ_1, θ_2)

Algorithm 8 shows the pseudocode of IK algorithm. Figure 2.19 displays an example of MATLAB inverse kinematics for the simple 2D manipulator by using

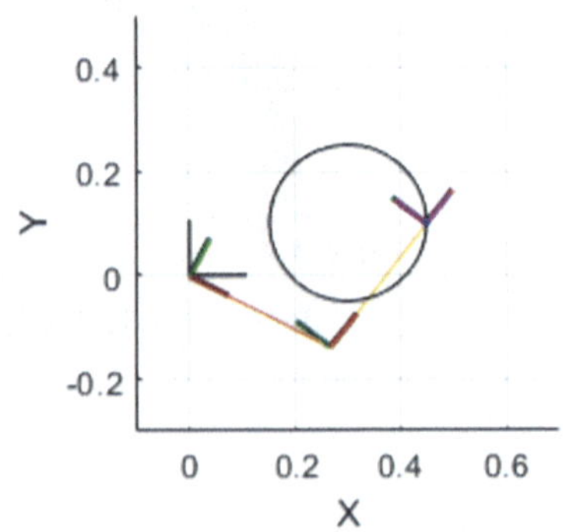

Fig. 2.19 MATLAB 2D path tracing with inverse kinematics (IK)

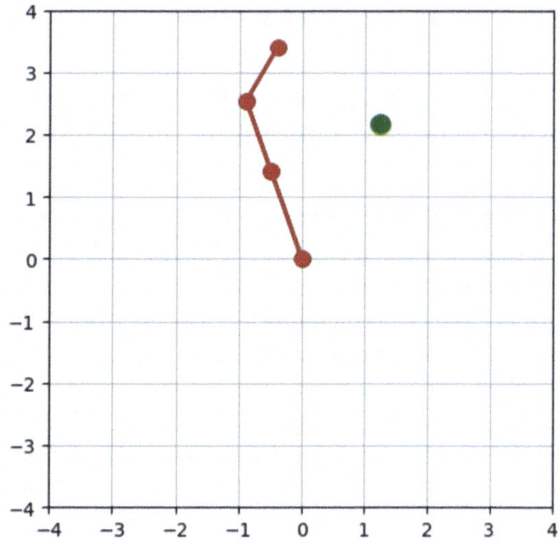

Fig. 2.20 A demo of inverse kinematics (IK) using Google Colab

```
# Inverse Kinematics calculation for 3-link arm
def inverse_kinematics(target_x, target_y):
    # Initialize angles (0 radians for all joints)
    angles = np.zeros(len(L))

    # Iterate through each joint starting from the last joint
    for i in range(len(L) - 1, -1, -1):
        if i == len(L) - 1:
            # Last joint directly points to the target
            angles[i] = np.arctan2(target_y, target_x)
        else:
            # Calculate the position of the end of the current link
            x_end = sum(L[j] * np.cos(angles[j]) for j in range(i, len(L)))
            y_end = sum(L[j] * np.sin(angles[j]) for j in range(i, len(L)))

            # Calculate the difference vector
            diff_x = target_x - x_end
            diff_y = target_y - y_end
            distance = np.sqrt(diff_x**2 + diff_y**2)

            # Update the angle using the atan2 function
            if distance > L[i]:
                angles[i] = np.arctan2(diff_y, diff_x)
            else:
                angles[i] = angles[i + 1]  # Retain the previous angle if target is too close

    return angles
```

Fig. 2.21 The inverse kinematics in Python

inverse kinematics (IK). The manipulator of a robot is a simple 2-DoF planar manipulator with revolute joints. A circular trajectory is created in a 2D plane which provides points to the inverse kinematics solver. The solver calculates the joint positions to achieve this trajectory. The robot is animated to show the robot configurations that achieve the circular trajectory.

Figure 2.20 shows a demonstration of inverse kinematics in Python with three links. The source code is given in Fig. 2.21.

2.6 Dynamics and Control

Robot dynamics are the relationship between the forces acting on a robot and the motion of the robot [20]. Robotics usually combines three aspects of design work to create robot systems:

- **Mechanical construction**: A frame, form, or shape which was designed to achieve a particular task. The payload, gravity, weights, and materials are taken into consideration, correspondingly. The forces and torques are the sources for each link with the purpose of supporting robot working.
- **Electrical components**: The components encapsulate power to control the machinery. Electrical motors (DC or AC) are thought as the most important component for control the robots and provide power to drive the robot working.
- **Software**: a program for a robot to decide when or how to conduct actions. The important software for robot working is ROS, no matter for one robot or a swarm of robots to coordinate working together.

Dynamics for robot control are related to these fundamental components:

- **Electric motors**: DC motors in portable robots or AC motors in industrial robots, where electric current flows in two ways as an alternating current (AC) or direct current (DC).
- **Actuators**: Actuator converts stored energy into movement, in most of the time, we make use of electric motors as the "muscle" to drive robots working.
- **Sensors**: Sensors provide real-time information to indicate the states of robots. The sensors are not only applied to localization, positioning, and navigation but also provide temperature, air humanity, and battery states.
- **Manipulation**: Manipulation is the control of robot's environment through selective touch or contact.
- **The operation**: Pick and place is the typical one of manipulations; basically the pick-and-place operation is based on translations and rotations of robot components in 3D space.
- **End-effector**: The device is located at the end of a robotic arm. The end-effector was designed to interact with the environment, and most of the time, it will replace human hands and fingers. Although the design is not perfect, the end-effector will be taken great values in the operation.

The interaction between human control and machine motions in the incremental HRI (i.e., human and robot Interactions) is listed as follows:

- **Teleoperation**: A human controls each component and movement, and the corresponding machine actuator is specified by the operator through wireless communications or mobile computing. The instructions will be understood and analyzed for robot moving or working.
- **Supervisory**: A human specifies general moves or position changes, and the machine understands the instructions and decides specific movements of its actuators to get the destination or location with the specified states.

- **Autonomy**: The operator specifies only the task, and the robot manages itself to completion [12]. Usually, a series of instructions of these tasks will be thought as one unit or package, and the batch instructions will be executed till the end of these tasks. Robots have the ability to deal with errors or mistakes during the execution.
- **Full autonomy**: The machine will create and complete all the tasks without human interactions [32]. The robots have the ability to deal with any problems during the execution.

In dynamics and control of a serial-link manipulator, each link is supported by using a reaction force and torque from the preceding link, which is subject to its own weight, as well as the reaction forces and torques from the links. We have the joint torques and joint forces applied directly as a vector to each joint [46].

$$\mathbf{Q} = \mathbf{M}(q)\ddot{q} + \mathbf{C}(q, \dot{q})\dot{q} + \mathbf{G}(q) + \mathbf{J}(q)^{\top} \cdot \mathbf{F}_{Ext} \tag{2.25}$$

where $\mathbf{G}(q)$ is the gravity term, $\mathbf{M}(q)\ddot{q}$ is the inertia matrix, $\mathbf{C}(q, \dot{q})\dot{q}$ is centrifugal torques, $\mathbf{J}(q)^{\top} \cdot \mathbf{F}_{Ext}$ is the external force, and $\mathbf{J}$ is the Jacobian matrix of the end-effector [19]. In inverse dynamics, given the pose q, velocity $\dot{q}$, and acceleration $\ddot{q}$, Eq. (2.25) is applied to compute the required joint forces or joint torques.

2.7 Applications of Robotics

Robotics [20] encompasses robotic vision and robotic control. Robotic vision usually encapsulates camera collaboration, image formation, image processing, stereo vision, and 3D reconstruction. The relevant content was depicted in the previous sections of this book. Robotic control takes effect through the research areas such as machine intelligence [14, 25, 49], genetic algorithm (GA), reinforcement learning [22, 45], visual servoing, and imitation learning.

Visual servoing is quite advanced. Given a robot with its specifications and configuration, the robot is expected to work effectively. Payload refers to the amount that a robot can be lifted and carried. In the family of human robots, the members include Android (male) and Gynoid (female); human robot has two kinds, one is male, and the other is female. Furthermore, the robot family has other members such as mobile robots, arm-type robots, and flying robots that refer to drones [9, 54, 55].

Pertaining to arm-type robots, the Cartesian robot's arm has three axes with Cartesian coordinates. The tiny robots are possible to be installed in kitchens for the facilitation of cutting fruits and preparing for a cup of coffee which may take account of nutrition estimation [65, 69, 70].

The Cartesian/Gantry robot's arm has three prismatic joints, and the axes are coincident with a Cartesian coordinator. It has 3D prismatic, which means the arms are working along X, Y, and Z axes [9, 54, 55], the joints can move up and down and back and forth, and the arm-type robot is famous for its six degrees of freedom

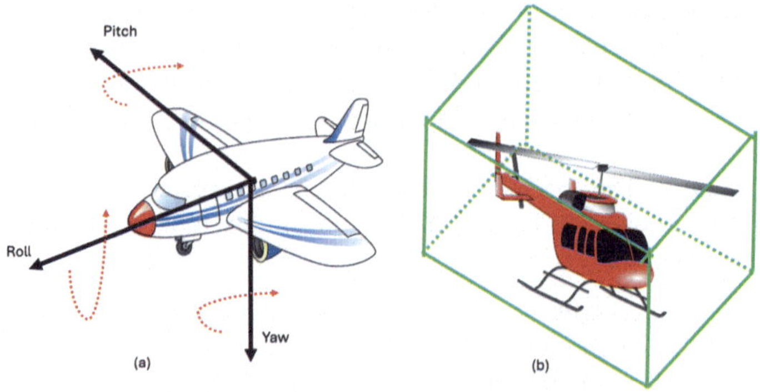

Fig. 2.22 An airplane and a helicopter. (**a**) The position of all three axes: roll, pitch, and yaw, with the right-hand rule for describing its rotations. (**b**) The work envelope of a helicopter

(DoF). Regarding the number of axes, roll, pitch, and yaw operations are required for full control of manipulator or end-effector as shown in Fig. 2.22. In robotics [40], regarding airplanes or drone systems [43], there are three rotations: pitch, yaw, and roll around the axes. The degree of freedom (DoF) and the number of joint points of robots are not the same [40].

The work envelope [60] refers to the region of space where a robot can work or layout. Suppose these robots have a 3D work envelope, and because a robot is made of iron and steel, we need to limit the motion of robots. In the work envelop, the robots are moving within the limited premise.

Robot kinematics is the study of how a robot's joints are connected and how they relate to the robot's spatial layout. It is a fundamental topic in robotics [40] that takes use of geometry to model the robot's links of rigid bodies [20]. Kinematics is related to the types of joints. Figure 2.23 shows a pick-and-place robot to pick up ping-pong balls [38, 50, 74–76, 78, 81] in our building.

The compliance refers to the measure of distance or angle of a robot joint. The speed includes angular or linear velocity. That means the robot moves not only transitional but also rotational. While moving from this angle to that angle like a space shuttle, there are velocity and acceleration limits, the maximum speed over short distance starts from zero. This process is called acceleration.

The power source includes electronic motors and hydraulics, i.e., two types of powers. Nowadays, it is completely electronic motor-based. One of the advantages is that electronic motors are quiet without noise.

Regarding robotic mapping, robots need a map and draw the map of the working place automatically. Robotic navigation leads the robots from one place to another by using map. When human communicates with robots, the robots can understand human intentions [30]. As well known, OpenAI ChatGPT is a multimodal model software, which showcases how many steps are needed if a task is expected to be completed.

Fig. 2.23 A wheeled robot is picking up table tennis balls with two cameras and one end-effector

Robots exactly follow human instructions. The whole process may be given through voices or talks. Given a prompt, a task or a job is completed on time. Currently, all robots are based on imitation learning. If robots learn from human's performance and experience, the operation will be much standard. If there has a competition contest whether human completes with robots, the outcome is that human cannot guarantee always beating robots in future. But the robots can ensure they will win our human sooner or later. Through Google software MediaPipe, it shows that robots can recognize human poses [17, 18, 67, 76] and reflect the key points from human body to the joint points of robots. Human facial emotion recognition [61, 71] can be implemented by using software. Human expression of emotions encloses angry, happy, and others [2, 48, 71].

The fundamental requirement in robotic vision [20] is to represent position and orientation of robots in an environment. Basically, the position and orientation are described by using its coordinate systems as shown in Fig. 2.24. A coordinate frame, or a Cartesian coordinate system, is a set of orthogonal axes that intersect at a point known as the origin. The position and the orientation of a coordinate frame are known as its pose which has shown graphically as a coordinate system [18]. A Cartesian coordinate system is a set of axes that intersect at support node as an origin. The origin is at the base of arm-type robots. If the system is initialized, the position and the orientation based on the origin of the coordinate frame are known, as shown in Fig. 2.25. That is the reason why the coordinate system is defined, and the important characteristics of relevant tools should be considered.

Fig. 2.24 The coordinate frame of robots in a scene. C_0, C_1, and C_2 are camera coordinate frames; R_1 and R_2 are robotic ordinate system

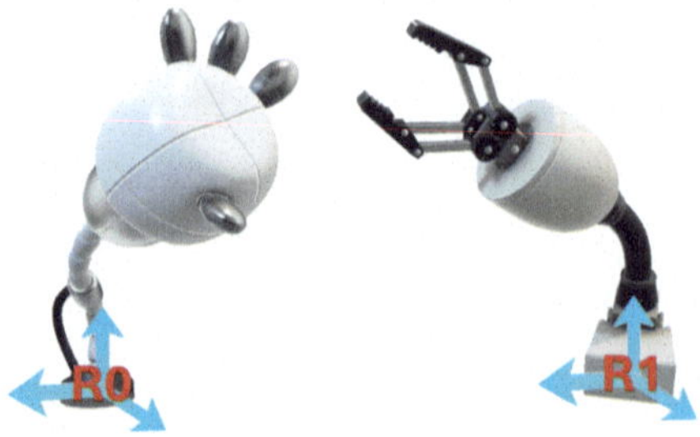

Fig. 2.25 Arm-type robots and the coordinate frames, where R_0 and R_1 are robotic coordinate frames on the bases

These characteristics are possible to be composed or compounded together. The world coordinates will be defined by using affine transformation in Eq. (2.26).

$$\begin{pmatrix} X' \\ Y' \\ Z' \end{pmatrix} = \begin{pmatrix} \alpha \cdot \cos(\theta) & -\sin(\theta) & \Delta X \\ \sin(\theta) & \beta \cdot \cos(\theta) & \Delta Y \\ 0 & \gamma & \Delta Z \end{pmatrix} \begin{pmatrix} X \\ Y \\ Z \end{pmatrix} \tag{2.26}$$

where $(\Delta X, \Delta Y, \Delta Z) \in \mathscr{R}^3$ is the shift, $\theta \in \mathscr{R}$ is the rotational angle, and $\alpha \in \mathscr{R}$, $\beta \in \mathscr{R}$, and $\gamma \in \mathscr{R}$ are the scaling factors between two coordinate systems. This equation transforms the 3D point $\mathbf{P} = (X, Y, Z)^\top \in \mathscr{R}^3$ in O_1 system to the point $\mathbf{P}' = (X', Y', Z')^\top$ in O_2 system.

The inverse transformation will transform the point $\mathbf{P}'$ back to $\mathbf{P}$. The inverse matrix $\mathbf{A}$ satisfies that $\mathbf{A}\mathbf{A}^{-1} = \mathbf{I}$, $\mathbf{I}$ is the identity matrix, and $\det(\mathbf{A}) \neq 0$. The affine transformations are shown in Fig. 2.26.

If a camera on the robot is fixed, this forms a basic relationship between the robot and the camera. A robot system must be kept in our mind fundamentally. There are many robots, cameras, and objects in the same environment. The occlusion of obstacles needs to be avoided in case that one blocks another [68], the position and orientation of the spatial object are related to a directed graph.

An alternative representation of spatial relationships is a directed graph. In an environment, we need to understand that there is a relationship between translation

Fig. 2.26 Affine transformation for the point **P** in two different coordinate systems O_1 and O_2

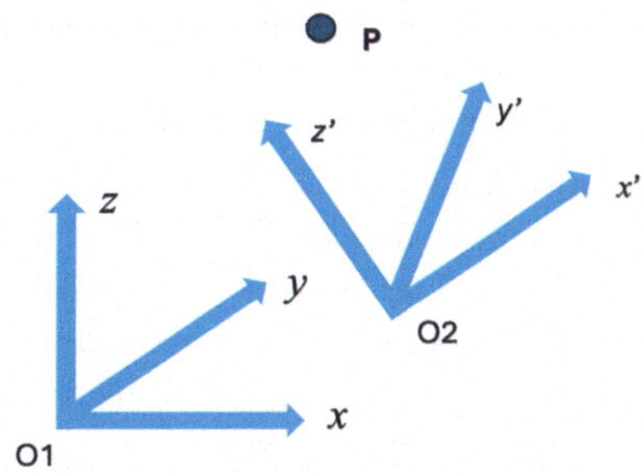

and orientation. Translation means shift from one place to another, rotation refers to rotations along X, Y, or Z axis, and it is 3D-based. Between the spaces, we have a transition matrix.

The object pose is varying as a function of time. With the difference, object pose will have different trajectory. Trajectory, the temporal sequence of poses, smoothly changes from an initial pose to a final pose. The trajectory is a temporary sequence of poses from one place to another, most changes from the initial pose to the final pose. Given a starting point and the end point, between them, the rate of change of positions is temporal derivative

$$\frac{ds}{dt} = \lim_{\Delta(t)\to 0} \frac{\Delta(s)}{\Delta(t)} \tag{2.27}$$

$$\frac{dw}{dt} = \lim_{\Delta(t)\to 0} \frac{\Delta(w)}{\Delta(t)} \tag{2.28}$$

The linear velocity is v_l, and the angular velocity is v_a. Correspondingly, we have linear acceleration a_l and angular acceleration a_a.

$$v_l = \frac{ds}{dt}; \; v_a = \frac{dw}{dt} \tag{2.29}$$

$$a_l = \frac{dv_l}{dt}; \; a_a = \frac{dv_a}{dt} \tag{2.30}$$

where s and w are the changes of positional translation and rotational angle.

We estimate the pose of moving objects. While the object is moving, the key issue is that this object has velocities of translation and rotation instead of only one kind of velocities. The velocity of a linear segment increases its duration time. Given measurements from linear velocity and angular velocity sensors, the pose for a moving object is estimated. As the velocity of linear segment increases, its duration decreases, and ultimately its duration would be zero. In fact, too high or too low speed, the maximum velocity will result in an infeasible trajectory. A path is a locus in space that leads from an initial pose to a final pose [27]. A trajectory is a path with specified timing. An important characteristic of a trajectory in robotics is smooth [57].

The trajectory has defined boundary conditions for position, velocity, and acceleration. Smoothness means that its first few temporal derivatives are continuous. Polynomials are simple to be computed that can easily provide the required smoothness and boundary conditions. There is a need to move smoothly along a path through one or more intermediates or via points without stopping. The trajectory has defined the boundary conditions for position, velocity, and acceleration. That means everything is under control.

Fundamentally, smoothness reflects that the first derivatives are existence and continuous. Polynomials are simple to be computed that can easily unveil the required smoothness and boundary conditions [57]. The simple way to control a robot is to harness polynomials. However, polynomials are hard to be controlled after degree 3 for interpolating purpose [40].

$$f(x) = a_0 + a_1 x + a_2 x^2 + \cdots + a_n x^n = a_0 + \sum_{i=1}^{n} a_i x^i \tag{2.31}$$

where $a_n \neq 0$, $a_i, x \in \mathscr{R}$, $n \in \mathscr{N}$. There is often a need to move smoothly along a path through one or more intermediates or via points without stopping. A trajectory is a piecewise curve [27, 73]. These points can control the curve, and the degree cannot be greater than four.

2.8 Lab Session: Mobile Arm with MATLAB

Interactive design for a mobile manipulator with four omnidirectional wheels [59] is split into four sections:

- Define a robot and environment
- Create a task and trajectory scheduler
- Add core manipulator dynamics and design a controller
- Verify complete workflow of the robot and environment

MATLAB provides the interactive design for mobile manipulator. The manipulator provides Link1, Link2, and Link3. In most of the factories, we use robots to move the object from one place to another. MATLAB has provided such a robot, and the basic operations include:

- The first move position and the open grips
- Close the ribs, and move the position to the place
- Approach the position, and move to the place position
- Open the grip, and start from here

Table 2.1 Lab report for robotic vision

Name	<First Name Last Name >
Email	<firstname.lastname@mailbox >
Lab date	<dd-mm-yy >
Submitted date	<dd-mm-yy >
Project title	Build Basic Rigid Body Tree Models
Lab objectives	The objective is to demonstrate how to construct a simple robot arm with five degrees of freedom (DoF) by using the components of the rigid body tree robot model
Configurations and settings	<The preferences, software, hardware, platforms, tools, etc. >
Methods	<The relevant scientific theories or concepts >
Workflow	<The step-by-step procedure for the experiment >
Datasets	<The data and materials for your experiments >
Input	<image filename, size, resolution >
Output	<image filename, size, resolution >
Testing steps	<Functional & non-functional testing methods step by step >
Bugs or problems	<The system error code, lines of the code >
Result analysis	<The tables, graphs, and figures, etc. >
Conclusion/reflection	<The strengths and weaknesses, or learned from this project >
References	https://au.mathworks.com/help/nav/ug/plan-mobile-robot-paths-usingrrt.html

Appendix: <Source codes with comments and line numbers >

The robot arms move to the designed position first, open the gripper, and close the grip. This is a standard operation of MATLAB examples, which has eight states. The last one was to verify the completed work for a robot.

At the end of this chapter, all readers are recommended to complete the lab report. Please fill in the form shown in Table 2.1 after each lab session (2 hours).

An example of this lab report is:

- **Project title**: Build basic rigid body tree models.
- **Project objectives**: In order to demonstrate how to construct a simple robot arm with five degrees of freedom (DoF) by using the components of the rigid body tree robot model. The model constructed in this example is a typical robot arm.
- **Configurations and settings**: MATLAB Online
- **Methods**: (1) Create a rigid Body Tree robot model. (2) Create a series of linkages as rigid body objects. (3) Create collision objects for each rigid body with different shapes and dimensions. (4) Add the collision bodies to the rigid body objects. (5) Set transformations of the joint attachment between bodies. (6) Create an object array for both the bodies and joints. (7) Visualize the robot model to confirm the dimensions. (8) Use the interactive GUI to move the model around. (9) View a list of the final tree information. (10) Move the interactive marker around to test different desired gripper positions.

- **Implementation steps**:
  1. Create Rigid Body Elements
  2. Attach Joints
  3. Assemble Robot
  4. Interact With Robot Model
- **Testing steps**:
  1. Verify Rigid Body Elements
  2. Test Joint Connections
  3. Validate Robot Assembly
  4. Interact with the Robot Model
  5. Simulation and Performance Testing
- **Result analysis**: The output images visually validate the creation, assembly, and interactive capabilities of the robot arm, enhancing the written descriptions and confirming the project's objectives have been met.
- **Conclusion/reflection**: The development of a basic rigid body tree model of a robot arm is shown by using MATLAB. The detailed step-by-step implementation and testing procedures highlight MATLAB's capabilities for robotic modeling and simulation. The absence of bugs or issues indicates a robust and well-executed experiment. Additionally, the integration of a GUI for interaction significantly enhances the model's practical applicability in real-world scenarios.
- **Readings**: https://au.mathworks.com/help/robotics/ug/build-basic-rigid-body-tree-models.html

2.9 Exercises

Question 2.1 Why the Braitenberg vehicle is the simplest robot? What are the features of Braitenberg vehicle?

Question 2.2 What is automaton in computer science?

Question 2.3 What are the differences between probabilistic road map and Voronoi road map?

Question 2.4 Why dead reckoning algorithm is still effective in the navigation for mobile robots?

Question 2.5 What is the full autonomy in robotics?

Question 2.6 Regarding robotic arm, how many degrees of freedom (DoF) of each joint at most has?

Question 2.7 What is the relationship between Forward Kinematics (FK) and Inverse Kinematics (IK)?

Question 2.8 How many numbers of axes is suitable for a humanoid robot?

Question 2.9 What are the differences between the number of axes and degree of freedom (DoF)?

References

1. Adiyatov O, Varol H (2017) A novel RRT-based algorithm for motion planning in dynamic environments. In: IEEE international conference on mechatronics and automation (ICMA), pp 1416–1421
2. Alexander R (2022) Human facial emotion recognition from digital images using deep learning. Master's Thesis, Auckland University of Technology, New Zealand
3. Al-Sarayreha M (2020) Hyperspectral imaging and deep learning for food safety. PhD Thesis. Auckland University of Technology, New Zealand
4. Al-Sarayreh M, Reis M, Yan W, Klette R (2017) Detection of adulteration in red meat species using hyperspectral imaging. In: Pacific-rim symposium on image and video technology, pp 182–196
5. Al-Sarayreh M, Reis M, Yan W, Klette R (2018) Detection of red-meat adulteration by deep spectral–spatial features in hyperspectral images. J Imag 4(5):63
6. Al-Sarayreh M, Reis M, Yan W, Klette R (2019) Deep spectral-spatial features of snapshot hyperspectral images for red-meat classification. In: International conference on image and vision computing New Zealand
7. Al-Sarayreh M, Reis M, Yan W, Klette R (2019) A sequential CNN approach for foreign object detection in hyperspectral images. In: International conference on information, communications and signal
8. Al-Sarayreha M, Reis M, Yan W, Klette R (2020) Potential of deep learning and snapshot hyperspectral imaging for classification of species in meat. Food Control 117:107332
9. Arnold RD, Yamaguchi H, Tanaka T (2018) Search and rescue with autonomous flying robots through behavior-based cooperative intelligence. J Int Humanit Action 3(1):18
10. Aurenhammer F, Klein R, Lee D (2013) Voronoi diagrams and delaunay triangulations. World Scientific, Singapore
11. Azevedo F, Cardoso JS, Ferreira A, Fernandes T, Moreira M, Campos L (2021) Efficient reactive obstacle avoidance using spirals for escape. Drones 5(2):51
12. Bedini S (1964) The role of automata in the history of technology. Technol Culture 5(1):24–42
13. Beggs J (1983) Kinematics. Taylor & Francis, Milton Park
14. Bengio Y, Lecun Y, Hinton G (2021) Deep learning for AI. Commun ACM 64(7):58–65
15. Bouzoualegh S, Guechi E-H, Kelaiaia R (2019) Model predictive control of a differential-drive mobile robot. Acta Universitatis Sapientiae Electr Mech Eng 10(1):20–41
16. Çabuk VU, Kubilay Şavkan A, Kahraman R, Karaduman F, Kırıl O, Sezer V (2018) Design and control of a tennis ball collector robot. In: International conference on control engineering and information technology (CEIT)
17. Cao X, Yan W (2022) Pose estimation for swimmers in video surveillance. In: Multimedia tools and applications, Springer, Berlin
18. Chen Z, Yan W (2023) Real-time pose recognition for billiard player using deep learning. In: Deep learning, reinforcement learning and the rise of intelligent systems, chap 10. IGI Global, Hershey, pp 188–208
19. Choset H, Hutchinson S, Lynch K et al (2005) Principles of robot motion: theory, algorithms, and implementation. MIT Press, Cambridge
20. Corke P Robotics, Vision and control, 2nd edn. Springer Nature, Berlin
21. Cormen T, Leiserson C, Rivest R, Stein C (2022) Introduction to algorithms, 4th edn. MIT Press, Cambridge

22. Dabney W et al (2020) A distributional code for value in dopamine-based reinforcement learning. Nature 577: 671–675
23. Dong K, Yan W (2024) Player performance analysis in table tennis through human action recognition. Computers 13(12):332
24. Elfes A (1989) Using occupancy grids for mobile robot perception and navigation. Computer 22(6):46–57
25. Ertel W (2019) Introduction to artificial intelligence. Springer International Publishing, Berlin
26. Farin G (1993) Curves and surfaces for computer-aided geometric design: a practical guide, 3rd edn. Academic, Cambridge
27. Farin G (1997) Curves and surfaces for computer-aided geometric design. Elsevier, Amsterdam. ISBN 978-01-22490-54-5
28. Farin G (2002) Curves and surfaces for CAGD: a practical guide, 5th edn. Morgan Kaufmann, Burlington
29. Fraenkel GS, Gunn DL (1961) The orientation of animals. Kineses, taxes and compass reactions. Dover Publications, Garden City
30. Gao X, Liu Y, Nguyen M, Yan W (2024) VICL-CLIP: enhancing face mask detection in context with multimodal foundation models. In: ICONIP
31. Gong X, Gao Y, Wang F, Zhu D, Zhao W, Wang F, Liu Y (2024) A local path planning algorithm for robots based on improved DWA. Electronics 13(15):2965
32. Hopcroft J, Motwani R, Ullman J (2001) Introduction to automata theory, languages, and computation. Addison-Wesley, Boston
33. Humpherys J (2012) A fresh look at the Kalman Filter. SIAM Rev 54(4):801–823
34. Jonathan V (2021) Tech explained: Ackermann steering geometry. Racecar Engineering
35. Kang J, Lim D, Choi Y, Jang W, Jung J (2021) Improved RRT-connect algorithm based on triangular inequality for robot path planning. Sensors 21(2):333
36. Kavraki LE, Svestka P, Latombe J-C, Overmars MH (1996) Probabilistic roadmaps for path planning in high-dimensional configuration spaces. IEEE Trans Rob Autom 12(4):566–580
37. Klette R (2014) Concise computer vision: an introduction into theory and algorithms. Springer-Verlag London, London
38. Li H, Wu H, Lou L, Kühnlenz K, Ravn O (2012) Ping-pong robotics with high-speed vision system. In: International conference on control automation robotics & vision (ICARCV), pp 106–111
39. Lu J (2016) Empirical approaches for human behavior analytics. Master's Thesis, Auckland University of Technology, New Zealand
40. Lynch K, Park F (2017) Modern robotics: mechanics, planning, and control. Cambridge University Press, Cambridge, MA
41. Maybeck PS (1990) The Kalman filter: an introduction to concepts. In Autonomous robot vehicles, Springer, Berlin, pp 194–204
42. Mehtab S (2022) Deep neural networks for road scene perception in autonomous vehicles using LiDARs and vision sensors. PhD Thesis, Auckland University of Technology, New Zealand
43. Meng Q, Yan W, et al (2025) Optimization of Sassafras tzumu leaf color quantification with UAV RGB imaging and Sassafras-net. Information processing in agriculture
44. Ming Y, Li Y, Zhang Z, Yan W (2021) A survey of path planning algorithms for autonomous vehicles. In: International journal of commercial vehicles
45. Mnih V et al (2015) Human-level control through deep reinforcement learning. Nature 518:529–533
46. Murphy R (2019) Introduction to AI robotics, 2nd edn. Bradford Books, Bradford
47. Muscat J (2014) Functional analysis. Springer, Berlin
48. Nguyen M, Yan W (2023) From faces to traffic lights: a multi-scale approach for emotional state representation. In: IEEE international conference on smart city
49. Norvig P, Russell S (2016) Artificial intelligence: a modern approach, 3rd edn. Prentice Hall, Upper Saddle River

50. Peng D (2025) Vision perception optimization and adaptive control for resource-constrained platform: a ping-pong ball pickup & place system. Master's Thesis, Auckland University of Technology, New Zealand
51. Peng D, Yan W (2025) Test-time training with adaptive memory for traffic accident severity prediction. Computers 14:186
52. Perera S, Barnes N, Zelinsky A (2014) Exploration: simultaneous localization and mapping (SLAM). In: Computer vision: a reference guide. Springer US, Berlin, pp 268–275
53. Phillips J (2007) Freedom in machinery. Cambridge University Press, Cambridge
54. Piacentini C, Bernardini S, Beck JC (2019) Autonomous target search with multiple coordinated UAVs. J Artif Int Res 65(1):519–568
55. Queralta JP, Raitoharju J, Gia TN, Passalis N, Westerlund T (2020) AutoSOS: towards multi-UAV systems supporting maritime search and rescue with lightweight AI and edge computing. arXiv preprint arXiv:2005.03409
56. Rashid H, Turuk A (2015) Dead reckoning localisation technique for mobile wireless sensor networks. IET Wirel Sensor Syst 5(2):87–96
57. Ravankar A, Ravankar AA, Kobayashi Y, Hoshino Y, Peng C-C (2018) Path smoothing techniques in robot navigation: state-of-the-art, current and future challenges. Sensors 18(9):3170
58. Se S et al (2001) Vision-based mobile robot localization and mapping using scale-invariant features. In: The international conference on robotics and automation (ICRA)
59. Siegwart R, Nourbakhsh I, Scaramuzza D (2004) Introduction to autonomous mobile robots. MIT Press, Cambridge
60. Singh CD, He B, Fermüller C, Metzler C, Aloimonos Y (2024) Minimal perception: enabling autonomy in resource-constrained robots. Front Robot AI 11:143182
61. Song C, He L, Yan W, Nand P (2019) An improved selective facial extraction model for age estimation. In: IEEE IVCNZ
62. Stentz A (1994) Optimal and efficient path planning for partially-known environments. In: International conference on robotics and automation, pp 3310–3317
63. Stentz A (1995) The focussed D* algorithm for real-time replanning. In: International joint conference on artificial intelligence, pp 1652–1659
64. Sugihara T (2011) Solvability-unconcerned inverse kinematics by the Levenberg–Marquardt method. IEEE Trans Robot 27(5):984–991
65. Tang S, Yan W (2024) Utilizing RT-DETR model for fruit calorie estimation from digital images. Information 15(8):469
66. Tang Y, Zakaria MA, Younas M (2025) Path planning trends for autonomous mobile robot navigation: a review. Sensors 25(4):1206
67. Tantiya R (2025) Design and implementation of a high DoF robot arm. Master's Thesis, Auckland University of Technology, New Zealand
68. Tokunaga S, Premachandra C, Premachandra HWH, Kawanaka H, Sumathipala S, Sudantha BS (2021) Autonomous spiral motion by a small-type robot on an obstacle-available surface. Micromachines 12(4):375
69. Xia Y, Nguyen M, Yan W (2023) Kiwifruit counting using KiwiDetector and KiwiTracker. In: Intelligent systems, pp 629–640
70. Xiao B, Nguyen M, Yan W (2023) Fruit ripeness identification using transformers. Appl Intell 53:22488–22499
71. Xu G, Yan W (2023) Facial emotion recognition using ensemble learning. In: Deep learning, reinforcement learning, and the rise of intelligent systems
72. Yan WQ (2019) Computational methods for deep learning, 2nd edn. Springer, Berlin
73. Yan W, Ding W, Qi D (2001) Rational many-knot spline interpolating curves and surfaces. J Image Graph 6(6):568–572
74. Yang G (2025) ChatPPG: multi-modal alignment of large language models for time-series forecasting in table tennis. Master's Thesis, Auckland University of Technology, New Zealand
75. Yang Y, Kim D, Choi D (2023) Ball tracking and trajectory prediction system for tennis robots. J Comput Design Eng 10(3):1176–1184

76. Yang G, Nguyen M, Yan W, Li X (2025) Foul detection for table tennis serves using deep learning. Electronics 14(1):27
77. Zarchan P, Musoff H (2000) Fundamentals of kalman filtering: a practical approach. American Institute of Aeronautics and Astronautics, Reston
78. Zhang Y, Zhao Y, Xiong R, Wang Y, Wang J, Chu J (2014) Spin observation and trajectory prediction of a ping-pong ball. In: IEEE international conference on robotics and automation (ICRA), pp 4108–4114
79. Zhao J, Badler N (1994) Inverse kinematics positioning Using nonlinear programming for highly articulated figures. ACM Trans Graph 13(4):313–336
80. Zhao H, Xu S, Yan W, Xu D (2025) Design and optimization of target detection and 3D localization models for intelligent muskmelon pollination robots. Horticulturae 11(8):905
81. Zhao Y, Wu J, Zhu Y, Yu H, Xiong R (2017) A learning framework towards real-time detection and localization of a ball for robotic table tennis system. In: IEEE international conference on real-time computing and robotics (RCAR), pp 97–102
82. Zhou Z, Guo J, Zhu Z, Guo H (2024) Uncalibrated visual servoing based on Kalman filter and mixed-kernel online sequential extreme learning machine for robot manipulator. Multimedia Tools Appl 83(7):18853–18879

Chapter 3
Image Processing for Robotics

Abstract In this chapter, robotic vision is elucidated from the aspects of camera calibration, digital image formation, and image processing. Starting from image formation of digital cameras, we form the images and explore their properties, and finally image processing at semantic level is detailed. The significance of this chapter is that we depict computer vision with image processing for robotics.

3.1 Fundamentals of Image Formation

In human vision, our eyes are a type of effective sensors for object detection and recognition, robotic navigation, obstacle avoidance, etc. [16]. Compared to our ears, our human eyes are more critical organ which can receive over 75% information. Cameras mimic the function of human eyes. In robotics, digital cameras are harnessed as robotic eyes [10], and cameras are taken into account to create vision-based competencies for robots [16]. We take into consideration of digital images to detect and recognize objects and navigate robots within the given real world. While robots are moving around world [27], the world is sensed by using robotic vision [16] to obtain real reality, and visual objects are sought on the images [19]. Robots armed with vision and intelligence could greatly reduce our human labors [22], such as the operation: pick and place. The technological development has made this feasible for robots to facilitate with cameras. A group of new emerging algorithms, cheap sensors, and plentiful computing power make cameras as a practical and applicable sensor.

Vision takes its effect through natural light. Generally, electromagnetic radiation (EMR) is classified by wavelength into radio waves, microwaves, infrared, the visible spectrum that our eyes perceive as light, ultraviolet, X-rays, and gamma rays. The light spans the visible spectrum which is usually defined as having wavelengths in the range of 400–700 nanometers (nm) as shown in Fig. 3.1. The frequencies of infrared rays are up to 1,050 nm; children and young adults may perceive ultraviolet wavelengths down to about 310–313 nm.

Our human eyes see colors in the limited range of wavelength with visible reflection light and visible object. If ultraviolet (UV) and infrared rays could not

W. Q. Yan, *Robotic Vision*, Advances in Computer Vision and Pattern Recognition,
https://doi.org/10.1007/978-981-95-4360-1_3

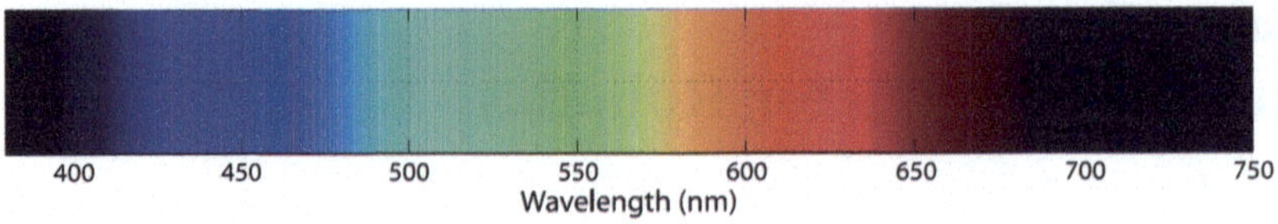

Fig. 3.1 The visible spectrum

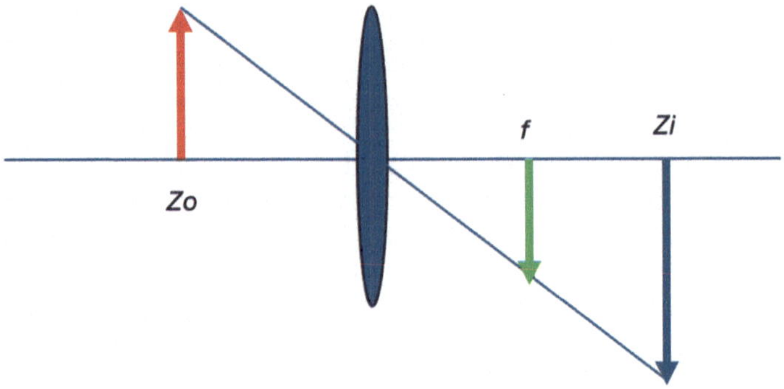

Fig. 3.2 The formation of images in geometry optics

be viewed by digital cameras or robotic vision, the image will be rendered by using visualization [28, 32]. In robot and human perception, the information such as size, shape, and position of visual objects, as well as other characteristics such as color and texture [10], is deduced. The colors enclose binary color, grayscale color, and real color. Binary color only has two colors: black and white [23–25]. In grayscale images, the intensities of red color, green color, and blue color are the same or similar. Color and texture are thought as visual features of digital images. Nowadays, the images from digital cameras are with real colors at retina level.

A simple pinhole is able to create an inverted image on the wall of a darkened room. When the sun rays pass through a hole, it will form an image on wall. In a digital camera, a glass or a plastic lens forms an image by using its semiconductor chip with an array of light-sensitive devices to convert light to an image. The chips are valuable, and there are challenges to develop new chips. The process of image formation involves a projection of the 3D world onto a 2D surface. In the real world, all objects are three-dimensional, but on images, the objects are two-dimensional only. On the given images, the depth information is disappeared. It is not possible to observe from the image whether the object is a large one in distance or a small one which is closer to the real object. From optic physics, z coordinate of an object and its image are formed by using the lens law as shown in Fig. 3.2.

$$\frac{1}{z_o} + \frac{1}{z_i} = \frac{1}{f} \tag{3.1}$$

where $z_o \in \mathscr{R}^+$, $z_o \neq 0$ is the distance to the object, $z_i \in \mathscr{R}^+$, $z_i \neq 0$, is the distance to the image, and $f \in \mathscr{R}^+$, $f \neq 0$, is the focal length of the lens. The coordinate frame of cameras is with z-axis defining the center of the field of view (FoV). Our human eyes usually perceive a view within the limited field. A point at the world coordinates $(X, Y, Z) \in \mathscr{R}^3$ is projected to the image plane $(x, y) \in \mathscr{R}^2$, after taken a photograph by using Eq. (3.2).

$$\begin{cases} x = f\frac{X}{Z} \\ y = f\frac{Y}{Z} \end{cases} \tag{3.2}$$

where (x, y) is the pixel location on the given image, (X, Y, Z) is a point of visual object in 3D space, and $Z \neq 0$ is the depth.

3.2 Camera Calibration

Regarding robotic vision [16], we set up a group of cameras and gauge the 3D space [10]. Camera calibration is a conventional way to sense and measure the 3D world. The calibration is the process of determining the camera's intrinsic parameters and the extrinsic parameters with respect to the world coordinate system. It relies on a set of world points whose relative coordinates are obtained and whose corresponding image plane coordinates are also gained. Camera calibration establishes a correspondence between real-world space and image space. The intrinsic parameters, including distortion parameters, can be harnessed to estimate the relative pose of chessboard in each image. However, classical calibration demands a 3D target or 3D object. Hence,

$$[x, y, z]^\top = \mathbf{R} \cdot [X, Y, Z]^\top + \mathbf{T} \tag{3.3}$$

$$\mathbf{m}' = [x', y']^\top = [x/z + c_x, y/z + c_y]^\top \tag{3.4}$$

$$s \cdot \mathbf{m}' = [u, v]^\top = [f_x \cdot x', f_y \cdot y']^\top \tag{3.5}$$

where $\mathbf{R}$ is the rotation matrix, $\mathbf{T}$ is the translation matrix, and $[\mathbf{R}|\mathbf{T}]$ is called the rotation-translation matrix. Hence,

$$s \cdot \mathbf{m}' = \mathbf{A} \cdot [\mathbf{R}|\mathbf{T}]\mathbf{M}' \tag{3.6}$$

where $(X, Y, Z) \in \mathscr{R}^3$ is the coordinate of a 3D point in the world space; $(u, v) \in \mathscr{R}^2$ is the coordinate of projection point in pixels; $(c_x, c_y) \in \mathscr{R}^2$ is a principal point, namely the image center; $(f_x, f_y) \in \mathscr{R}^2$ is the focal lengths expressed in pixel-related units; and $\mathbf{A}$ is a camera matrix or a matrix of intrinsic parameters. The joint

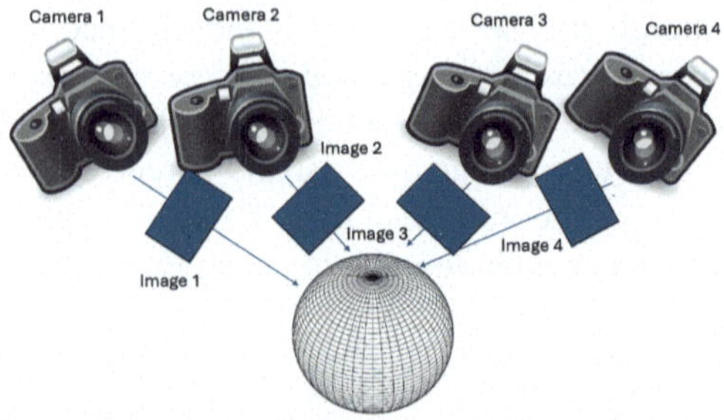

Fig. 3.3 A multiple cameras environment for camera calibration

Fig. 3.4 Our chessboard for camera calibration

rotation-translation matrix [**R**|**T**] is named as a matrix of extrinsic parameters. The steps of camera calibration for correcting image distortion are listed as follows:

- Corner extraction
- Point ordering
- Point correspondences
- Bundle adjustments

If we have four images from four cameras, namely images I_1, I_2, I_3, and I_4 are from cameras C_1, C_2, C_3, and C_4, respectively, the problem is still about how to find the parameters of cameras and parameters of 3D objects.

In the environment as shown in Fig. 3.3, no matter how the objects move or no matter how the cameras shift, the locations are promptly acquired from the environment. Especially in camera calibration, we should have a chessboard with a grid layout as shown in Fig. 3.4.

In camera calibration, the first step is for corner extraction. The corners are the intersection between edges. A corner in an image is detected at a pixel location where two edges of different directions intersect [17]. Corners usually lie on high-contrast regions of image. A corner pixel has surroundings varying from all of its near neighbors in omni-directions. If the corners are attained, the points are sorted in a proper sequence. Thus, the correspondences of these corners are earned.

From a robot's view, what our human sees is not matched with what the camera captured [29]. As the summery, the camera calibration in pseudocode is shown in Algorithm 9.

Algorithm 9: Camera calibration

Input: A set of N images of a known calibration pattern (e.g., chessboard)
Output: Camera intrinsic matrix K, distortion coefficients D, extrinsic parameters for each image

for *each image* $i = 1$ *to* N **do**
  Detect the 2D coordinates of the pattern corners in the image
  Store the corresponding 3D world coordinates of the corners

Use the set of 2D-3D correspondences to estimate the camera parameters:
Estimate the intrinsic matrix K (focal length, principal point, skew)
Estimate distortion coefficients D (radial and tangential)
Estimate extrinsic parameters (rotation and translation for each image)
Optimize all parameters using nonlinear least squares (e.g., Levenberg–Marquardt)
return K, D, and the set of extrinsic parameters

3.3 Essentials of Image Processing

After camera calibration, image processing [10] will be conducted. A digital image is a rectangular array of picture pixels. Robots always gather imperfect images of the world with artifacts due to noise, shadow, reflection, uneven illumination [22], etc. The image processing algorithms operate pixelwise on a single image or a pair of images or on a group of pixels within an image [21, 31, 33]. The image processing has two categories:

- *Monadic operations*: Each output pixel is based on a function of corresponding input pixel. For example, histogram normalization only takes pixel intensities into consideration, the results of statistics show how the values of pixels are distributed on the range from 0 to 255, and the number with the same values of pixels will be counted. In histogram normalization, all the values of histograms will be mapped to the interval [0, 1].
- *Spatial operations*: Each pixel in the output image is a function of all pixels in a region surrounding the corresponding pixel in the input image; a typical example is convolution operation [30]. The convolution is a linear spatial operation, and the kernel of convolution operation usually is a standard Gaussian distribution.

$$\mathbf{O}[u, v] = \sum_{(i,j)\in W} \mathbf{I}(u + i, v + j)\mathbf{K}(i, j), \forall (u, v) \in \mathbf{I} \tag{3.7}$$

where **K** is the convolution kernel, and W is the image window. Hence,

$$\mathbf{O} = \mathbf{I} \otimes \mathbf{K} \tag{3.8}$$

where $\otimes$ is the convolution operator. Gaussian kernel is symmetric:

$$G(x, y) = \frac{1}{2\pi\sigma^2} e^{-\frac{x^2+y^2}{2\sigma^2}} \tag{3.9}$$

where $\sigma \in \mathscr{R}$ is the parameters of standard deviation.

Filters are designed to respond to a variety of edges at any arbitrary angle of digital images. For example, Sobel kernel is considered as an image edge detector.

$$\mathbf{G}_x = \begin{bmatrix} +1 & 0 & -1 \\ +2 & 0 & -2 \\ +1 & 0 & -1 \end{bmatrix} * \mathbf{I} \tag{3.10}$$

$$\mathbf{G}_y = \begin{bmatrix} +1 & +2 & +1 \\ 0 & 0 & 0 \\ -1 & -2 & -1 \end{bmatrix} * \mathbf{I} \tag{3.11}$$

where **I** is the source image, $\mathbf{G}_x$ and $\mathbf{G}_y$ are two matrices which at each point contain the horizontal and vertical derivative approximations, respectively, and "*" denotes the 2D convolution operation.

Canny edge detector [9] is an edge detection operator that takes use of a multistage algorithm to detect a wide range of edges in images which was developed in 1986 [18]. The advantages of Canny edge detector are (1) detection of edge with low error rate, (2) the point detected from the operator could accurately localize on the center of edges, and (3) the image noise should not create false edges. Gaussian filter is employed to smooth the image in order to remove noise. A 5×5 Gaussian filter is given as

$$\mathbf{T}_{5\times5} = \begin{bmatrix} 2 & 4 & 5 & 4 & 2 \\ 4 & 9 & 12 & 9 & 4 \\ 5 & 12 & 15 & 12 & 5 \\ 4 & 9 & 12 & 9 & 4 \\ 2 & 4 & 5 & 4 & 2 \end{bmatrix}, \mathbf{T} = \mathbf{T}^\top \tag{3.12}$$

Hence, the gradient and the direction of edges are determined by using Eqs. (3.13) and (3.14).

$$|\mathbf{G}| = \sqrt{{\mathbf{G}_x}^2 + {\mathbf{G}_y}^2} \tag{3.13}$$

where $\nabla \mathbf{G} = (\mathbf{G}_x, \mathbf{G}_y)^\top$ is the gradient of each pixel (x, y) in image $\mathbf{I}(x, y)$, $x = 1, 2, \ldots, W$ and $y = 1, 2, \ldots, H$. $W \in \mathscr{N}$ and $H \in \mathscr{N}$ are the width and the height of image $\mathbf{I}$.

$$\theta = \text{atan2}\left(\mathbf{G}_y, \mathbf{G}_x\right) \tag{3.14}$$

where $\mathbf{G}$ is the gradient magnitude, computed by using the Pythagorean addition operator. $atan2(\cdot)$ is the arctangent function for calculating the edge direction angle θ which is rounded to one of the four angles representing vertical, horizontal, and two diagonals, namely 0°, 45°, 90°, and 135°. The Canny detector [9] applies double threshold to determine potential edges and finalizes the detection of edges by suppressing all other edges that are weak and not connected to strong edges.

In computer vision and image processing, blob detection methods aim at detecting regions in a digital image that differ in properties, such as brightness or color, compared to surrounding regions [20]. The most popular method for blob detection is implemented by using convolution operations. There are two main classes of blob detectors: (1) the differential methods based on derivatives of the function with respect to position and (2) the local extrema methods based on finding the local maxima and minima of the function. Blob detection is often employed in object detection and recognition, medical imaging, and key point detection.

A silhouette refers to a solid and shape-based representation of an object or subject, typically shown as a dark shape on a lighter background. A silhouette image is represented as a solid shape of a single color which is related to image binarization in image processing [14]. The interior of a silhouette is featureless. Silhouette sequences are applied to object tracking, shape matching, 3D reconstruction, and action classification.

In image template matching, it is easy to find which parts of the input image are most similar to the template [34]. Each pixel in the output image is rendered by using

$$\mathbf{O}(u, v) = s(\mathbf{T}, W) \tag{3.15}$$

where $\mathbf{T}$ is the template, and W is the window centered at $(u, v) \in \mathscr{R}^2, u, v \in \mathscr{R}$, in the input image $\mathbf{I}$. The function $s(\mathbf{I}_1, \mathbf{I}_2)$ is a scalar measure that describes the similarity of two equally sized images $\mathbf{I}_1$ and $\mathbf{I}_2$. The difference between two images is the sum of absolute differences (SADs) as shown in Eq. (3.16) or the sum of squared differences (SSDs) as shown in Eq. (3.17). These metrics are zero if the images are identical. The similarity NCC (Normalized Cross-Correlation) is calculated by using Eq. (3.18).

$$S = \sum_{(x,y)\in I} |\mathbf{I}_1(x, y) - \mathbf{I}_2(x, y)| \tag{3.16}$$

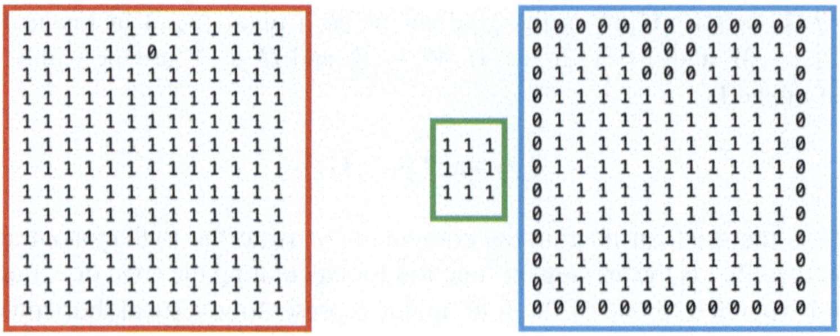

Fig. 3.5 The erosion operation of images

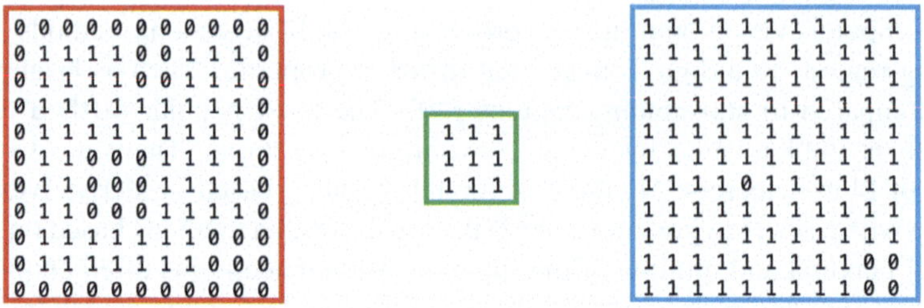

Fig. 3.6 The dilation operation of images

$$S = \sum_{(x,y)\in I} |\mathbf{I}_1(x, y) - \mathbf{I}_2(x, y)|^2 \tag{3.17}$$

$$S = \frac{\sum_{(x,y)\in I} \mathbf{I}_1(x, y) \cdot \mathbf{I}_2(x, y)}{\sqrt{\sum_{(x,y)\in \mathbf{I}} \mathbf{I}_1^2(x, y) \sum_{(x,y)\in \mathbf{I}} \mathbf{I}_1^2(x, y)}} \tag{3.18}$$

3.4 Image Morphology

Image morphology is concerned with the form or shape of visual objects in an image (binary color) [8]. In morphological operations, eroded image is marked in blue as shown in Fig. 3.5. If B (Green) is completely contained by A (Red), the pixel is retained or else deleted.

In morphological operations [8], the dilated image is marked in blue. Each pixel in $\mathbf{A}$ (red) with "1" will be superimposed with B (Green). All pixels after superimposed with $\mathbf{B}$ (green) are encapsulated in the dilation (blue) (Fig. 3.6).

In morphological operations, the sequence of operations, namely erosion then dilation, is known as opening. The sequence in the inverse order, dilation and then erosion, is the closing procedure as shown in Fig. 3.7.

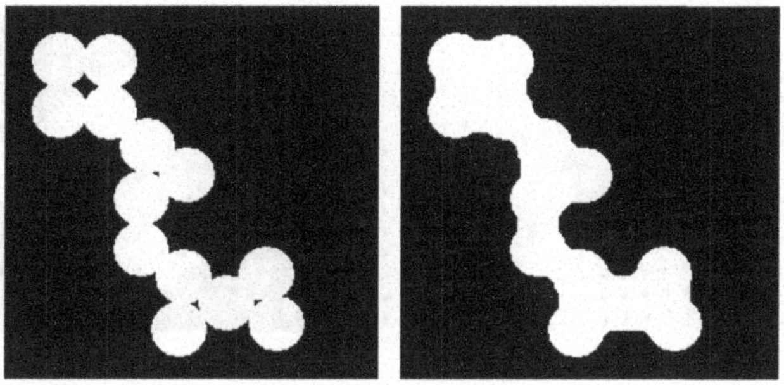

(a) (b)

Fig. 3.7 The closing operation of images

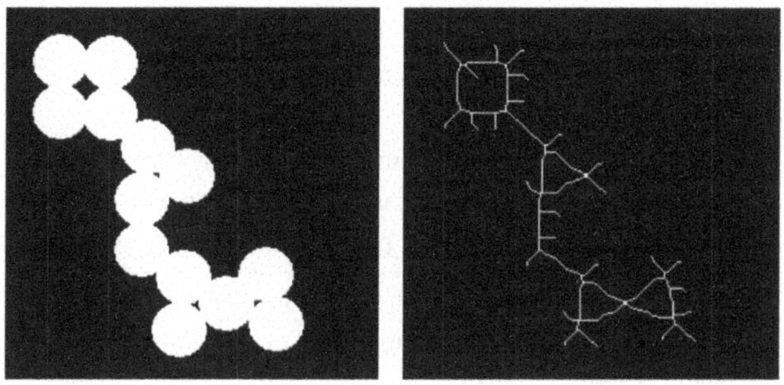

(a) (b)

Fig. 3.8 The skeletonization operation of images

Image skeletonization extracts the center line while preserving the topology of visual objects, as shown in Fig. 3.8. Image transformation is employed iteratively with a variety of structuring elements to conduct operations such as skeletonization and linear feature detection.

Image warping is a transformation of pixel coordinates as shown in Fig. 3.9. Mathematically, the image warping is based on bilinear interpolation. The interpolation as a whole is not linear but rather quadratic in the sample location.

In image processing, bilinear interpolation [13] is employed to resample images and textures. The algorithm is applied to map an image pixel location to a corresponding point on the texture map. Assume we have the four points (i.e., top-left point, bottom-left point, top-right point, and bottom-right point) of image $\mathbf{I}_1$: $\mathbf{P}_{TL}$, $\mathbf{P}_{BL}$, $\mathbf{P}_{TR}$, and $\mathbf{P}_{BR}$, and the other image I_2 has the corresponding points: $\mathbf{P}'_{TL}$, $\mathbf{P}'_{BL}$, $\mathbf{P}'_{TR}$, and $\mathbf{P}'_{BR}$. Hence, the correspondences are established.

$$\mathbf{P}_{st} = t \cdot [s \cdot \mathbf{P}_{TR} + (1-s) \cdot \mathbf{P}_{BR}] + (1-t) \cdot [s \cdot \mathbf{P}_{TL} + (1-s) \cdot \mathbf{P}_{BL}] \quad (3.19)$$

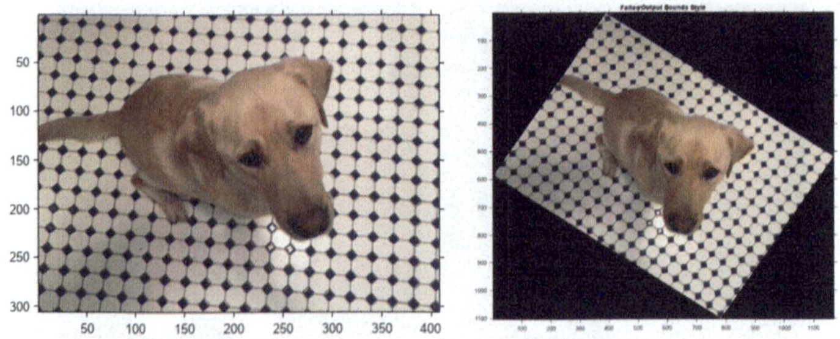

Fig. 3.9 The warping operation of images

and

$$\mathbf{P}'_{st} = t \cdot [s \cdot \mathbf{P}'_{TR} + (1-s) \cdot \mathbf{P}'_{BR}] + (1-t) \cdot [s \cdot \mathbf{P}'_{TL} + (1-s) \cdot \mathbf{P}'_{BL}] \tag{3.20}$$

where $\mathbf{P}_{st}$ and $\mathbf{P}'_{st}$ are the corresponding points on the two images, respectively, $s \in [0, 1]$, $t \in [0, 1]$. Thus, we render a pixel based on the color of the other image. The corresponding pseudocode is shown in Algorithm 10.

Algorithm 10: Bilinear interpolation for image pixel mapping

Input: Image I of size $H \times W$, floating-point coordinate (x, y)
Output: Interpolated value v at (x, y)

if $x < 0$ *or* $x > W - 1$ *or* $y < 0$ *or* $y > H - 1$ **then**
  return 0; `// Out of bounds`
`// Compute integer neighbors`
$x_1 \leftarrow \lfloor x \rfloor, \quad x_2 \leftarrow \min(x_1 + 1, W - 1)$
$y_1 \leftarrow \lfloor y \rfloor, \quad y_2 \leftarrow \min(y_1 + 1, H - 1)$
`// Compute distances`
$dx \leftarrow x - x_1, \quad dy \leftarrow y - y_1$
`// Fetch pixel values`
$Q_{11} \leftarrow I[y_1][x_1], \quad Q_{21} \leftarrow I[y_1][x_2]$
$Q_{12} \leftarrow I[y_2][x_1], \quad Q_{22} \leftarrow I[y_2][x_2]$
`// Interpolate horizontally`
$R_1 \leftarrow Q_{11} \cdot (1 - dx) + Q_{21} \cdot dx$
$R_2 \leftarrow Q_{12} \cdot (1 - dx) + Q_{22} \cdot dx$
`// Interpolate vertically`
$v \leftarrow R_1 \cdot (1 - dy) + R_2 \cdot dy$
return v

3.5 Feature Extraction for Object Detection and Recognition

In terms of visual features such as object size, position, and shape related to robotics, all features could be written in vectors for computing [10], and thus we have the following:

Bounding Box is the smallest rectangle that encloses the region and the position of visual object. Intersection over Union (IoU), also known as Jaccard index, is a metric to evaluate the accuracy of object detection and recognition, as well as image segmentation algorithms by measuring the overlap between predicted and ground truth regions.

Moment is a computationally cheap class of image features that describe region size and location as well as shape in invariant way. In a grayscale image with pixel intensity $\mathbf{I}(x, y)$, $(x, y) \in \mathscr{R}^2$, raw image moments M_{ij} are calculated by

$$M_{ij} = \sum_x \sum_y x^i y^j \mathbf{I}(x, y) \tag{3.21}$$

If $\bar{x} = \frac{M_{10}}{M_{00}}$ and $\bar{y} = \frac{M_{01}}{M_{00}}$, $(\bar{x}, \bar{y})$ is the centroid, the central moments are

$$M_{ij} = \sum_x \sum_y (x - \bar{x})^i (y - \bar{y})^j \mathbf{I}(x, y) \tag{3.22}$$

The moments are well known for applications in image analysis, since they are employed to derive invariants with respect to specific transformations [14]. The invariance is that the shape of an object is invariant to image operations such as image translation, image rotation, and image scaling.

The typical examples of invariance are interest points and corners of images. An interest point of image is the intersection of edges that has a high gradient in orthogonal directions. Corners are computed from image gradients and robust to offsets in illumination, and the structure is invariant to the rotation of visual objects. Relative positions between corners in the scenes should not change. Corners are invariant to scaling, orientation, and distortions. They are robust and scarcely affected in computer vision [19].

Hough transform estimates the direction of lines by fitting the lines to the edge pixels [11]. There are numerous lines passing through that point. If the points could vote for these lines [12], then each possible line passing through the point would receive one vote [7]. In Fig. 3.10, the distance is calculated from the origin to the straight line, and the slope is calculated because the two lines are perpendicular. MATLAB provides the Hough transform algorithm [15].

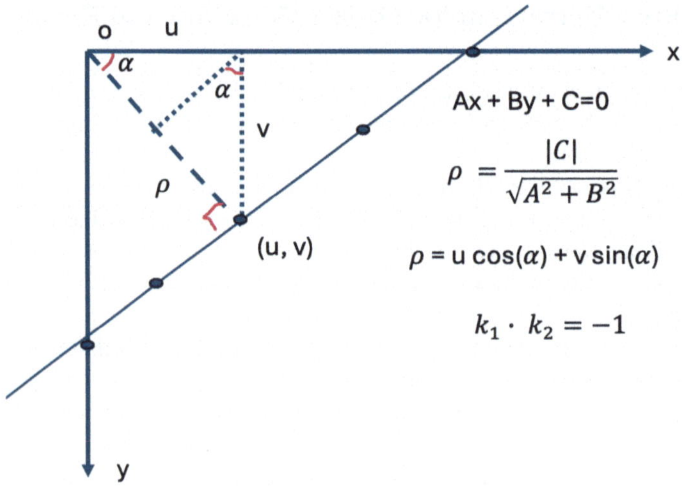

Fig. 3.10 Hough transform

Algorithm 11: Hough transform for line detection

Input: Edge image E
Output: Detected lines in (ρ, θ) space

Initialize an accumulator array $A[\rho, \theta] \leftarrow 0$
for *each edge pixel* (x, y) *in* E **do**
  for θ *from* 0 *to* 180° **do**
    Compute $\rho = x \cdot \cos(\theta) + y \cdot \sin(\theta)$
    Increment $A[\rho, \theta] \leftarrow A[\rho, \theta] + 1$

Find peaks in accumulator array $A[\rho, \theta]$
for *each peak in A above threshold* **do**
  Add corresponding line (ρ, θ) to the result set
return *Set of detected lines*

Figure 3.11 shows the algorithm for line detection by using Hough transform in the platform OpenCV. More generally, the Hough transform algorithm for line detection is depicted in Algorithm 11. Figure 3.13 shows the algorithm for circle detection [7]. The source code in Python for implementing the circle detection by using Hough transform is shown in Fig. 3.12.

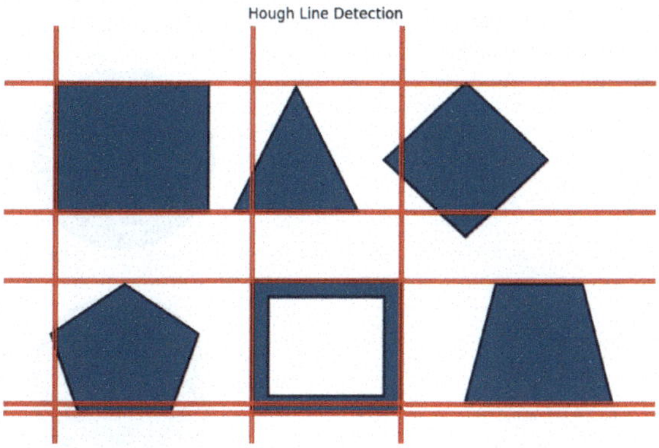

Fig. 3.11 Line detection using Hough transform in OpenCV

```
import cv2
import numpy as np
import matplotlib.pyplot as plt
from google.colab import files

# Step 1: Upload your image
uploaded = files.upload()

# Step 2: Read the uploaded image (you can replace 'your_image.jpg' with the uploaded file name)
image_path = list(uploaded.keys())[0]  # Get the uploaded image file name
image = cv2.imread(image_path)

# Step 3: Convert the image to grayscale
gray = cv2.cvtColor(image, cv2.COLOR_BGR2GRAY)

# Step 4: Apply Gaussian Blur to reduce noise and improve edge detection
blurred = cv2.GaussianBlur(gray, (9, 9), 2)

# Step 5: Use Hough Circle Transform to detect circles
circles = cv2.HoughCircles(
    blurred,                # Input image (blurred grayscale)
    cv2.HOUGH_GRADIENT,     # Detection method
    dp=1.2,                 # Inverse ratio of the accumulator resolution to the image resolution
    minDist=30,             # Minimum distance between detected centers
    param1=100,             # Upper threshold for Canny edge detection
    param2=30,              # Threshold for center detection
    minRadius=15,           # Minimum circle radius
    maxRadius=100           # Maximum circle radius
)
```

Fig. 3.12 The source code in Python for circle detection using Hough transform in OpenCV

3.6 Image Processing with MATLAB

MATLAB image processing is a set of techniques for manipulating and analyzing 2D images and 3D volumes [15]. It is employed in various industries, such as photography, medicine, robotics, and remote sensing. MATLAB Image Processing Toolbox assists us to enhance, filter, denoise, register, and segment images and volumes with cloud computing supports. MATLAB Online is cloud-based software, and it has no such problems as system configurations, script files copying, and datasets moving.

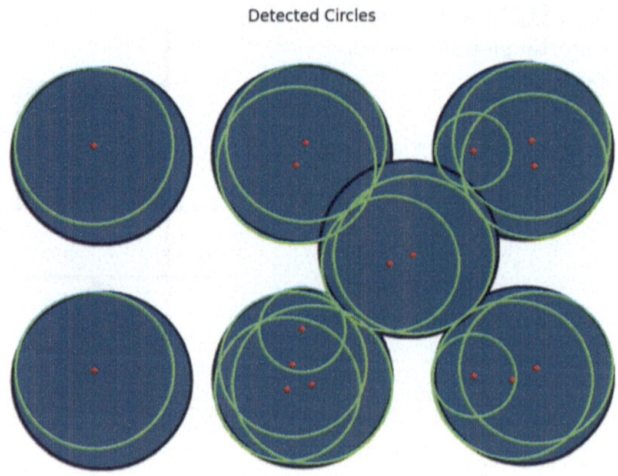

Fig. 3.13 Circle detection using Hough transform in OpenCV

In binary images, image data is stored as logical matrix, and its values 0 and 1 are interpreted as colors black and white, respectively. In indexed images, image data is stored as numeric matrix, and the elements are direct indices in a color map. In grayscale images, image data are stored as a numeric matrix, and its elements specify intensity values. In true color images, image data are stored as numeric array whose elements are from the intensity values of one of the three color channels, i.e., red (R), green (G), and blue (B).

In multispectral images and hyperspectral images [1–6, 26], image data is stored as an $m \times n \times c$ numeric array, where c is the number of color channels. In labeled images, the image data are stored as the numeric matrix of nonnegative integers.

Regarding image dilation in MATLAB, with respect to a binary image, a pixel is set to 1 if any of the neighboring pixels have the value 1. Pertaining to image erosion, in a binary image, a pixel is set to 0 if any of the neighboring pixels have the value 0. In image opening, the opening operation erodes an image and then dilates the eroded image by using the same structuring element for both operations. In image closing, the closing operation dilates an image and then erodes the dilated image by using the same structuring element for both operations.

In MATLAB, camera calibration is the process of estimating camera parameters by using images that contain a calibration pattern. The camera parameters are applied to remove distortion effects from an image, measure planar objects, reconstruct 3D scenes from multiple cameras, etc. The steps for camera calibration in MATLAB include:

- Prepare camera and capture images for camera calibration [29].
- Add image pairs and select camera model.
- Calibrate multiple cameras.
- Evaluate the calibration results.
- Improve the calibration if necessary.
- Export the camera parameters.

3.7 Lab Session: Implmenting Camera Calibration with MATLAB

At the end of this chapter, we would like to recommend all readers complete the lab report. Please fill in the form shown in Table 3.1 after each lab session (2 hours).

An example of this lab report is:

- **Project title**: Assessing and Enhancing Camera Calibration Accuracy
- **Project objectives**: (1) Plot the relative locations of the camera and the calibration pattern. (2) Calculate the re-projection errors. (3) Calculate the parameter estimation errors.
- **Configurations and settings**: (1) Modify calibration settings. (2) Exclude images that have high re-projection errors and recalibrate. (3) Modify calibration settings.
- **Methods**: Camera calibration is the process of estimating parameters of the camera by using the images of a special calibration pattern. The parameters include camera intrinsics, distortion coefficients, and camera extrinsics. Once a camera is calibrated, there are multiple ways to evaluate the accuracy of the estimated parameters: (1) Plot the relative locations of the camera and the calibration pattern. (2) Calculate the re-projection errors. (3) Calculate the parameter estimation errors.

Table 3.1 Lab report for robotic vision

Name	<First Name Last Name >
Email	<firstname.lastname@mailbox >
Lab date	<dd-mm-yy >
Submitted date	<dd-mm-yy >
Project title	Assessing and Enhancing Camera Calibration Accuracy
Lab objectives	The objective is to calculate the re-projection errors and the parameter estimation errors
Configurations and settings	<The preferences, software, hardware, platforms, tools, etc. >
Methods	<The relevant scientific theories or concepts >
Workflow	<The step-by-step procedure for the experiment >
Datasets	<The data and materials for your experiments >
Input	<image filename, size, resolution >
Output	<image filename, size, resolution >
Testing steps	<Functional & non-functional testing methods step by step >
Bugs or problems	<The system error code, lines of the code >
Result analysis	<The tables, graphs, and figures, etc. >
Conclusion/reflection	<The strengths and weaknesses, or learned from this project >
References	https://au.mathworks.com/help/vision/ug/evaluating-the-accuracy-of-single-camera-calibration.html

Appendix: <Source codes with comments and line numbers >

- **Implementation steps**:
  1. Capture calibration images.
  2. Detect calibration pattern.
  3. Generate world coordinates.
  4. Estimate camera parameters.
  5. Evaluate calibration accuracy.
  6. Re-projection errors.
  7. Estimation errors.
  8. Improve calibration.
- **Testing steps**:
  1. Check Extrinsics: looking for logical camera and pattern positions
  2. Analyze Re-projection Errors: ensuring errors; exclude images with high errors
  3. Review Estimation Errors: confirming errors within acceptable limits
- **Result analysis**: We improve calibration accuracy; whether or not a particular re-projection or estimation error is acceptable depends on the precision requirements of particular application. (1) Modify calibration settings. (2) Take more calibration images. (3) Exclude images that have high re-projection errors and recalibrate.
- **Conclusion/reflection**: Accurate camera calibration is vital for reliable measurements; regular evaluation and refinement ensure precision in computer vision tasks.
- **Readings**: https://au.mathworks.com/help/vision/ug/evaluating-the-accuracy-of-single-camera-calibration.html.

3.8 Exercises

Question 3.1 What is the relationship between camera calibration and stereo vision?

Question 3.2 Why do we study image morphology?

Question 3.3 Why robots cannot always gather imperfect images from the real world?

Question 3.4 Why Kalman filtering essentially is a linear algorithm?

Question 3.5 In camera calibration, how many images at least we need to collect?

References

1. Al-Sarayreha M (2020) Hyperspectral imaging and deep learning for food safety. PhD Thesis. Auckland University of Technology, New Zealand
2. Al-Sarayreh M, Reis M, Yan W, Klette R (2017) Detection of adulteration in red meat species using hyperspectral imaging. In: Pacific-rim symposium on image and video technology, pp 182–196
3. Al-Sarayreh M, Reis M, Yan W, Klette R (2018) Detection of red-meat adulteration by deep spectral–spatial features in hyperspectral images. J Imag 4(5):63
4. Al-Sarayreh M, Reis M, Yan W, Klette R (2019) Deep spectral-spatial features of snapshot hyperspectral images for red-meat classification. In: International conference on image and vision computing new Zealand
5. Al-Sarayreh M, Reis M, Yan W, Klette R (2019) A sequential CNN approach for foreign object detection in hyperspectral images. In: International conference on computer analysis of images and patterns, pp 271–283
6. Al-Sarayreha M, Reis M, Yan W, Klette R (2020) Potential of deep learning and snapshot hyperspectral imaging for classification of species in meat. Food Control 117:107332
7. Ballard DH (1981) Generalizing the Hough transform to detect arbitrary shapes. Pattern Recog 13(2):111–122
8. Boomgaard R, van Balen R (1992) Methods for fast morphological image transforms using bitmapped binary images. Graph Models Image Process 54(3):252–258
9. Canny JA (1986) Computational approach to edge detection, IEEE Trans Pattern Analy Mach Intell 8(6):679–698
10. Corke P (2017) Robotics, vision and control, 2nd edn. Springer Nature, Berlin
11. Duda RO, Hart PE (1972) Use of the Hough transformation to detect lines and curves in pictures. Comm ACM 15:11–15
12. Fernandes F, Oliveira M (2008) Real-time line detection through an improved Hough transform voting scheme. Pattern Recogn 41(1):299–314
13. Foley van D (1996) Computer graphics: principles and practice, 2nd edn. Addison-Wesley, Boston
14. Gonzalez R, Woods R (2001) Digital image processing. Prentice Hall, Upper Saddle River
15. Gonzalez R, Woods R, Eddins S (2020) Digital image processing using MATLAB. Gatesmark Publishing, Knoxville
16. Haralick RM, Shapiro L (1992) Computer and robot vision. Addison-Wesley Longman, London
17. Harris C, Stephens M (1988) A combined corner and edge detector. In: Proceedings of the 4th Alvey vision conference, pp 147–151
18. Hu X (2017) Frequency based texture feature descriptors. PhD Thesis, Auckland University of Technology, New Zealand
19. Klette R (2014) Concise computer vision: an introduction into theory and algorithms. Springer-Verlag London, London
20. Lindeberg T (1993) Detecting salient blob-like image structures and their scales with a scale-space primal sketch: a method for focus-of-attention. Int J Comput Vision 11(3):283–318
21. Liu Z, Yan W, Yang B (2018) Image denoising based on a CNN model. In: International conference on control, automation and robotics
22. Murphy R (2019) Introduction to AI robotics, 2nd edn. Bradford Books, Bradford
23. Pan C, Yan W (2018) A learning-based positive feedback in salient object detection. In: International conference on image and vision computing New Zealand.
24. Pan C, Yan W (2020) Object detection based on saturation of visual perception. Multimedia Tools Appl 79(27–28):19925–19944
25. Pan C, Liu J, Yan W, Zhou Y (2021) Salient object detection based on visual perceptual saturation and two-stream hybrid networks. IEEE Trans Image Process 30:4773–4787

26. Reisa M, Beersd R, Al-Sarayreh R, Shortenb R, Yan W, Saeysd W (2018) Chemometrics and hyperspectral imaging applied to assessment of chemical, textural and structural characteristics of meat. Meat Sci 144:100–109
27. Siegwart R, Nourbakhsh I, Scaramuzza D (2004) Introduction to autonomous mobile robots. MIT Press, Cambridge
28. Wang Y, Yan W (2022) Colorising grayscale CT images of human lungs using deep learning methods. Springer Multimedia Tools Appl 81:37805–37819
29. Yan WQ (2019) Introduction to intelligent surveillance: surveillance data capture, transmission, and analytics. Springer, Berlin
30. Yan WQ (2023) Computational methods for deep learning: theory, algorithms, and implementations, 2nd edn. Springer, Berlin
31. Yan W, Kankanhalli M (2002) Detection and removal of lighting & shaking artifacts in home videos. In: ACM international conference on multimedia, pp 107–116
32. Yan W, Kankanhalli M (2003) Colorizing infrared home videos. In: International conference on multimedia and expo, pp 97–100
33. Yan W, Kankanhalli M, Wang J (2005) Analogies-based video editing. Multimedia Syst 11(1):3–18
34. Zhao H, Xu S, Yan W, Xu D (2025) Design and optimization of target detection and 3D localization models for intelligent muskmelon pollination robots. Horticulturae 11(8):905

Chapter 4
Stereo Vision and 3D Reconstruction

Abstract Our living world is 3D naturally, and our human beings use eyes to percept this world, which are equivalent to stereo cameras in cyberspace. In this chapter, three concepts are introduced with the fundamental knowledge: stereo camera, stereo vision, and 3D reconstruction. Finally, the 3D scene is constructed by using sensors to observe this environment. The significance of this chapter is that we reconstruct the 3D scene and take advantage of stereo vision for probing robotic view.

4.1 Stereo Camera and Stereo Vision

In this section, we see how cameras are applied to capture images [31, 32], how 3D space is understood through these images, how our human eyes watch the world, and how the robots sense the environment using visual sensors [4].

Figure 4.1 shows a 3D stereo camera made by Fuji film. The first digital camera was manufactured by Sony Cooperation in 1981. It is called CCD camera, namely charge-coupled device. By using this digital camera, the key function is to convert natural light to pixel signals. That is the reason why CCD cameras can capture the image from our real world. Then, it has been designed and made with color accuracy. A right color is sensed with the CCD chips, and it has no or has less coloring bias or mistakes.

Digital camera lens has not distortion problem. Like our mobile phones, usually our photographs are taken with an aspect ratio, usually 4:3 or 16:9. The aspect ratio is the ratio between the width and the height of a given image [36]. This aspect ratio is closely related to image resolution. Currently, a video resolution is 1,080 lines, which is the standard 1K resolution. With the development of video technology, we have 4K and 8K display technology because the screen size is large enough. A large screen can display images clearly. If the resolution is low, the details of images will be lost. Previously, our TV sets are 18 inches or 24 inches, and up to date, most of them are more than 100 inches.

In color expression, the concept "bit depth" shows how many bits are adopted to store the color values of one pixel. A pixel color usually has 256 options, and the bit

W. Q. Yan, *Robotic Vision*, Advances in Computer Vision and Pattern Recognition,
https://doi.org/10.1007/978-981-95-4360-1_4

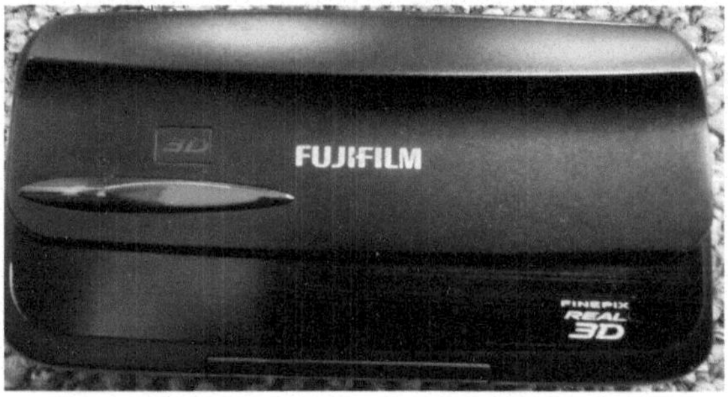

Fig. 4.1 Fuji film stereo camera

depth is 8, i.e., $2^8 = 256$. That means we have 256 colors to be shown on an image concurrently. Thus, the bit depth indicates the display capability of a screen [41].

Dynamic range refers to our cameras which can display various colors in a short time. In one image, the colors may be completely white; in another image, the colors may be completely dark. Thus, no matter how an image is completely white or dark [42], the dynamic range colors can be displayed by using spectrum wave length.

A digital camera may have the functions: pan, tilt, and zoom, and we call the camera as pan–tilt–zoom camera or PTZ camera. Panning means the direction of our camera can point from left to right or from right to left. Naturally, the direction of our camera can scan up or down. In surveillance, the cameras are automatically controlled by using panning and zooming; zooming encapsulates zooming in and zooming out. The functions of cameras are implemented in hardware [40, 41].

Digital cameras can sense the colors ranging from the visible wave length. Our human eyes cannot see infrared rays and ultraviolet (UV) light. The images from the UV and infrared rays can be visualized by using specific algorithms. No matter which digital camera is utilized to take a photograph, the central projection must be followed. If a camera is utilized to take a photograph, the pixel location on the image will have the corresponding point in 3D space. In central projection,

$$x_u = \frac{f \cdot X_s}{Z_s}, \; y_u = \frac{f \cdot Y_s}{Z_s} \tag{4.1}$$

where $(X_s, Y_s, Z_s)^\top \in \mathscr{R}^3$, $X_s, Y_s, Z_s \in \mathscr{R}$, $Z_s \neq 0$, is a visible point in the real world, namely 3D space. $(x_u, y_u)^\top \in \mathscr{R}^2$, $x_u, y_u \in \mathscr{R}$ is the pixel location on the image, correspondingly, and $f \in \mathscr{R}$ is the focal length. $X_s \in \mathscr{R}$ and $Y_s \in \mathscr{R}$ are symmetric, and in central projection, they are the same.

If a camera has two lenses, this camera is called a stereo camera. Usually, there are two images, one is the left image, and the other is the right one as shown in Fig. 4.2. The two images have identical size and parallel optic axes. The two optic axes are pointed in the same direction. The two coplanar images have the identical size, and the two lenses in stereo camera have the parallel optic axes. The angle between the two axes is zero. The two lenses have the identical focal length. The

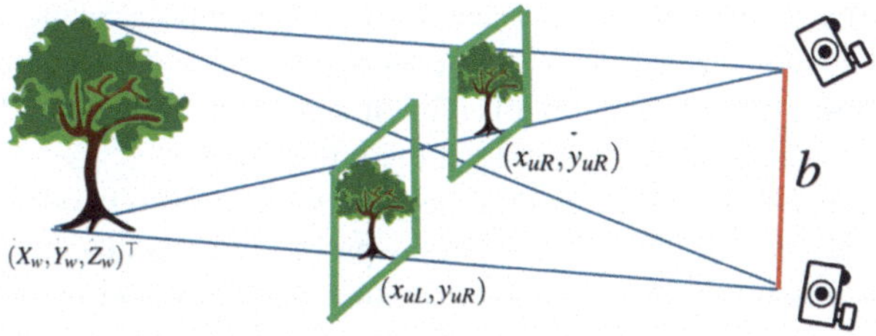

Fig. 4.2 The stereo vision from stereo cameras

two images have the collinear image rows, which means the y coordinate of two corresponding pixels in the two images should be the same.

$$(x_{uL}, y_{uL}) = \left(\frac{f \cdot X_s}{Z_s}, \frac{f \cdot Y_s}{Z_s}\right) \tag{4.2}$$

and

$$(x_{uR}, y_{uR}) = \left[\frac{f \cdot (X_s - b)}{Z_s}, \frac{f \cdot Y_s}{Z_s}\right] \tag{4.3}$$

where $b \in \mathscr{R}$ is the base distance of the stereo system, $(X_s, Y_s, Z_s)^\top$ is a visible point in the world, (x_u, y_u) is the pixel location, (x_{uR}, y_{uR}) for the pixel on the right image and $(x_{uL}, y_{uR})^\top \in \mathscr{R}^2$ for the pixel on the left image, and f is the focal length. In 3D transformation, $(X_w, Y_w, Z_w)^\top \in \mathscr{R}^3$ is the coordinates of a 3D point, and we have

$$(X_s, Y_s, Z_s)^\top = \mathbf{R} \cdot [(X_w, Y_w, Z_w)^\top + \mathbf{T}] \tag{4.4}$$

where $\mathbf{R}$ is the rotation matrix, and $\mathbf{T}$ is the translation vector. A point $(X_w, Y_w, Z_w)^\top$ in the 3D scene is projected onto an image; it is visible at an image point $(x, y)^\top \in \mathscr{R}^2, x, y \in \mathscr{R}$ in xy coordinate system.

$$\begin{pmatrix} x - x_c \\ y - y_c \\ f \end{pmatrix} = \begin{pmatrix} x_u \\ y_u \\ f \end{pmatrix} = f \cdot \begin{pmatrix} X_s/Z_s \\ Y_s/Z_s \\ 1 \end{pmatrix} \tag{4.5}$$

where $(x_c, y_c, 0)^\top \in \mathscr{R}^3, x_c, y_c \in \mathscr{R}$, is the shift to principal point in undistorted image.

Intrinsic (internal) parameters enclose focal length, aspect ratio, radial distortion parameters, scaling factors, coordinates of the principal point, etc. Extrinsic parameters encompass poses of camera [6], such as location and direction. In camera calibration [2, 39, 42], epipolar geometry indicates the two cameras with associated coordinate frames and image planes. It represents the case of two cameras simultaneously by viewing the same scene [40]. In the epipolar plane, a world point is projected onto the image planes of the two cameras at two pixel coordinates, respectively, known as conjugate pixels. Given a point in one image, the conjugate pixels are constrained to lie along a line in the other image.

Stereo vision is employed for estimating 3D structure from two images by using two different viewpoints with approaches: sparse stereo and dense stereo [15]. Sparse stereo is a natural extension about feature matching and recovers the world coordinate for each corresponding point pair. Dense stereo recovers the world coordinate for every pixel in the image. A stereo pair is taken by using two cameras, generally with parallel optical axes, and separated by using a known distance referred to the camera baseline. The camera baseline means that there is a distance between the two cameras.

For the parallel-axis camera geometry, the epipolar lines are parallel and horizontal, and the conjugate pixels have the same vertical coordinate. The displacement along the horizontal epipolar line is called disparity. The disparity is an important concept in stereo vision [37]. The epipolar constraint means that only 1D search is needed for the corresponding point. Our search is limited in x-axis direction with the fixed y. The design of a stereo vision system [37] has three constraints: (1) baseline distance, (2) disparity search range, and (3) template size.

In anaglyphs, human stereo perception of depth works well because each eye views the scene from a unique viewpoint. The key in all 3D display is to take the images from two cameras, with a similar baseline to human eyes and present those images to the corresponding eyes. The advantage of anaglyphs is that the images can be printed on paper or projected onto ordinary movie film, while being viewed with simple and cheap glasses. Stereo cameras are built accurately to ensure that the optical axes of the cameras are parallel.

In robotic vision [10], a robot moves on a plane. A particular feature point lies on the ground or the top of a doorway, such as a vacuum robot. The view is upward [4, 29]. The magnitude of camera translational motion, at each time, is estimated from essential matrix and the ground truth. In a camera coordinate system, the unknown visible point $(X_s, Y_s, Z_s)^\top \in \mathscr{R}^3$ is recovered by using the undistorted image coordinates $(x_{uL}, y_{uL})^\top \in \mathscr{R}^2$, $x_{uL}, y_{uL} \in \mathscr{R}$, and $(x_{uR}, y_{uR})^\top \in \mathscr{R}^2$, $x_{uR}, y_{uR} \in \mathscr{R}$ as input, where $y_{uL} = y_{uR} = y_u \in \mathscr{R}$ and $x_{uR} \leq x_{uL}$, the base line distance is $b > 0$, and $f \in \mathscr{R}$ is the unified focal length. Ultimately, we get the coordinates of a 3D point $(X_s, Y_s, Z_s)^\top$. Because

$$Z_s = \frac{f \cdot X_s}{x_{uL}} = \frac{f \cdot (X_s - b)}{x_{uR}} \tag{4.6}$$

therefore,

$$X_s = \frac{b \cdot x_{uL}}{x_{uL} - x_{uR}}; \tag{4.7}$$

$$Y_s = \frac{b \cdot y_{uL}}{y_{uL} - y_u}; \tag{4.8}$$

$$Z_s = \frac{b \cdot f}{x_{uL} - x_{uR}} \tag{4.9}$$

$$(X_s, Y_s, Z_s)^\top = \left(\frac{b \cdot x_{uL}}{x_{uL} - x_{uR}}, \frac{b \cdot y_u}{x_{uL} - x_{uR}}, \frac{b \cdot f}{x_{uL} - x_{uR}} \right)^\top \tag{4.10}$$

where $d = x_{uL} - x_{uR} \neq 0, d \in \mathscr{R}$ is the disparity, and $b \in \mathscr{R}$ is the base distance. In the camera coordinate system, we recover unknown visible point by using

$$(X_s, Y_s, Z_s)^\top = \left(\frac{b \cdot x_{uL}}{x_{uL} - x_{uR}}, \frac{b \cdot y_u}{x_{uL} - x_{uR}}, \frac{b \cdot f}{x_{uL} - x_{uR}} \right)^\top \tag{4.11}$$

Therefore, if $d = x_{uL} - x_{uR} = 0$, then $(X, Y, Z)^\top$ is an infinity point (∞). Larger b and f support an increase in depth level but reduce the number of pixels that have corresponding pixels in the second image. An increase in image resolution is a way to improve the accuracy of depth levels. Since the XYZ system can be transformed into the $(X_L, Y_L, Z_L)^\top \in \mathscr{R}^3$ and (X_R, Y_R, Z_R) by translating $(X - \frac{b}{2}, Y, Z)^\top$ and $(X + \frac{b}{2}, Y, Z)^\top$,

$$\begin{pmatrix} X_L \\ Y_L \\ Z_L \end{pmatrix} = \begin{bmatrix} \cos(\theta) & 0 & \sin(\theta) \\ 0 & 1 & 0 \\ -\sin(\theta) & 0 & \cos(\theta) \end{bmatrix} \begin{pmatrix} X - \frac{b}{2} \\ Y \\ Z \end{pmatrix} \tag{4.12}$$

and

$$\begin{pmatrix} X_R \\ Y_R \\ Z_R \end{pmatrix} = \begin{bmatrix} \cos(\theta) & 0 & -\sin(\theta) \\ 0 & 1 & 0 \\ \sin(\theta) & 0 & \cos(\theta) \end{bmatrix} \begin{pmatrix} X + \frac{b}{2} \\ Y \\ Z \end{pmatrix} \tag{4.13}$$

Moreover,

$$\begin{aligned} x_{uL} &= \tfrac{f \cdot X_L}{Z_L}, Z_L \neq 0 \\ y_{uL} &= \tfrac{f \cdot Y_L}{Z_L} = y_{uR}, Z_L \neq 0 \\ x_{uR} &= \tfrac{f \cdot X_R}{Z_R}, Z_R \neq 0 \end{aligned} \tag{4.14}$$

Stereo pairs are already geometrically rectified and preprocessed for reducing brightness issues. Corresponding pixels are expected to be in the left and right images at the same image row. Regarding a pixel $(x, y) \in \mathscr{R}^2$ in a base image **B**, we search for a corresponding pixel $(x + d, y), d \in \mathscr{R}$, in the match image **M**, based on the same epipolar line identified by row y. The two pixels are corresponding if they are projections of the same point $(X, Y, Z)^\top$, where $d > 0$ is the disparity. We initiate a search by selecting the point (x, y) in $\mathbf{B}$. This defines the search interval of point $(x + d, y)$ in $\mathbf{M}$ with $\max(x - d, 1) \leq x + d$. With regard to identify corresponding points, a straightforward idea is to compare neighborhoods, namely rectangular windows for simplicity, such as 8×8 or 16×16 around a pixel $\mathbf{p}$ in the image $\mathbf{I}$.

- Global matching (GM): An area is approximated by using time-expensive control structure of a stereo matcher.
- Local matching (LM): An area of influence is bounded by using fixed constant.
- Semi-global matching: We take more pixels into account than the local approach, but not yet as much as a global approach.

The complexity of semi-global matching is between global matching and local matching [38], The third-eye method includes mapping a reference image of a pair of stereo camera into the pose of a third camera, measuring the similarity between created virtual image and the actually recorded third image. The outline of the third-eye method is as follows:

- Record stereo data with two cameras, and calculate disparities.
- Have a third calibrated camera looking into the same space as the other two cameras [13].
- Use the calculated disparities for mapping the recorded image of the left camera into the image plane of the third camera, and create a virtual image.
- Compare the virtual image with the image recorded by using the third camera.
- If the virtual images from the third camera basically coincide, then the stereo matcher provides "useful" disparities [13].

By using the third-eye method, the disparity map and the depth map of the given scene are calculated and shown in Algorithm 12.

Algorithm 12: The third-eye stereo vision algorithm for depth estimation

Input: Rectified images I_L, I_C, I_R (left, center, right), camera calibration parameters
Output: Disparity map D, depth map Z

foreach *pixel* (x, y) *in* I_C **do**
  for *disparity* $d \in [d_{\min}, d_{\max}]$ **do**
    Compute matching cost $C_L \leftarrow \text{cost}(I_C(x, y), I_L(x - d, y))$;
    Compute matching cost $C_R \leftarrow \text{cost}(I_C(x, y), I_R(x + d, y))$;
    Aggregate cost: $C(d) \leftarrow w_L \cdot C_L + w_R \cdot C_R$;
  Find disparity: $d^* \leftarrow \arg\min_d C(d)$;
  Set $D(x, y) \leftarrow d^*$;
Compute depth map: $Z(x, y) \leftarrow \frac{f \cdot B}{D(x,y)}$;
return D, Z;

A point $(X, Y, Z)^\top \in \mathscr{R}^3$ mapped into a pixel $(x, y)^\top \in \mathscr{R}^2$ in the left image corresponds to a point $(x_T, y_T)^\top \in \mathscr{R}^2$, $x_T, y_T \in \mathscr{R}$ in the third image, and (x_T, y_T) is expressed in terms of (x, y) by using the calibrated translation $(t_X, t_Y, t_Z)^\top \in \mathscr{R}^3$, $t_X, t_Y, t_Z \in \mathscr{R}$ [11]. The base distance $b \in \mathscr{R}$, the focal length $f_T \in \mathscr{R}$, and the disparity $d > 0$ are provided by using the given stereo matcher:

$$(X_T, Y_T, Z_T)^\top = (X - t_X, Y - t_Y, Z - t_Z)^\top \tag{4.15}$$

and

$$(x_T, y_T) = f_T \cdot \left(\frac{X_T}{Z_T}, \frac{Y_T}{Z_T}\right), Z_T \neq 0 \tag{4.16}$$

Therefore,

$$(x_T, y_T) = f_T \cdot \left(\frac{X - t_X}{Z - t_Z}, \frac{Y - t_Y}{Z - t_Z}\right), Z \neq t_Z \tag{4.17}$$

If $X = \frac{b \cdot x}{d}$, $Y = \frac{b \cdot y}{d}$, $Z = f \cdot \frac{b}{d}$, $d \neq 0$, then

$$x_T = f_T \cdot \frac{b \cdot x - d \cdot t_X}{f \cdot b - d \cdot t_Z} \tag{4.18}$$

and

$$y_T = f_T \cdot \frac{b \cdot y - d \cdot t_Y}{f \cdot b - d \cdot t_Z} \tag{4.19}$$

where $f \cdot b - d \cdot t_Z \neq 0$.

Let $\Omega_t \in \mathscr{R}$ be the set of pixels that are employed for the comparison with regard to video frames at time $t \in \mathscr{R}$. The means are μ_V and μ_T, respectively, and the standard variations are σ_V and σ_T for the virtual $V(p)$ and the third image $T(p)$ at time t, respectively. Hence, the Normalized Cross-Correlation (NCC) is calculated as shown in Eq. (4.20). The NCC is employed to compare the performance of stereo matches based on long sequences.

$$M_{NCC}(V, T) = \frac{1}{|\Omega_t|} \sum_{p \in \Omega_t} \frac{[T(p) - \mu_T][V(p) - \mu_V]}{\sigma_T \sigma_V} \tag{4.20}$$

4.2 3D Reconstruction

The surface S is known as border of the existing 3D object in the real world; we usually have two kinds of gap-free smooth surfaces: (1) Continuous derivatives exist

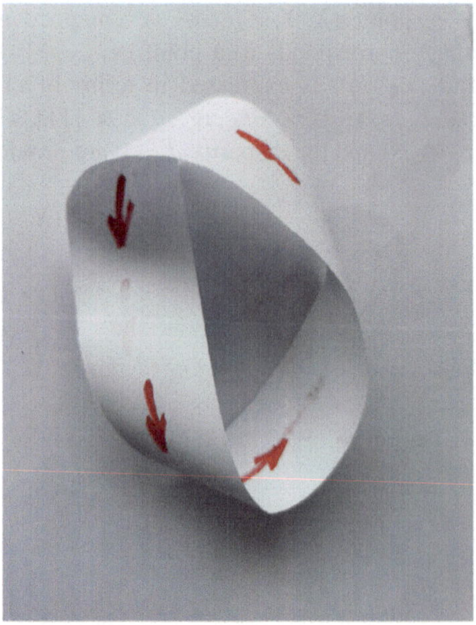

Fig. 4.3 The smooth surface: Möbius strip

and (2) the existence of a neighborhood in S. The typical one is the Möbius strip as shown in Fig. 4.3, and the derivatives exist everywhere.

Gap-free polyhedral surfaces have two groups: (1) discontinuities at edges and (2) the existence of a neighborhood in S. The typical one is the tetrahedron. The explicit representation of function $F(\cdot)$ is $Z = F(X, Y),\ X, Y, Z \in \mathscr{R}$. The equation of a straight line is $y = ax + b,\ a, b \in \mathscr{R}$. The implicit representation is $F(X, Y, Z) = 0$, for the straight line, and the equation is $Ax + By + C = 0$, $A, B, C \in \mathscr{R}$. The gradient of a surface $Z = F(X, Y)$ is the vector given by

$$\nabla Z = \mathbf{grad}(Z) = \left(\frac{\partial Z}{\partial X}, \frac{\partial Z}{\partial Y} \right) \tag{4.21}$$

In the case of plane $aX + bY + Z = c$,

$$\mathbf{n} = \left(\frac{\partial Z}{\partial X}, \frac{\partial Z}{\partial Y}, 1 \right)^\top = (a, b, 1)^\top \tag{4.22}$$

The normalized vector is

$$\mathbf{n}^\circ = (n_1, n_2, n_3)^\top = \frac{\mathbf{n}}{\|\mathbf{n}\|_2} = \frac{(a, b, 1)^\top}{\sqrt{a^2 + b^2 + 1}} \tag{4.23}$$

Fig. 4.4 A sphere rendered by using Lambert cosine law in Python

Let $\mathbf{P} = (a, b, 1)^\top$ be the surface normal vector of a visible and illuminated surface at point P

$$\cos\alpha = \frac{\mathbf{s}^\top \mathbf{n_p}}{\|\mathbf{s}^\top\|_2 \|\mathbf{n_p}\|_2} \tag{4.24}$$

On one surface [7], there are numerous norm vectors. The emitted light at the point $\mathbf{P}$ is scaled by

$$\eta(\mathbf{P}) = \rho(\mathbf{P}) \cdot \frac{E_l}{\pi} \tag{4.25}$$

where $E_L \in \mathscr{R}$ was defined as a light source energy, which is reflected at $\mathbf{P}$ uniformly into all directions of a hemisphere.

$$R(\mathbf{P}) = \eta(\mathbf{P}) \frac{\mathbf{s}^\top \mathbf{n_p}}{\|\mathbf{s}^\top\|_2 \|\mathbf{n_p}\|_2} \tag{4.26}$$

where $R(\mathbf{P}) \geq 0$ is the reflectance function.

Lambert's cosine law is employed to render a geometric model as shown in Fig. 4.4. In this law, only norms are considered in this model [8]. There are two kinds of surfaces, i.e., mirror surface and rough surface. These surfaces are related to surface materials. The source code in Python for generating Fig. 4.4 is shown in Fig. 4.5. The corresponding pseudocode is shown in Algorithm 13.

For an example, if the light color is $\mathbf{C} = (255, 255, 255)$, computing with Lambert's cosine law, $\alpha = \frac{\pi}{3}$, the reflectance $\mathbf{C}_R = \mathbf{C} \cdot \cos(\frac{\pi}{3})$ is obtained. The light intensity is $\mathbf{C}_R = (127.5, 127.5, 127.5)$ if $\eta(\mathbf{P}) = 1.0$.

```python
import numpy as np
import matplotlib.pyplot as plt

# Define the sphere's parameters
radius = 1.0  # Sphere radius
light_dir = np.array([0, 0, 1])  # Direction of the light (from z-axis)
light_dir = light_dir / np.linalg.norm(light_dir)  # Normalize the light direction

# Create a grid of points representing the sphere's surface
theta = np.linspace(0, np.pi, 100)  # Polar angle
phi = np.linspace(0, 2 * np.pi, 100)  # Azimuthal angle
theta, phi = np.meshgrid(theta, phi)

# Convert spherical coordinates to Cartesian coordinates
x = radius * np.sin(theta) * np.cos(phi)
y = radius * np.sin(theta) * np.sin(phi)
z = radius * np.cos(theta)

# Calculate normals at each point on the sphere's surface
normals = np.stack((x, y, z), axis=-1)
normals = normals / np.linalg.norm(normals, axis=-1, keepdims=True)

# Apply Lambert's Cosine Law: intensity = max(0, normal · light_dir)
intensity = np.maximum(0, np.sum(normals * light_dir, axis=-1))

# Plot the sphere with intensity values as colors
fig = plt.figure(figsize=(8, 8))
ax = fig.add_subplot(111, projection='3d')
ax.plot_surface(x, y, z, facecolors=plt.cm.viridis(intensity), rstride=1, cstride=1, linewidth=0, antialiased=False)

# Adjust plot appearance
ax.set_box_aspect([1, 1, 1])  # Equal aspect ratio
ax.set_axis_off()  # Turn off axis lines
plt.show()
```

Fig. 4.5 The source code of Lambert cosine law in Python

Algorithm 13: Lambertian reflectance for diffuse shading

Input: Surface normal vector $\vec{N}$, light direction vector $\vec{L}$, light intensity I, diffuse color C_d

Output: Diffuse shading color C

Normalize the surface normal: $\vec{N} \leftarrow \frac{\vec{N}}{\|\vec{N}\|}$;

Normalize the light direction: $\vec{L} \leftarrow \frac{\vec{L}}{\|\vec{L}\|}$;

Compute dot product: $D \leftarrow \vec{N} \cdot \vec{L}$;

Clamp to non-negative: $D \leftarrow \max(0, D)$;

Compute final color: $C \leftarrow I \cdot C_d \cdot D$;

return C;

4.3 Applications of Stereo Vision

Stereo vision plays a crucial role in robotic navigation[16], robotic planning, and scene understanding, offering depth perception and 3D spatial awareness [46]. The applications in these fields are listed as below.

4.3.1 Applications of Robot Navigation

Stereo vision [30, 31] provides depth information that helps robots deeply understand the environment, make plans, design routines, and navigate effectively. The key applications include:

In obstacle avoidance, robots can detect obstacles and estimate their distance, allowing for real-time path planning in cluttered environment [28]. If a map has been generated, the obstacle avoidance is assumed to be relatively easy. By using localization and mapping (SLAM), stereo cameras contribute to 3D map generation and aid autonomous navigation. In outdoor environments, based on scene understanding, for example, stereo vision assists us to estimate road surface for safe travel.

In stereo vision [31–34], the problem is human-robot interaction, it needs to detect humans actions and their movements, and it enables the interaction in shared spaces. The principle of human-robot interaction (HRI) revolves the designing issues that can effectively and safely collaborate with humans.

4.3.2 Applications in Deep Scene Understanding

The interfaces of ChatGPT (OpenAI) and Gemini (Google) have extremely attracted our eyeballs. In the latest design, how to make use of chatbot software to control robots is an interesting research direction. In scene understanding, the stereo vision will set a knowledge base, and it conveys robots what the environment is and how can set up such a conversion environment by using chatbots such as Gemini or ChatGPT. The corresponding Chain-of-Thought (CoT) is established. The outputs of chatbots could be filtered and utilized to control agents. Furthermore, the unknown world will be explored and understood by using conversations. Figure 4.6 shows the interface of Google Gemini. From Google image search, we obtain the results as shown in Fig. 4.7. This example shows chatbots have the ability to explore much broader content based on visual information, while search engines could not completely understand the assigned tasks.

Chatbots are distinctive from soft robots [5, 35, 43]. Soft robotics, inspired by biology [12], concerns the design, control, and fabrication of robots composed of compliant materials [14]. The goal of soft robotics is the design and construction of robots with physically flexible bodies and electronics. All soft robots facilitate an actuation system to generate reaction forces, and it is admitted for movement and interaction with its environment. Soft robots are much safer for human and robot interaction and for internal deployment inside a human body [1, 3] for medical applications [44, 45].

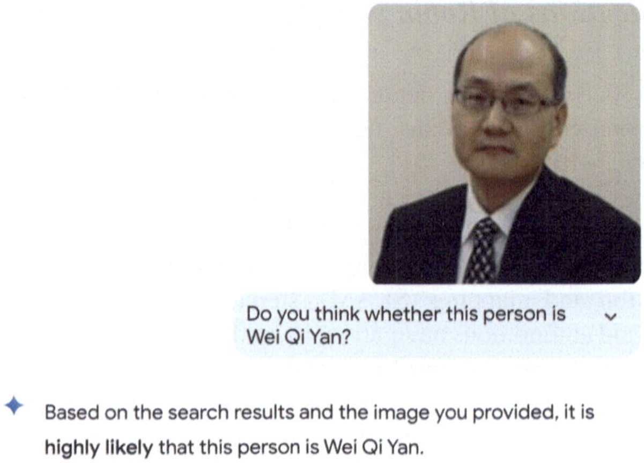

Fig. 4.6 The interface of chatbot: Google Gemini

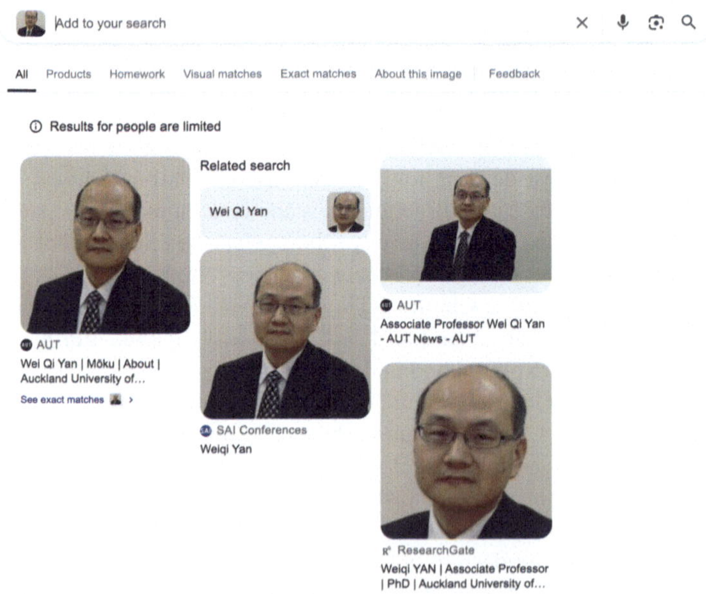

Fig. 4.7 The interface of Google image search

Fig. 4.8 The scene of 3D vehicles with depth

4.3.3 Applications in Visual Object Recognition

Stereo vision enhances visual object recognition by providing 3D shape and depth information [9], improving accuracy over 2D image processing from all aspects or multiple views. The basic applications should include 3D object detection and recognition [17–20]. The depth assists us to differentiate objects from the background and classify them more reliably [21–23]. An example of 3D vehicle scene [24–27] is shown in Fig. 4.8.

Another application is robotic path planning, grasping, and manipulation [28]. Robots make use of stereo vision to estimate visual distance, position, and shape for accurate pick-and-place tasks. In autonomous vehicles, stereo vision is applied to detect pedestrians, vehicles, and road obstacles outside of the moving robots.

In augmented reality and robotics [31–34], stereo vision transfers human experience and spatial understanding to interactive AR/VR applications in real time with the unknown world. By merging with 3D animations having the same view angle, robotic vision will combine the real world and virtual one together.

4.4 Lab Session: Implementing Stereo Vision Systems with MATLAB

At the end of this chapter, we would like to recommend all readers complete the lab report. Please fill in the form shown in Table 4.1 after each lab session (2 hours). An example of this lab report is:

- **Project title**: Depth Estimation from Stereo Video
- **Project objectives**: The objective is to detect people and the distance to the camera from a video taken with a calibrated stereo camera.
- **Configurations and settings**: MATLAB Online
- **Methods**: Use of disparity map to determine 3D core coordinates corresponding to each pixel.
- **Implementation steps**:

  1. Stereo Camera Setup: Calibrate the camera pair.
  2. Rectify Video Frames: Correct video frames for parallel alignment.
  3. Compute Disparity Map: Calculate pixel disparities.

Table 4.1 Lab report for robotic vision

Name	<First Name Last Name >
Email	<firstname.lastname@mailbox >
Lab date	<dd-mm-yy >
Submitted date	<dd-mm-yy >
Project title	Depth Estimation from Stereo Video
Lab objectives	The objective is to detect people and the distance to the camera from a video with a calibrated stereo camera
Configurations and settings	<The preferences, software, hardware, platforms, tools, etc. >
Methods	<The relevant scientific theories or concepts >
Workflow	<The step-by-step procedure for the experiment >
Datasets	<The data and materials for your experiments >
Input	<image filename, size, resolution >
Output	<image filename, size, resolution >
Testing steps	<Functional & non-functional testing methods step by step >
Bugs or problems	<The system error code, lines of the code >
Result analysis	<The tables, graphs, and figures, etc. >
Conclusion/reflection	<The strengths and weaknesses, or learned from this project >
References	https://au.mathworks.com/help/vision/ug/evaluating-the-accuracy-of-single-camera-calibration.html

Appendix: <Source codes with comments and line numbers >

4. 3D Reconstruction: Reconstruct the scene in 3D.
5. Object Detection and Recognition: Identify objects and measure distances.

- **Testing steps**:

1. Load the parameters of the stereo camera.
2. Create video file readers and the video player.
3. Read and rectify video frames.
4. Compute disparity.
5. Reconstruct the 3D scene.
6. Detect people in the left image.
7. Determine the distance of each person to the camera.
8. Process the rest of the video.

- **Result analysis**: (1) Accuracy: The system accurately estimates depth based on the quality of the disparity map. (2) 3D Reconstruction: The 3D scene reconstruction closely matches the real scene. (3) Object Detection and Recognition: The system reliably detects objects and measures distances. (4) Performance: The system's robustness varies under various conditions (lighting, camera angles, and textures).

- **Conclusion/reflection**: The project demonstrates effective depth estimation, though performance may vary based on environmental factors.
- **Readings**:
https://au.mathworks.com/help/vision/ug/depth-estimation-from-stereo-video.html

4.5 Exercises

Question 4.1 How to accelerate stereo matching?

Question 4.2 What are the differences by using LiDAR and computer vision for 3D reconstruction?

Question 4.3 What is image disparity? How to calculate the disparity?

Question 4.4 In Lambert cosine model, how can we make the algorithm more perfect?

Question 4.5 What are the relationships between computer graphics and computer vision?

Question 4.6 How to verify the depth available from the 3D reconstruction in stereo Vision?

References

1. Abidi H, Cianchetti M (2017) On intrinsic safety of soft robots. Frontiers in Robotics and AI. 4.
2. Chen Z, Si X, Wu D, Tian F, Zheng Z, Li R (2024) A novel camera calibration method based on known rotations and translations. Comput Vision Image Understand 243:103996
3. Cianchetti M, Ranzani T, Gerboni G et al (2014) Soft robotics technologies to address shortcomings in today's minimally invasive surgery: the STIFF-FLOP approach. Soft Rob. 1(2):122–131
4. Corke P (2017) Robotics, vision and control, 2nd edn. Springer Nature, Berlin
5. Crawford M (2019) Soft robots are essential for future space exploration. American Society of Mechanical Engineers (ASME), New York City
6. Ding W, Tan W, Liu G, Zhang H, Wang W (2024) Adaptive adjustment of brightness and blur of the camera for high precision internal parameter calibration. Measurement 231:114637
7. Foley van D (1996) Computer graphics: principles and practice, 2nd edn. Addison-Wesley, Boston
8. Gonzalez R, Woods R, Eddins S (2020) Digital image processing using MATLAB. Gatesmark Publishing, Knoxville
9. Gu Q, Yang J, Kong L, Yan W, Klette R (2017) Embedded and real-time vehicle detection system for challenging on-road scenes. Opt Eng 56(6):063102
10. Haralick RM, Shapiro L (1992) Computer and robot vision. Addison-Wesley Longman Publishing, London

11. Huang W, Miao H, Jiao S, Miao W, Xiao C, Wang Y (2024) A planar constraint optimization method to improve camera calibration for imperfect planar targets. Opt Lasers Eng 180:108273
12. Kim S, Laschi C, Trimmer B (2013) Soft robotics: a bio-inspired evolution in robotics. Trends Biotechnol 31(5):287–294
13. Klette R (2014) Concise computer vision: an introduction into theory and algorithms. Springer-Verlag London, London
14. Laschi C, Calisti M (2021) Soft robot reaches the deepest part of the ocean. Nature 591(7848):35–36
15. Lazaros N, Sirakoulis G, Gasteratos A (2008) Review of stereo vision algorithms: From software to hardware. Int J Optomechatr 2(4):435–462
16. Le R (2022) Synthetic data annotation for enhancing the experiences of augmented reality application based on machine learning, PhD Thesis. Auckland University of Technology, New Zealand
17. Liu X (2019) Vehicle-related scene understanding using deep learning. Master's Thesis, Auckland University of Technology, New Zealand
18. Liu X, Nguyen M, Yan W (2019) Vehicle-related scene understanding using deep learning. In: Asian conference on pattern recognition workshop, pp 61–73
19. Liu X, Yan W, Kasabov N (2020) Vehicle-related scene segmentation using CapsNets. In: International conference on image and vision computing New Zealand, pp 1–6
20. Liu X, Yan W (2022) Depth estimation of traffic scenes from image sequence using deep learning. In: Pacific-rim symposium on image and video technology, pp 186–196
21. Liu X, Yan W (2022) Vehicle-related distance estimation using customized YOLOv7. In: International conference on image and vision computing New Zealand (IVCNZ), pp 91–103
22. Liu X, Yan W, Kasabov N (2023) Moving vehicle tracking and scene understanding: a hybrid approach. Multimedia Tools Appl 83:51541–51558
23. Liu X, Yan W (2024) Vehicle detection and distance estimation using improved YOLOv7 model. In: Deep learning, reinforcement learning and the rise of intelligent systems. IGI Global, Hershey, pp 173–187
24. Mehtab S (2022) Deep neural networks for road scene perception in autonomous vehicles using LiDARs and vision sensors. PhD Thesis, Auckland University of Technology, New Zealand
25. Mehtab S, Yan W (2021) FlexiNet: fast and accurate vehicle detection for autonomous vehicles-2D vehicle detection using deep neural network. In: International conference on control and computer vision, pp 43–49
26. Mehtab S, Yan W (2022) Flexible neural network for fast and accurate road scene perception. Multimedia Tools Appl 81:7169–7181
27. Mehtab S, Yan W, Narayanan A (2022) 3D vehicle detection using cheap LiDAR and camera sensors. In: International conference on image and vision computing New Zealand
28. Ming Y, Li Y, Zhang Z, Yan W (2021) A survey of path planning algorithms for autonomous vehicles. In: International journal of commercial vehicles
29. Murphy R (2019) Introduction to AI robotics, 2nd edn. Bradford Books, Bradford
30. Nguyen M, Yan W, Gong R, Delmas P (2015) Toward a real-time belief propagation stereo reconstruction for computers, robots, and beyond. In: International conference on image and vision computing New Zealand (IVCNZ)
31. Nguyen M, Le R, Yan W (2017) A personalized stereoscopic 3D gallery with virtual reality technology on smartphone. In: International conference on image and vision computing New Zealand (IVCNZ)
32. Nguyen M, Le H, Yan W, Dawda A (2018) A vision aid for the visually impaired using commodity dual-rear-camera smartphones. In: International conference on mechatronics and machine vision
33. Nguyen M, Lai P, Le R, Yan W (2019) A web-based augmented reality platform using pictorial QR code for educational purposes and beyond. In: ACM symposium on virtual reality software and technology
34. Nguyen M, Le R, Yan W (2020) Red-green-blue augmented reality tags for retail stores. In: International conference on advanced concepts for intelligent vision systems

35. Rus D, Tolley M (2015) Design, fabrication and control of soft robots. Nature 521(7553):467–475
36. Siegwart R, Nourbakhsh I, Scaramuzza D (2004) Introduction to autonomous mobile robots. MIT Press, Cambridge
37. Steinman S, Steinman B, Garzia R (2000) Foundations of binocular vision: a clinical perspective. McGraw-Hill Medical, Columbus
38. Tychola KA, Tsimperidis I, Papakostas GA (2022) On 3D reconstruction using RGB-D cameras. Digital 2(3):401–421
39. Wang J, Wan Y (2018) A new camera calibration method based on two vertical lines. In: International conference on communications, circuits and systems (ICCCAS), pp 399–402
40. Yan WQ (2019) Introduction to intelligent surveillance: surveillance data capture, transmission, and analytics, 3rd edn. Springer, Berlin
41. Yan WQ (2023) Computational methods for deep learning: theory, algorithms, and implementations, 2nd edn. Springer, Berlin
42. Yan W, Kankanhalli M (2002) Detection and removal of lighting & shaking artifacts in home videos. In: ACM international conference on multimedia, pp 107–116
43. Yasa O, Toshimitsu Y, Michelis M, Jones L, Filippi M, Buchner T, Katzschmann R (2023) An overview of soft robotics. Ann Rev Control Rob Auton Syst 6(1):1–29
44. Younas F, Usman M, Yan W (2022) A deep neural network ensemble framework for colorectal polyp classification. Multimedia Tools Appl 82:18925–18946
45. Younas F, Usman A, Yan W (2022) A deep ensemble learning method for colorectal polyp classification with optimized network parameters. Appl Intell 53:2410–2433
46. Zhao H, Xu S, Yan W, Xu D (2025) Design and optimization of target detection and 3D localization models for intelligent muskmelon pollination robots. Horticulturae 11(8):905

Chapter 5
Deep Learning for Robotic Vision

Abstract Deep learning is related to a series of the state-of-the-art methods in contemporary artificial intelligence. In this chapter, our deep learning methods mainly include CNN and RNN models. In CNN models, YOLO models are especially emphasized, while in RNN models, we stress on transformer models for time series analysis along with LSTM. The transformer models are still large, active, and effective in our research projects, especially the diffusion transformer models for generative AI (GenAI). In this chapter, our focus is on vision transformer (ViT) for robotic scene understanding. The significance of this chapter is that the state-of-the-art knowledge in deep learning is mingled with the knowledge of robotic vision for developing autonomous systems.

5.1 Overview of Deep Learning Architectures for Vision

Deep learning offers a new way for exploring robotic vision by using the state-of-the-art (SOTA) models such as YOLO series and transformer models [61]. The robotic vision is not limited to object detection and recognition and object tracking. The moving cameras mounted on mobile robots are able to freely select viewpoints and sense much broader world. Hence, robots are able to understand holistic scenes naturally. The latest developed chatbots such as ChatGPT (OpenAI), DeepSeek (DeepSeek), Gemini (Google), Copilot (Microsoft), Qwen (Alibaba), etc. are beyond the limitations. They inspire deep scene understanding based on visual data.

Therefore, YOLO models and transformer models only accommodate visual information and knowledge for chatbots. We thus fuse visual information and knowledge for deep scene understanding. The cameras on tripods only capture a limited scene from one view. Hence, we need to move tripods and cameras back and forth for capturing holistic view. Thus, the cameras on mobile robots overcome these shortcomings, and they are able to deeply understand much wider field of view (FoV).

The chain of thought (CoT) is a method that allows large language models (LLMs) to resolve a complicated problem as a series of intermediate steps before

W. Q. Yan, *Robotic Vision*, Advances in Computer Vision and Pattern Recognition,
https://doi.org/10.1007/978-981-95-4360-1_5

offering the final answer [49]. The CoT method improves reasoning ability by inducing the model to answer a multistep question with a series of steps of reasoning. Tree of thoughts (ToT) generalizes the CoT to generate one or more "possible next steps" and executes the model on each of the possible steps by using breadth-first search [53] or other methods of tree search.

Dify (https://docs.dify.ai/) is an open-source platform for docking AI applications to streamline the development of generative AI solutions. Dify can create innovative AI applications that solve CoT problems. ComfyUI (www.comfy.org) is an open-source and node-based program to generate images from a series of text prompts. It makes use of free diffusion models [13] as the base with each tool being represented by using a node. Each node has a function. The function can be applied to calculate the confidence score of LLM outputs, hence controlling the ethics problems. ComfyUI supports multiple text-to-image models.

Ollama, short for Omni-Layer Learning Language Acquisition Model, is a cutting-edge platform designed to simplify the process of running large language models (LLMs) on local machines. The transcripts generated from deep learning and computer vision models, such as YOLO models and transformer models, will be added into the Ollama for conversation. In the initialization stage, a group of designated prompts will assist the system to avoid any problems related to ethics.

The LLM interface, like OpenAI ChatGPT, Google Gemini, and Microsoft Copilot, escapes the simple phrase matching, and it also avoids the difficulties of Google search without proper keywords. The chatbot systems, like Qwen and DeepSeek, accommodate a solution for answering questions and reasoning the information from deep scene understanding from knowledge base.

Retrieval-Augmented Generation (RAG) is a method that allows large language models (LLMs) to retrieve and incorporate additional information before generating responses [27], and it minimizes the hallucination problem. RAG allows LLMs for information indexing, information retrieval, information augmentation, and new information generation. RAG can be simply deployed and integrated with open-source models such as DeepSeek and Ollama on web pages. Furthermore, RAG can lower the computational costs for running LLM-powered chatbots.

5.2 Convolutional Neural Networks (CNNs) and YOLO Models

5.2.1 CNN Models

OpenAI ChatGPT was developed based on transformer models. GPT means generative pretrained transformer. "T" refers to transformer. In this chapter, we emphasize on Vision Transformer (ViT) and Diffusion Transformer (DiT) [20].

Deep learning is a type of machine learning approaches in which a deep learning model is trained to perform pattern classification from the end-to-end point of view. In deep truth, deep learning is a probability-based classification method, and its performance has surpassed our human's ability [41]. Deep learning is usually implemented by using neural network architecture. Previous artificial neural networks are neurons-based, which were fully connected networks; now the neural networks are layer-based. The multiple layer networks are called deep neural networks or deep nets. The term "deep" refers to the number of layers in the layered neural networks, while the simple neural networks with few number of layers are called "shallow" nets.

Conventional neural networks or ConvNets contain only a few layers; now deep learning or deep nets can have more and many. The state-of-the-art (SOTA) methods are to access massive sets of labeled data [3]. Because there are sufficient labeled datasets, deep learning algorithms are easy to implement. Another reason is the increased computing power (e.g., GPU, FPGA, etc.). GPU is a hardware unit for graphics processing, e.g., NVIDIA GPUs. In matrix multiplications and vector computations, GPUs accelerate the computations by operating on the corresponding elements simultaneously. Parallel computing accelerates arithmetic operations in infrastructure. A famous demo is that the picture Mona Lisa was displayed on a big screen within 1 second by using GPU computing. Pretrained models were created by experts. Transfer learning [34] transfers parameters from one model to another [32]. With more data samples to be added, the deep learning models will be better regarding precision and recall in pattern classifications.

In deep learning, the end-to-end methods have been adopted. The feature map from convolution and pooling operations with hierarchical structure has been utilized. Softmax function has been deployed to the final stage of the classification. The classification is based on probabilities; the one with the highest probability is selected as the output of this net.

$$\sigma(\mathbf{z})_i = \frac{e^{z_i}}{\sum_{j=1}^{K} e^{z_j}} \tag{5.1}$$

where $\sigma \in [0, 1]^K$ is the softmax function, $\mathbf{z} = (z_1, z_2, \cdots, z_K)^\top \in \mathscr{R}^K$ is the input vector, e^{z_i} is the standard exponential function for input vector, and $K \in \mathscr{N}$ is the number of classes in multiclass classifier.

Convolution operations and pooling operations are employed to extract features in deep learning [21, 25]. We have the terms related to deep learning [22, 24]:

- *Convolution* puts the input through a set of convolutional filters [21].
- *Pooling* simplifies the output through nonlinear downsampling to reduce the number of parameters that the network needs to be trained.
- *ReLU* (Rectified Linear Unit) is associated with fast and effective training by mapping negative values to zero and maintaining positive ones.

A fully connected layer (FC) outputs a vector of k dimensions where k is the number of classes that the deep net is able to predict. The vector contains the probabilities for each class of any images being classified. The final layer of CNN architecture makes use of a softmax function to generate the classification output. ConvNets are inspired from the biological structure of a visual cortex or human vision system, and it contains arrangements of simple and complex neurons. In order to simulate a neuron, there is an activation function between input and output of each neuron. The input and output of the neuron may be a scalar or a vector. The transfer function is the composition of activation functions by using the output of the last layer as the input of the next layer in deep nets.

Deep learning work was awarded Nobel Prize in Physics. Professor Geoffrey Hinton received the ACM Turing Award 2018 in 2019 and Novel Prize in Physics in 2024. This work simulated the mechanism of human visual system. A light ray travels and passes through our iris and left the impression on our retina. These cells are stimulated based on the subregions of a visual field, i.e., **receptive field**. Receptive field is a region of the original image corresponding to a pixel on the feature map. Our left eye is linked to right half brain; meanwhile, our right eye is connected to the left half brain.

Feature map is the output of convolution operations in hierarchical structure [21]. A ConvNet reduces a number of parameters with the number of connections and shared weights. A ConvNet consists of multiple layers, such as convolutional layers, max pooling layers or average pooling layers, and fully connected layers [21].

The input layer defines the size of inputs of a convolutional neural network and contains raw values of the input. Among all deep learning models, we have visible layer (input layer or output layer), invisible layers, or latent layers. A convolutional layer consists of neurons that connect to subregions of the inputs or the outputs of the layer; it extracts the features localized by these regions. A set of weights is related to a filter or a kernel, and the filter moves along the input image vertically and horizontally and repeats the same computation. Batch normalization normalizes the activation and gradients propagating through a neural network, and it makes network training as an easier optimization problem [11, 28]. Basically, it refers to normalization of output between 0 and 1 [23]. In the context of artificial neural networks [16, 30], a ReLU function is a typical activation function [11]. The ReLU function performs a threshold operation to each element.

$$y = \max(x, 0) = \begin{cases} x & x > 0, \\ 0 & x \leq 0 \end{cases} \tag{5.2}$$

where $x, y \in \mathscr{R}$, x is the input to a neuron, and y is the output.

Leaky ReLUs have a small and positive gradient [28] when the unit is not active. A leaky ReLU layer multiplies input values, and it allows negative inputs to “leak” into the output.

$$y = \max(\alpha \cdot x, 0) = \alpha \cdot \max(x, 0) = \begin{cases} x & x > 0, \\ \alpha \cdot x & x \leq 0 \end{cases} \tag{5.3}$$

where $x, y, \alpha \in \mathscr{R}$, $0 \leq \alpha$, is a constant.

Pooling operations are grouped in two categories: max pooling and average pooling. The max pooling layer returns the maximum pixel intensity of the given rectangular regions. The average pooling layer outputs the average pixel intensity of the given rectangular regions. All neurons in a fully connected layer connect to all the neurons in the previous layer [37]. This layer combines all of the features extracted by the previous layers across the image to identify the larger patterns.

The softmax function after normalization, i.e., normalized exponential function, is the output function. A regression output layer must follow the fully connected layer. The default loss function for a regression layer is Mean Squared Error (MSE). A full pass through the whole dataset is called *epoch*. The iteration in deep learning is the number of batches needed to complete one epoch. What a larger *learning rate* is gradually reduced during the optimization time enables smaller steps toward the optimum value [38]. The decay function is

$$\mathbf{w}_{i+1} = \mathbf{w}_i + \eta \cdot \frac{\partial f(\mathbf{w}, \mathbf{x})}{\partial \mathbf{w}} \tag{5.4}$$

where $\mathbf{w}_i \in \mathscr{R}^n$ is the weight at step $i \in \mathscr{Z}^+$, $\eta \in \mathscr{R}$ is the learning rate of this decay function, and $f(\cdot)$ is the cost function or loss function [40].

Performing *validation* check at regular intervals during model training can determine whether the network is *overfitting* over the training data. Hence, *training loss* and *accuracy* are compared. The most important concept in deep learning is accuracy. Along with the number of iterations, accuracy has been applied as the termination condition. The termination condition is to check whether the computations are converge or not and decide when the iterations should be halted.

5.2.2 YOLO Models

YOLO is a single neural network that predicts bounding boxes and class probabilities directly from full images [39]. The bounding boxes refer to object position. YOLO is trained based on full images which directly optimizes model performance. The class probabilities refer to the output class label. YOLO models adopt the entire image during training and testing time so that it encodes contextual information of all classes. YOLO models segment the input image into grids [6], typically 3×3 or 5×5. Each grid cell predicts the bounding boxes and confidence scores for those objects. The confidence scores refer to the test process with ground truth. Each bounding box consists of five parameters $x, y, w, h \in \mathscr{R}$ and confidence $c \in \mathscr{R}$ in percentage. Each grid cell is harnessed to predict conditional class probabilities, usually 3×3 or 5×5. YOLO predicts what objects present and where they are. A single convolutional network simultaneously estimates multiple bounding boxes and class probabilities for those boxes.

YOLO is highly generalizable which is less likely to break down when applied to new domains or unexpected inputs. It is fast and makes use of regression with

45 frames per second. In the YOLO model, a picture is segmented into 7×7 blocks; visual objects with confidence and coordinates are detected in each block. YOLOv2 makes use of *anchor boxes* to detect visual objects in an image. In order to find anchor boxes, Intersection over Union (IoU) is harnessed to predict the objectiveness score which is calculated by using

$$IoU = \frac{|A \cap B|}{|A \cup B|} \in [0, 1] \tag{5.5}$$

where A is the region of ground truth and B is the detected region of visual object. $A \cap B$ is the intersection between region A and region B. $A \cup B$ is the union of region A and region B. $| \cdot |$ is the area of the region of the given image.

Anchor box offset is to refine the anchor box. Class probability is to predict the class label assigned to each anchor box. Anchor boxes are a set of predefined bounding boxes. Each anchor box is tiled across the image. The use of anchor boxes enables a network to detect multiple objects, visual objects with multiple scales, and the overlapping objects. The advantages of using anchor boxes are that anchor boxes eliminate the need to scan an image with a sliding window, and it computes a prediction at every potential position. The use of anchor boxes replaces and drastically reduces the cost of the sliding windows. Through anchor boxes, visual object detectors are designed with three stages, namely object detection, feature encoding, and pattern classification.

YOLOv3 improves upon YOLOv2 by adding object detection at multiple scales so as to detect smaller objects. The loss function of YOLOv3 is separated into mean squared error for bounding box regression, while binary cross-entropy is employed for visual object classification, and it improves the detection accuracy [8]. YOLOv3 detector utilizes anchor boxes to have better initial priors and predict the boxes accurately.

YOLOv4 is a one-stage object detection network that is composed of three parts: backbone, neck, and head. The backbone of YOLOv4 network acts as the feature extraction network that computes feature maps from the input images. The neck connects the backbone and the head, and it is composed of a spatial pyramid pooling (SPP) module and a path aggregation network (PAN). The head processes the aggregated features and predicts the bounding boxes, objectness scores, and classification scores. MATLAB provides the Deep Learning Toolbox including YOLOv1 to YOLOv4 models with source codes [47].

YOLOv5 [56] was developed in the base framework with the objective of reducing the complexity and improving the performance of the network. This constitutes a benchmark with the aim of improving the implementability. The YOLO network partitions the input image into a grid of cells. The grid cells are employed to predict bounding boxes; each of the cells contains a target. In essence, the output of YOLOv5 comprises predictive information for each grid cell. This encompasses the parameters like class predictions with the bounding boxes of each grid cell.

During the evolution of YOLO series [50], YOLOv6 [12], YOLOv7 [48], and YOLOv8 [19] have promoted industrial applications. YOLOv6 combines processes such as EfficientRep, self-distillation [60], and advanced quantification. It provides a deployable network with customizable architecture and effectively balances computing accuracy and speed. YOLOv7 is an enhanced version of YOLOv6. YOLOv7 [48] focuses on the training process and introduces strategies such as reparameterization modules and model scaling. YOLOv8 [19] was evolved from YOLOv5. Together, these releases showcase significant advances in the performance and efficiency of object detection.

YOLOv9 [33] has taken significant advances in the field of object detection by using deep learning. The proposed concept of programmable gradient information (PGI) was employed to cope with the variations required for deep neural networks with multiple goals. YOLOv10 introduces an approach to real-time object detection, addressing both the post-processing and model architecture deficiencies found in previous YOLO versions. By eliminating non-maximum suppression (NMS) and optimizing various model components, YOLOv10 achieves the performance with significantly reduced computational overhead. YOLOv11 [4, 55, 57] was selected for its high efficiency in detecting small and fast-moving objects, and it is suitable for identifying a small object in each frame. In order to optimize YOLOv11 for the specific challenges, a plethora of modifications were implemented to improve its accuracy in detecting small objects. YOLOv12 is based on the attention-centric YOLO framework that matches the speed of previous CNN-based ones while harnessing the performance benefits of attention mechanisms [44]. YOLOv13 is an accurate and lightweight object detector with a hypergraph-based Adaptive correlation Enhancement (HyperACE) mechanism that achieves efficient global cross-location and cross-scale feature fusion.

In CNNs [43], there are the exploding gradient problems and the vanishing gradient problems [5, 14] due to the uncertain existence of gradients or derivatives of the loss surfaces [17, 28]. RNNs including LSTM and transformer models are thought as one of the solutions to resolve these problems.

5.3 RNNs, Transformers, and Multimodal Approaches

5.3.1 RNNs

RNNs are a family of artificial neural networks for processing sequential data, which is a dynamical system [7]. It is possible to use the same transition function with the same parameters at every time step. LSTM is a model for long short-term memory, and the model can be lasted for a long period of time [43]. An LSTM unit consists of four gates: input gate, cell, forget gate, and output gate. LSTM is well suited to classify, process, and predict time series given time lags of unknown size and duration between important events. It is the same with CNNs, but it has memory cells. The cells store a value of state, for either long or short time periods. LSTM gates compute an output by using the logistic function, see Eq. (5.6).

$$f(x) = \frac{1}{1+e^x}, x \in \mathscr{R} \tag{5.6}$$

The advantage of LSTM model is that LSTM was developed to deal with the exploding and vanishing gradient problems [5, 23]. An LSTM network is a type of RNN models that can learn long-term dependencies between time steps of sequence data. A sequence input layer inputs sequence or time series data into the network. An LSTM layer learns long-term dependencies between time steps of sequence data. To predict class labels, the network ends with a fully connected layer, a softmax layer, and a classification output layer. It is the same as CNN models, but it has memory.

OpenAI GPT models refer to Generative Pretrained Transformer (GPT), and GPT shows how a generative model of language is able to acquire knowledge and process long-range dependencies by pretraining on a diverse corpus with long stretches of contiguous text [9, 36, 51, 52]. The famous software such as Microsoft PowerPoint provided real-time translation between two languages by using transformer models [29, 42]. Transformer is a deep learning model, and it makes use of the mechanism of self-attention, deferentially weighting the significance of each part of the input data. Transformer is based solely on attention mechanisms, dispensing with recurrence and convolutions entirely [46]. Transformers were introduced in 2017 by Google Brain for NLP problems, so as to replace RNN models (LSTM). The Google BERT model refers to Bidirectional Encoder Representations from Transformers (BERT), and BERT was pretrained based on two tasks: (1) language modeling and (2) the next sentence prediction [54].

Recently, DeepSeek [1] has been developed, which was funded by the Chinese hedge fund High-Flyer in 2023. DeepSeek's success has been described as "upending AI." DeepSeek-R1 provides responses comparable to other contemporary large language models. The training cost was reported to be significantly lower than other LLMs. This breakthrough in reducing expenses while increasing efficiency and maintaining the model's performance in AI industry sent "shockwaves" through the market. The release history of DeepSeek is listed as:

- **January 2025**: DeepSeek chatbot
- **December 2024**: the base model DeepSeek-V3-Base and the chat model DeepSeek-V3
- **June 2024**: DeepSeek Coder V2
- **April 2024**: DeepSeek-Math models: Base, Instruct, and RL
- **January 2024**: DeepSeek-MoE models (Base and Chat)
- **November 2023**: DeepSeek-LLM
- **November 2023**: DeepSeek Coder

DeepSeek-R1 improves model reasoning capabilities by using pure reinforcement learning (RL). It explores the potential of LLMs without any supervised data, focusing on the self-evolution through a pure reinforcement learning process.

DeepSeek-R1 incorporates a small amount of cold-start data and a multistage training pipeline, after collecting thousands of cold-start data to conduct fine-tuning operations on the DeepSeek-V3-Base model. After the fine-tuning operations, the checkbot underwent an additional reinforcement learning process by taking into account of prompts from all scenarios [59]. DeepSeek directly applies reinforcement learning to the base model without relying on supervised fine-tuning operations (SFT).

In deep learning, fine-tuning is a method of transferring knowledge [54], and the parameters of a pretrained neural network model are trained based on new data. Low-rank adaptation (LoRA) algorithm is an adapter-based method for efficiently compressing large models. If a matrix $\mathbf{A}_{n\times n}$ has $n \times n$ elements, $n \in \mathscr{N}$, it will be decomposed into the multiplication of two smaller matrices $\mathbf{B}_{n\times m}$ and $\mathbf{C}_{m\times n}$, $m \in \mathscr{N}$,

$$\mathbf{A}_{n\times n} = \mathbf{B}_{n\times m} \cdot \mathbf{C}_{m\times n} \tag{5.7}$$

where m satisfies $n \times n \geq n \times m + m \times n$, matrix B and matrix $\mathbf{C}$ are expected to have less elements in total than that of matrix A. Therefore, matrix $\mathbf{A}$ is replaced in fine-tuning process by using $\mathbf{B} \cdot \mathbf{C}$. The pseudocode of LoRA method is shown in Algorithm 14.

Algorithm 14: Low-rank adaptation (LoRA) for compressing large models

Input : Pre-trained model with weight matrix $W_0 \in \mathscr{R}^{d\times k}$
Training data $\mathscr{D} = \{(x_i, y_i)\}_{i=1}^{N}$
Rank r, learning rate η

Output: Fine-tuned model with adapted weights

1 **Initialize** $A \in \mathscr{R}^{d\times r}$, $B \in \mathscr{R}^{r\times k}$ *such that* $W = W_0 + \Delta W$, *where* $\Delta W = A \cdot B$
2 *Initialize* A *and* B *randomly, freeze* W_0
3 **foreach** *mini-batch* (x, y) *in* $\mathscr{D}$ **do**
4 Forward pass using $W = W_0 + A \cdot B$
5 Compute loss $\mathscr{L}(x, y; W)$
6 Backpropagate gradients w.r.t. A and B
7 Update $A \leftarrow A - \eta \cdot \nabla_A \mathscr{L}$
8 Update $B \leftarrow B - \eta \cdot \nabla_B \mathscr{L}$
9 **return** $W_0 + A \cdot B$ *as the adapted weight matrix*

The reasoning patterns of larger models can be distilled into smaller models [1, 60]. DeepSeek conducted compressing operations on a few dense models, and the distilled smaller dense models perform exceptionally well. DeepSeek-R1 applies reinforcement learning method starting from a checkpoint fine-tuned with thousands of long chain-of-thought (CoT) examples [45]. It distills the reasoning capability from a large spare model to small dense models. The reasoning capabilities are significantly improved through large-scale reinforcement learning. The performance is further enhanced with the inclusion of a small amount of cold-start data.

In DeepSeek, the integration of reward signals and diverse data enables us to train a model that excels in reasoning. In machine learning, distillation is the process of transferring knowledge from a large model or a teacher model to a smaller one [60] or a student model. Distilling more powerful models into smaller ones yields excellent results. The distillation strategies are both economical and effective.

The strategies in deep learning for model simplifications usually comprise model pruning and model quantization including model distillation. The main task of model quantization is to convert high-precision floating-point numbers of the parameters of neural networks into low-precision numbers. The quantization methods reduce the size of the given models; thereby they diminish memory consumption. The increase of the speed on processors is capable of performing faster low-precision calculations.

5.3.2 Vision Transformers

Vision transformer models are trained for image classification in supervised learning with labels. The labels are related to image sequence. Transformers could not be generalized well when trained on insufficient amounts of data. In vision transformer (ViT), an image is treated as a sequence of patches, and it is processed by using a standard transformer encoder. The first layer of ViT projects the flattened patches into a lower dimensional space. Flattened means the rows will be linked together. After the projection, a position embedding is added to patch representations. Self-attention allows ViT to integrate information across the entire image in the lowest layers. Transformers show impressive performance from the scalability and self-supervised pretraining. Image inpainting and image outpainting are two examples of the scalability. ViT matches or exceeds the state of the art on image datasets, but relatively cheap to be pretrained. MATLAB has developed the ViT example.

In the field of machine learning [2, 18], a confusion matrix is a specific table layout that allows visualization of the performance of an algorithm, typically a supervised learning one; in unsupervised learning, it is usually called as a matching matrix.

5.3.3 Diffusion Transformers

In machine learning, diffusion models [15] are a class of latent variable generative models. The goal of diffusion models is to learn a diffusion process, and it generates the probability distribution of a given dataset. The diffusion models are employed to image denoising, inpainting, superresolution, and image generation.

Diffusion models train a neural network to sequentially denoise images blurred with Gaussian noise. The model is trained to reverse the process of adding noise to an image. After the training, the diffusion models are employed for image generation by starting with an image composed of random noise. Diffusion models can be applied to perform upscaling. Cascading diffusion model stacks multiple diffusion models one after another. The famous software DALL·E 2 is a cascaded diffusion model; it generates images from text.

A new group of diffusion models is explored based on transformer architecture. The scalability of Diffusion transformers (DiT) is analyzed through the lens of forward pass complexity as measured by using Gflops. DiTs with higher Gflops consistently have lower FID (Fréchet Inception Distance) [10], through increasing transformer depth/width or increasing the number of input tokens. The diffusion models are well-poised to benefit by inheriting best practices and training recipes from other domains, as well as retaining favorable properties. The attributes include scalability, robustness, and efficiency. DiTs [35] adhere to the best practices of Vision Transformers (ViTs). They are more effective for visual recognition than traditional convolutional neural networks. There is a strong correlation between the network complexity (measured by Gflops) and sample quality (measured by FID [10]).

Transformers have replaced domain-specific architectures across natural language, machine vision, reinforcement learning [59], and metalearning [26]. Transformers have been explored in Denoising Diffusion Probabilistic Models (DDPMs) to synthesize nonspatial data, e.g., to generate CLIP image embeddings in DALL·E 2. The Gaussian diffusion model adopts a forward noising process, and it gradually applies noise to real data $x_0 \in \mathscr{R}$

$$q(x_t|x_0) = \mathscr{N}[x_t; \sqrt{\alpha_t}x_0, (1-\alpha_t)\mathbf{I}] \tag{5.8}$$

where $\alpha_t \in \mathscr{R}$ is a hyperparameter, and $x_t = \sqrt{\alpha_t}x_0 + \sqrt{(1-\alpha_t)}\varepsilon_t$, $\varepsilon_t \sim \mathscr{N}(0, \mathbf{I})$.

Diffusion models are trained to learn the reverse process

$$p_\theta(x_{t-1}|x_t) = \mathscr{N}[\mu_\theta(x_t), \Sigma_\theta(x_t)] \tag{5.9}$$

where deep neural networks are employed to predict $p_\theta \in [0, 1] \in \mathscr{R}$.

In order to train diffusion models with a learned reverse process, we have $\varepsilon(\theta)$ with $\mathscr{L}_{simple}$

$$\mathscr{L}_{simple}(\theta) = \|\varepsilon_\theta(x_t) - \varepsilon_t\|_2^2 \tag{5.10}$$

We train $\sum_\theta$ with the full $\mathscr{L}(\theta)$.

$$\mathscr{L}(\theta) = -p(x_0|x_1) + \sum_t \mathscr{D}_{KL}[q^*(x_{t-1}|x_t, x_0)\|p_\theta(x_{t-1}|x_t)] \tag{5.11}$$

Once $p_\theta \in [0, 1] \in \mathscr{R}$ is trained, new images are sampled by initializing $x_{t_{max}} \sim \mathscr{N}(0, \mathbf{I})$ and sampling $x_{t-1} \sim p_\theta(x_{t-1}, x_t)$. By interpreting the output of diffusion models as the score function, the DDPM sampling procedure is guided to sample x with $p(x|c) \in [0, 1]$ by using

$$\hat{\varepsilon}_\theta(x_t, c) \triangleq \varepsilon_\theta(x_t, \phi) + s \cdot \nabla_x \log[p(c|x)] \tag{5.12}$$

where

$$p(c|x) \cdot p(x) = p(x|c) \cdot p(c) \tag{5.13}$$

and

$$\log[p(c|x)] \propto \log[p(x|c)] - \log[p(x)] \tag{5.14}$$

Hence,

$$\nabla_x \log[p(c|x)] \propto \nabla_x \log[p(x|c)] - \nabla_x \log[p(x)] \tag{5.15}$$

The DDPM sampling procedure is guided to sample x with $p(x|c) \in [0, 1] \in \mathscr{R}^+$ by using

$$\hat{\varepsilon}_\theta(x_t, c) \triangleq \varepsilon_\theta(x_t, \phi) + s \cdot \nabla_x \log[p(c|x)] \tag{5.16}$$

Simply,

$$\hat{\varepsilon}_\theta(x_t, c) \propto \varepsilon_\theta(x_t, \phi) + s \cdot [\varepsilon_\theta(x_t, c) - \varepsilon_\theta(x_t, \phi)] \tag{5.17}$$

$$\hat{\varepsilon}_\theta(x_t, c) \propto (1 - s)\varepsilon_\theta(x_t, \phi) + s \cdot \varepsilon_\theta(x_t, c), s \geq 0 \tag{5.18}$$

$$\hat{\varepsilon}_\theta(x_t, c) \propto \begin{cases} \varepsilon_\theta(x_t, c), & s = 1 \\ \varepsilon_\theta(x_t, \phi), & s = 0 \\ \varepsilon_\theta(x_t, \phi), & c = \phi \end{cases} \tag{5.19}$$

A diffusion model is trained with the representations $z = \mathbf{E}(x)$. New images can be generated by sampling a representation z and subsequently decoding it to an image $x = \mathbf{D}(z)$. DiT is based on Vision Transformer (ViT) architecture, and it is operated on sequences of patches. A smaller patch size results in a longer sequence length. "Patchify" converts the spatial input into a sequence of tokens. The number of tokens created by patchify is determined by the patch size. The input tokens are processed by using a sequence of transformer blocks. The transformer block is modified to include an additional multi-head cross attention layer following the multi-head self-attention block. The complete DiT design space is patch size, transformer block architecture, and model size. Scaling the transformer backbone yields better generative models across all model sizes and patch sizes. The scaling performance is measured by using Fréchet Inception Distance (FID), the standard metric for evaluating generative models of images. In mathematics, Fréchet distance [10] is a measure of similarity between curves that takes into account the location and ordering of the points along the curves. FID is a metric to assess the quality of images created by using a generative model. For two multidimensional Gaussian distributions $\mathcal{N}(\mu, \Sigma)$ and $\mathcal{N}(\mu', \Sigma')$,

$$d_F[\mathcal{N}(\mu, \Sigma), \mathcal{N}(\mu', \Sigma')] = \|\mu - \mu'\|^2 + tr[\Sigma + \Sigma' - 2(\Sigma\Sigma')^{\frac{1}{2}}] \tag{5.20}$$

Inception Score (IS) is an algorithm to assess the quality of images created by using a generative image model. Inception score only evaluates the distribution of generated images, and the FID compares the distribution of generated images with the distribution of a set of real images ("ground truth").

$$IS(P_{gen}, P_{dis}) = \exp[\mathbf{E}_{x \sim P_{gen}} D_{KL}(P_{gen}, P_{dis})] \tag{5.21}$$

$$D_{KL}(P_{gen}, P_{dis}) = D_{KL}[P_{dis}(\cdot|x) \| \mathbf{E}_{x \sim P_{gen}} P_{dis}(\cdot|x)] \tag{5.22}$$

Scaling the transformer backbone yields better generative models across all model sizes and patch sizes. Increasing model size and decreasing patch size yield considerably improved diffusion models. Larger DiT models take use of large computes more efficiently. Scaling both model size and the number of tokens yields notable improvements in visual quality. Diffusion transformers (DiTs) inherit the excellent scaling properties of the transformer model [31, 58], and the DiT model can be distilled by using the pseudocode supplied in Algorithm 15.

Algorithm 15: Distillation algorithm for DiT model

Input: Teacher model T, Student model S, dataset D, noise scheduler β_t, loss weights α, β

Output: Trained student model S

foreach *epoch e in* $1 \dots E$ **do**
  foreach *batch x in D* **do**
    `// Sample random timestep and noise`
    $t \sim \mathcal{U}\{1, T_{\max}\}$
    $\varepsilon \sim \mathcal{N}(0, I)$
    `// Noisy input according to diffusion process`
    $\tilde{x}_t \leftarrow \sqrt{\bar{\alpha}_t} \cdot x + \sqrt{1 - \bar{\alpha}_t} \cdot \varepsilon$
    `// Teacher prediction (no gradient)`
    $\hat{\varepsilon}_T \leftarrow T(\tilde{x}_t, t)$
    `// Student prediction`
    $\hat{\varepsilon}_S \leftarrow S(\tilde{x}_t, t)$
    `// Compute distillation loss`
    $L_{\text{KD}} \leftarrow \|\hat{\varepsilon}_S - \hat{\varepsilon}_T\|_2^2$
    `// Compute ground-truth denoising loss`
    $L_{\text{GT}} \leftarrow \|\hat{\varepsilon}_S - \varepsilon\|_2^2$
    `// Total loss`
    $L \leftarrow \alpha \cdot L_{\text{KD}} + \beta \cdot L_{\text{GT}}$
    `// Backpropagation and update`
    Backpropagate L and update S

return S

5.4 Lab Session: Training a Vision Model with MATLAB

At the end of this chapter, we would like to recommend all readers complete the lab report. Please fill in the form shown in Table 5.1 and submit it timely after each lab session (2 hours).

An example of this lab report is:

- **Project title**: Vision Transformer for Image Classification
- **Project objectives**: The objective of using transfer learning with a pretrained Vision Transformer (ViT) is to enhance image classification by adapting a model trained on large datasets to a new task, improving accuracy, and reducing training time through fine-tuning on specific data.
- **Configurations and settings**: MATLAB Online
- Methods: ViT is a neural network model that uses the transformer architecture to encode image inputs into feature vectors. The network consists of two main components: backbone and head. The pretrained ViT network has learned a strong feature representation for images.
- **Datasets**: The flowers dataset has a size of about 218 MB and contains 3670 images of flowers belonging to five classes: Daisy, Dandelion, Rose, Sunflower, and Tulip.

Table 5.1 Lab report for robotic vision

Name	<First Name Last Name >
Email	<firstname.lastname@mailbox >
Lab date	<dd-mm-yy >
Submitted date	<dd-mm-yy >
Project title	Vision Transformer for Image Classification
Lab objectives	The objective is to detect people and the distance to the camera from a video with a calibrated stereo camera
Configurations and settings	<The preferences, software, hardware, platforms, tools, etc. >
Methods	<The relevant scientific theories or concepts >
Workflow	<The step-by-step procedure for the experiment >
Datasets	<The data and materials for your experiments >
Input	<image filename, size, resolution >
Output	<image filename, size, resolution >
Testing steps	<Functional and non-functional testing methods step by step >
Bugs or problems	<The system error code, lines of the code >
Result analysis	<The tables, graphs, and figures, etc. >
Conclusion/reflection	<The strengths and weaknesses, or learned from this project >
References	https://au.mathworks.com/help/vision/ug/evaluating-the-accuracy-of-single-camera-calibration.html

Appendix: <Source codes with comments and line numbers >

- **Implementation steps**:
  1. Load a pretrained ViT network by using the vision transformer function.
  2. Download and extract the training data.
  3. Replace the classification head with a new one that maps the extracted features to prediction scores for the new set of classes in order to train the neural network to classify images across those classes.
  4. Specify the training options.
  5. Train the neural network by using the trainnet function.
  6. Evaluate the accuracy of the network by using the test data.
  7. Make predictions using the test data.
  8. Use the trained neural network to make a prediction using the first image in the test data.
- **Testing steps**:
  1. Make predictions using the test data.
  2. To convert the prediction scores to class labels, use the onehotdecode function.
  3. Use the trained neural network to make a prediction by using the first image in the test data.
- **Result analysis**: The output images visually validate the creation, assembly, and interactive capabilities of the robot arm, enhancing the written descriptions and confirming the project's objectives have been met.
- **Conclusion/reflection**: The ViT model demonstrates efficient adaptation for image classification tasks with reduced training time and improved accuracy, proving effective for complex vision applications through transfer learning and data augmentation. **Readings**: https://au.mathworks.com/help/vision/ug/transfer-learning-using-pretrained-vit-network.html.

5.5 Exercises

Question 5.1 Can YOLOs detect small visual objects?

Question 5.2 In deep learning, how to select a suitable algorithm for object detection? What balance should we take into consideration?

Question 5.3 Why transformers are better than other deep learning methods?

Question 5.4 How to simplify a large transformer model in deep learning?

Question 5.5 What are the differences between model pruning and model distillation in deep learning?

References

1. An W, Bi X, Chen G et al (2024) Fire-flyer AI-HPC: A cost-effective software-hardware co-design for deep learning. In: International conference for high performance computing, networking, storage and analysis. IEEE, pp 1–23
2. Alpaydin E (2009) Introduction to machine learning. MIT Press, Cambridge
3. Badrinarayanan V, Handa A, Cipolla R (2017) SegNet: a deep convolutional encoder-decoder architecture for robust semantic pixel-wise labelling. IEEE Trans Pattern Analy Mach Intell 39(12):2481–2495
4. Çabuk VU, Kubilay Şavkan A, Kahraman R, Karaduman F, Kırıl O, Sezer V (2018) Design and control of a tennis ball collector robot. In: International conference on control engineering and information technology (CEIT)
5. Caruana R, Lawrence S, Giles CL (2001) Overfitting in neural nets: backpropagation, conjugate gradient, and early stopping. In: Advances in neural information processing systems, pp 402–408
6. Chen LC, Papandreou G, Kokkinos I, Murphy K, Yuille AL (2018) DeepLab: semantic image segmentation with deep convolutional nets, atrous convolution, and fully connected CRFs. IEEE Trans Pattern Analy Mach Intell 40(4):834–848
7. Collobert R, Weston J (2008) A unified architecture for natural language processing: dEEP neural networks with multitask learning. In: International conference on machine learning, pp 160–167
8. Cover T, Thomas J (1991) Elements of information theory. Wiley, Hoboken
9. Dosovitskiy A et al (2021) An image is worth 16×16 words: transformers for image recognition at scale. In: International conference on learning representations
10. Dowson D, Landau B (1982) The Fréchet distance between multivariate normal distributions. J Multivar Analy 12 (3):450–455
11. Dunne RA, Campbell NA (1997). On the pairing of the softmax activation and cross-entropy penalty functions and the derivation of the softmax activation function. In: Australasian conference on neural networks, vol 181, p 185
12. Gao X, Nguyen M, Yan W (2024) HFM-YOLO: a novel lightweight and high-speed object detection model. In: Optimization, machine learning, and fuzzy logic: theory, algorithms, and applications. IGI Global, Hershey
13. Guo Y et al (2024) AnimateDiff: Animate your personalized text-to-image diffusion models without specific tuning. In: International conference on learning representations
14. He K, Zhang X, Ren S, Sun J (2016). Identity mappings in deep residual networks. In: European conference on computer vision, pp 630–645
15. Ho J, Jain A, Abbeel P (2020) Denoising diffusion probabilistic models. In: Advances in neural information processing systems
16. Hopfield JJ (1988). Artificial neural networks. IEEE Circuits Devices (Magazine) 4(5):3–10
17. Huang G, Liu Z, Weinberger KQ, van der Maaten L (2017). Densely connected convolutional networks. In: IEEE CVPR, vol 1, no 2, p 3
18. Jordan MI, Mitchell TM (2015) Machine learning: Trends, perspectives, and prospects. Science 349(6245):255–260
19. Ju RY, Cai W (2023). Fracture detection in pediatric wrist trauma X-ray images using YOLOv8 algorithm. Sci Rep 13(1):20077
20. Klette R (2014) Concise computer vision: an introduction into theory and algorithms. Springer, London
21. LeCun Y, Bengio Y (1995). Convolutional networks for images, speech, and time series. In: The handbook of brain theory and neural networks, vol 3361, no 10
22. LeCun Y, Boser B, Denker JS, Henderson D, Howard RE, Hubbard W, Jackel LD (1989) Backpropagation applied to handwritten zip code recognition. Neural Comput 1(4):541–551
23. LeCun Y, Bottou L, Bengio Y, Haffner P (1998). Gradient-based learning applied to document recognition. Proc IEEE 86(11):2278–2324

24. LeCun Y, Bengio Y, Hinton G (2015) Deep learning. Nature 521:436–444
25. Lee CY, Gallagher PW, Tu Z (2016). Generalizing pooling functions in convolutional neural networks: mixed, gated, and tree. In: Artificial intelligence and statistics, pp 464–472
26. Lemke C, Budka M, Gabrys B, (2013). Metalearning: a survey of trends and technologies. Artif Intell Rev 44(1):117–130
27. Lewis P et al (2020) Retrieval-augmented generation for knowledge-intensive NLP tasks. In: Advances in neural information processing systems
28. Li X (2018) Preconditioned stochastic gradient descent. IEEE Trans Neural Netw Learn Syst 29(5):1454–1466
29. Liu Y, Nand P, Hossain A, Nguyen M, Yan W (2023) Sign language recognition from digital videos using feature pyramid network with detection transformer. Multimed Tools Appl 82:21673–21685
30. MacKay D (2003). Hopfield networks. In: Information theory, inference and learning algorithms. Cambridge University, Cambridge, p 508
31. Meng C, Rombach R, Gao R, Kingma D, Ermon S, Ho J, Salimans T (2023) On distillation of guided diffusion models. In: IEEE CVPR
32. Meznar S, Lavrac N, Skrlj B (2021) Transfer learning for node regression applied to spreading prediction. arXiv:2104.00088
33. Mi Z, Yan W (2024) Strawberry ripeness detection using deep learning models. Big Data Cogn Comput 8(8):92
34. Pan S, Yang Q (2010) A survey on transfer learning. IEEE Trans Knowl Data Eng 22(10):1345–1359
35. Peebles W, Xie S (2023) Scalable diffusion models with transformers. In: IEEE ICCV
36. Qi J, Nguyen M, Yan W (2022) Small visual object detection in smart waste classification using Transformers with deep learning. In: International conference on image and vision computing new zealand (IVCNZ).
37. Ramsauer H et al (2021). Hopfield networks is all you need. In: International conference on learning representations
38. Rao S (2009) Engineering optimization: theory and practice, 4th edn. Wiley, Hoboken. ISBN: 978-04-70183-52-6
39. Redmon J, Divvala S, Girshick R, Farhadi A (2016). You only look once: unified, real-time object detection. In: IEEE CVPR, pp 779–788
40. Rumelhart DE, Hinton GE, Williams RJ (1986) Learning representations by backpropagating errors. Nature 323(6088):533–536
41. Russakovsky O, Deng J, Su H, Krause J, Satheesh S, Ma S, Berg AC (2015) ImageNet large scale visual recognition challenge. Int J Comput Vision 115(3):211–252
42. Sarikaya R, Hinton GE, Deoras A (2014) Application of deep belief networks for natural language understanding. IEEE/ACM Trans Audio Speech Lang Process 22(4):778–784
43. Schmidhuber J (2015) Deep learning in neural networks: an overview. Neural Netw 61:85–117
44. Tian Y, Ye Q, Doermann D (2025) YOLOv12: attention-centric real-time object detectors. https://arxiv.org/abs/2502.12524
systems
45. Vallayil M, Nand P, Yan W, Allende-Cid H (2025) CARAG: a context-aware retrieval framework for fact verification, integrating local and global perspectives of explainable AI. Appl Sci 15:1970
46. Vaswani A et al (2017) Attention is all you need. In: The conference on neural information processing systems (NIPS)
47. Vedaldi A, Lenc K (2015) MatConvNet: convolutional neural networks for MATLAB. In: ACM international conference on multimedia, pp 689–692
48. Wang CY, Bochkovskiy A, Liao HYM (2023). YOLOv7: trainable bag-of-freebies sets new state-of-the-art for real-time object detectors. In: IEEE/CVF conference on computer vision and pattern recognition, pp 7464–7475

49. Wei J, Wang X, Schuurmans D, Bosma M, Ichter B, Xia F, Chi E, Le Q, Zhou D (2022) Chain-of-thought prompting elicits reasoning in large language models. In: Advances in neural information processing systems
50. Xia Y, Nguyen M, Yan W (2024) An improved YOLO algorithm for Kiwifruit detection. In: Optimization, machine learning, and fuzzy logic: theory, algorithms, and applications. IGI Global, Hershey
51. Xiao B, Nguyen M, Yan W (2023) Apple ripeness identification from digital images using transformers. In: Multimedia tools and applications. Springer Science and Business Media LLC, Berlin
52. Xiao B, Nguyen M, Yan W (2023) Fruit ripeness identification using transformers. In: Applied intelligence. Springer Science and Business Media LLC, Berlin
53. Yan WQ (2019) Introduction to intelligent surveillance: surveillance data capture, transmission, and analytics, 3rd edn. Springer, Berlin
54. Yan WQ (2023) Computational methods for deep learning: theory, algorithms, and implementations, 2nd edn. Springer, Berlin
55. Yang G (2025) ChatPPG: multi-modal alignment of large language models for time-series forecasting in table tennis. Master's Thesis, Auckland University of Technology, New Zealand
56. Yang X, Zhao W, Wang Y, Yan W, Li Y (2024) Lightweight and efficient deep learning models for fruit detection in orchards. Nat Sci Rep 14:26086
57. Yang G, Nguyen M, Yan W, Li X (2025) Foul detection for table tennis serves using deep learning. Electronics 14(1):27
58. Zhang Y, Long J, Li C (2025) Knowledge distillation for object detection with diffusion model. Neurocomputing 636:130019
59. Zhu D, Li T, Ho D, Wang C, Meng MQ-H (2018) Deep reinforcement learning supervised autonomous exploration in office environments. In: IEEE international conference on robotics and automation (ICRA), pp 7548–7555
60. Zhu W, Peng B, Yan W (2024) Dual knowledge distillation on multiview pseudo labels for unsupervised person re-identification. IEEE Trans Multimedia 26:7359–7371
61. Zhao H, Xu S, Yan W, Xu D (2025) Design and optimization of target detection and 3D localization models for intelligent muskmelon pollination robots. Horticulturae 11(8):905

Chapter 6
Robotic Perception and Intelligence

Abstract In this chapter, starting from machine intelligence and genetic algorithm (GA), our depiction expounds how to measure the intelligence of robots by using Turing test. Following this, our focus is on reinforcement learning, especially deep Q-learning and imitation learning such as inverse reinforcement learning (IRL) for robotic perception and autonomous systems. The significance of this chapter is to measure the intelligence of robots and deliver the knowledge of how to train robots in operations to reach the level of human intelligence.

6.1 Perception

In robotics, we acquire visual information of holistic scenes from our perception [50] by using sensors. The sensors include digital cameras, microphones, and other instruments, and the data is collected from our perceptible environment. With fusing information from multiple channels of sensors on robots, our observations are employed for robotic path planning [28], navigation, scene understanding, and obstacle avoidance [62].

LiDAR, namely, Light Detection and Ranging, or Laser Imaging, Detection, and Ranging, is a method for determining ranges by targeting an object or a surface with a laser, measuring the time for the reflected light to the receiver [22, 27]. LiDAR harnesses ultraviolet, visible, or near infrared light to image objects. The method is employed for measuring distances by using a laser on a target and measuring its reflection with a sensor. A LiDAR determines the distance of an object or a surface by using

$$d = \frac{c \cdot t}{2} \tag{6.1}$$

where $c \in \mathscr{R}$ is the speed of light, $d \in \mathscr{R}$ is the distance between a sensor and an object, and $t \in \mathscr{R}$ is the time spent for the laser light to pass and then travel back to the detector.

W. Q. Yan, *Robotic Vision*, Advances in Computer Vision and Pattern Recognition,
https://doi.org/10.1007/978-981-95-4360-1_6

A mobile robot uses its LiDAR system to percept our environment, understand surrounding scene, construct a map, and avoid obstacles [27]. LiDAR sensors are mounted on mobile platform, and they require instrumentation to determine the resolution, absolute position, and orientation of robots such as Global Positioning System (GPS) receiver and an Inertial Measurement Unit (IMU). LiDAR could provide the scanned 3D maps for robotic navigation and path planning [28].

Cameras provide image data to the robots for visual object detection and recognition, tracking, and manipulation. Different from LiDAR systems that only provide point clouds and shape information, digital cameras offer the details of visual objects, such as texture, color, and rotations, especially for rotating objects. Recently, Tesla cars discarded LiDAR sensors on the autonomous cars, and only digital cameras are adopted for obstacle avoidance, path planning, and driving navigation [28]. All Tesla vehicles are equipped with computers and cameras. Hence, digital cameras on robots are playing decisive roles in visual scene understanding and visual information processing.

An Inertial Measurement Unit (IMU) is an electronic device, and it measures and reports a robot's force, angular rate, and orientation of robot, by using a combination of accelerometers, gyroscopes, and magnetometers. IMUs are incorporated into Inertial Navigation Systems (INS), and they utilize the raw IMU measurements to calculate attitude, angular rates, linear velocity, and position related to a global reference frame. In robotics, an IMU can be integrated into GPS-based automotive navigation systems or robot tracking systems for the purposes of traffic collision analysis [36, 37]. An IMU sensor adopts information fusion to control robots.

6.2 Robotic Intelligence

Robots have intelligence. Firstly, we shed light on logic [3], which refers to Boolean logic in algebra. Logic only has two states: True and False or "1" and "0." The family of logic concepts includes first-order logic, fuzzy logic, predicative logic, propositional logic, etc. Computers have the ability to make smart decision [20] fundamentally.

Fuzzy logic is a form of many-valued logic in which the truth value of variables may be any real number between 0 and 1. By contrast, in Boolean logic, the truth values of variables may only be the integer value 0 or 1. Fuzzy logic is employed in control systems to allow experts to contribute vague rules [29].

AI consists of the parts like perception or observation [33–35], learning, presentation, and reasoning or inference. AI covers the fields of search, retrieval, mining, and reasoning and path planning [28]. In AI, the topics include uninformed search, informed (heuristic) search, adversarial search, etc. Robots can find the shortest path because of searching on maps.

Reasoning [57] is a verb, which conveys the understandings from the knowledge what we know to infer what we do not know. Reasoning has the approaches-based forward/backward chaining, probabilistic reasoning, Bayes' rule, dynamic Bayesian networks, etc. Bayes' rule, namely Bayes' theorem, is related to the prior, posterior, likelihood, and evidence. It is the base knowledge of modern machine learning [1, 18].

$$p(x, y) = p(x|y)p(y) = p(y|x)p(x) \in [0, 1] \tag{6.2}$$

where $x \in \mathscr{R}$ and $y \in \mathscr{R}$ are events, $p(x, y) \in [0, 1]$ is the joint probability, and $p(x|y) \in [0, 1]$ and $p(y|x) \in [0, 1]$ are conditional probabilities.

There are a number of ways to make decision [20], such as decision trees, decision networks, expert systems, sequential decision, game theory, etc. Decision tree is a typical method to make smart decision. Typically, the decision tree is a binary tree. The tree as one of the data structures already sorted data in order; thus the decision tree will save our time. Based on decision trees, decision forest [20] is considered to develop much complicated approaches for decision-making.

Expert system fully harnesses or clones our human experience [29]. In robotics, an expert system is a computer system emulating the decision-making ability of a human expert. An expert system is divided into two subsystems: knowledge base, which represents facts and rules, and inference engine that applies the rules to the known facts.

The nature-inspired computing refers to cellular automata, neural computations, and evolutionary computation. More recent computations include swarm intelligence [10], artificial immune systems, membrane computing, and amorphous computing. In machine intelligence [9, 47, 48], there are three types of algorithms.

Physics-inspired algorithms employ basic principles of physics based on deterministic principles, for example, Newton's laws and simulated annealing (SA) algorithm. Physics-inspired machine learning takes advantage of the obtained prior knowledge to train machine learning models. This means it will need fewer samples to train the model or make the training outcomes more accurate.

In chemistry, chemical reactions are written in the form of chemical formulas by using symbols representing chemical elements and molecules. The mechanisms of chemical reactions are quite similar to the mechanisms of selection and variation in evolutionary algorithms, and the algorithms lead to new concepts of search and optimization algorithms.

Bioinspired computing, short for biologically inspired computing, is a field of study which seeks to solve computer science problems by using models of biology [8, 52]. Bioinspired computing is employed to train a robot. A robot is navigated in an unknown terrain. Biology-based algorithms (BBAs) are classified into three groups: evolutionary algorithms (EA), brain-inspired algorithms (BIA), and swarm intelligence-based algorithms (SIA) [9].

Swarm intelligence is the collective behavior of decentralized and self-organized systems. A swarm is made up of multiple agents [32]. The agents are able to exchange heuristic information in the form of local interactions.

The fundamental idea of evolutionary algorithms is based on Darwin's theory of evolution; it gained momentum in the late 1950s after the publication of the book "Origin of Species" [4].

Brain-inspired computing refers to computational models and methods based on the mechanism of human brain [21]. The goal is to enable the machine to realize various cognitive abilities and coordination mechanisms of human beings in a brain-inspired manner and finally achieve or exceed human intelligence. Brain-inspired computing has been applied to deep learning [15, 23, 41], and the mechanism of our human brain is partially harnessed in artificial neural networks [26].

A genetic algorithm (GA) is a metaheuristic inspired by using the process of natural selection, and GA belongs to the larger class of evolutionary algorithms (EAs). A gene is devitalized in allele. An allele is a form of genes at a particular position (locus) on a chromosome. It is the bit of coding DNA at that place. Hence, we take advantage of genetic algorithms in logic way to process gene information. A typical genetic algorithm requires (1) a genetic representation of the solution domain and (2) a fitness function to evaluate the solution domain. The genetic algorithm (GA) has the following steps:

- **Initialization**: Create an initial population.
- **Evaluation**: Evaluate each member of the population, and calculate a "fitness" for the individual.
- **Selection**: Constantly improve populations' overall fitness.
- **Crossover**: Create new individuals by combining aspects of the selected individuals.
- **Mutation**: Add randomness into populations' genetics.
- **Repeat**: Start again until a termination condition is reached.

When we repeat this process, the termination conditions are:

- A solution is found that satisfies the minimum criteria.
- A fixed number of generations reached.
- An allocated budget (e.g., computational time, etc.) reached.
- The highest ranking solution's fitness has reached.
- A plateau no longer produces better results.
- Combinations of the above.

The pseudocode for the GA algorithm is shown in Algorithm 16. The Python code for GA algorithm is shown in Fig 6.1. The advantages of using the GA algorithm are global optimum, without continuity requirements, without derivatives, and without linearity limitation, etc. Based on GA algorithms, we are able to solve the optimization problems of the weights of an artificial neural network by using loss surfaces in deep learning [15, 23, 41]. Through using GA algorithm, it is possible to get rid of the vanishing gradient problem and the exploding gradient problem. Traditionally, RNNs such as LSTM [5] and GRU [49] have been applied to solve this weight optimization problem as shown in Fig. 6.2.

Human has IQ (i.e., Intelligence Quotient) and EQ (i.e., Emotional Quotient) [42]. An IQ is a total score derived from a set of standardized tests or subtests designed to assess human intelligence [32]. Raven's progressive matrices [40] have been applied to evaluate the IQ of an individual as shown in Fig. 6.3. Recent tests

Algorithm 16: Genetic algorithm

```
Input: Fitness function f, population size N, mutation rate m, crossover rate c, number of
       generations G
Output: Best individual found
// Initialize population
P ← Randomly initialize N individuals ;
for g ← 1 to G do
    // Evaluate fitness
    foreach i ∈ P do
        i.fitness ← f(i) ;
    // Selection
    M ← Select parents from P based on fitness (e.g., tournament or roulette wheel) ;
    // Crossover
    C ← {} ;                                                    // New offspring
    while |C| < N do
        Select parents p1, p2 from M ;
        if random() < c then
            (o1, o2) ← Crossover(p1, p2) ;
        else
            o1 ← p1,   o2 ← p2 ;
        Add o1, o2 to C ;
    // Mutation
    foreach i ∈ C do
        if random() < m then
            Mutate(i) ;
    // Create new generation (with elitism)
    P ← Best individual in P + top N − 1 from C ;
return Best individual in P
```

are based on WAIS-II (Wechsler Adult Intelligence Scale). In WAIS-II, two groups of tests will be conducted: Verbal IQ and Performance IQ.

IQ classification is the practice of categorizing human intelligence, as measured by intelligence quotient (IQ) tests. The Wechsler Adult Intelligence Scale (WAIS) [53] is an IQ test designed to measure intelligence and cognitive ability in adults and older adolescents. In the latest WAIS 5 (2024) test, the FSIQ (i.e., Full Scale IQ) is generated from seven subtests: similarities, vocabulary, block design, matrix reasoning, figure weights, digit span sequencing, and coding. The 15 ancillary index scores include general ability index. The test may be administered in the classic physical format or on a digital platform.

Turing test [7, 11] is a test of machine's ability to exhibit intelligent behavior, and it is equivalent to, or indistinguishable from, that of a human [16]. ChatGPT-4 passes a rigorous Turing test, diverging from average human behavior chiefly to be more cooperative [29]. ChatGPT is able to recognize CAPTCHA characters now, and CAPTCHA [14] stands for "Completely Automated Public Turing test to tell

```python
def genetic_algorithm(population_size, chromosome_length, generations, crossover_rate=0.7, mutation_rate=0.01):
    population = generate_population(population_size, chromosome_length)
    best_solution = None
    best_fitness = -float('inf')

    for generation in range(generations):
        fitness_scores = calculate_fitness(population)

        # Track the best solution
        current_best_index = np.argmax(fitness_scores)
        current_best_fitness = fitness_scores[current_best_index]
        if current_best_fitness > best_fitness:
            best_fitness = current_best_fitness
            best_solution = population[current_best_index]

        print(f"Generation {generation+1}: Best fitness = {best_fitness}")

        # Select individuals for the next generation
        population = select_individuals(population, fitness_scores)

        # Create the next generation via crossover and mutation
        new_population = []
        for i in range(0, population_size, 2):
            parent1 = population[i]
            parent2 = population[(i + 1) % population_size]
            offspring1, offspring2 = crossover(parent1, parent2, crossover_rate)
            new_population.append(mutate(offspring1, mutation_rate))
            new_population.append(mutate(offspring2, mutation_rate))

        population = np.array(new_population)

    return best_solution, best_fitness
```

Fig. 6.1 The Python code for GA algorithm

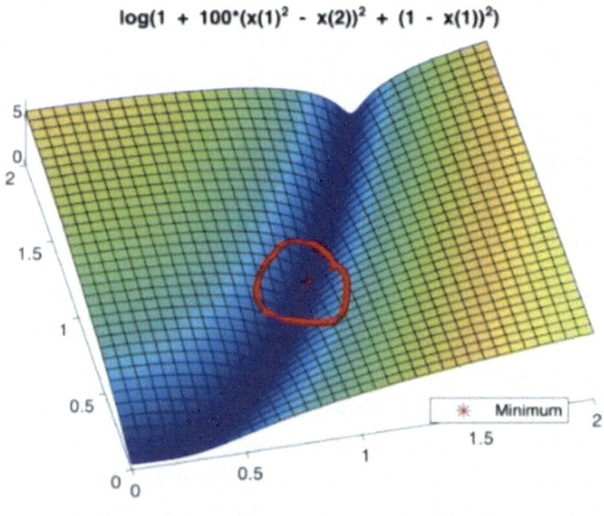

Fig. 6.2 The GA algorithm is employed for resolving optimization problems in deep learning

Computers and Humans Apart." Figure 6.4 provides an example of CAPTCHA character recognition by using ChatGPT.

Thus, robotic intelligence is realistic [9], it is one of the new research directions, and robotic intelligence is possible to be measured by using computational methods. We are able to use text and image pairs to measure the intelligence in multimodal way through deep learning models [11, 56].

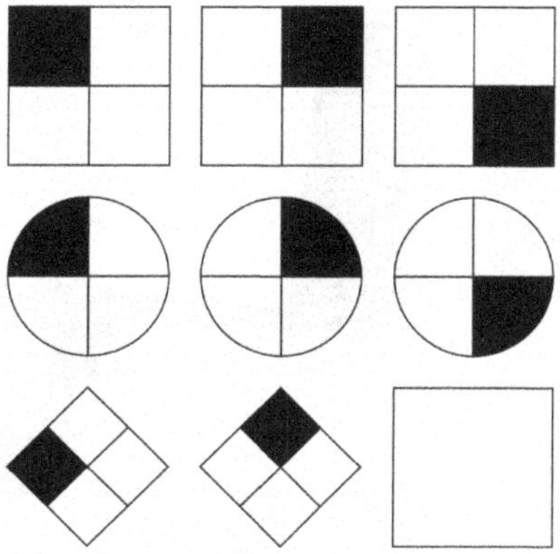

Fig. 6.3 An IQ test item in the style of a Raven's progressive matrices test

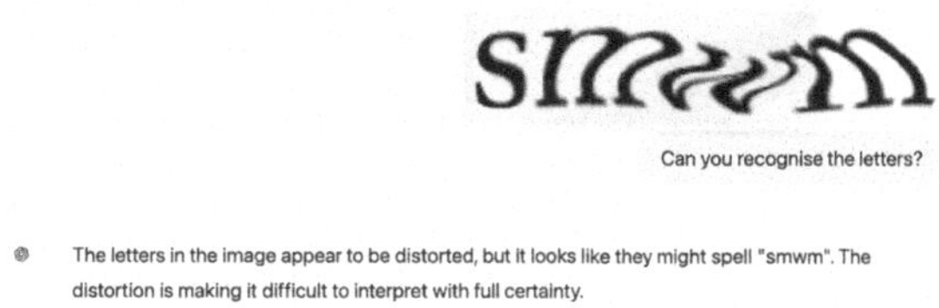

Fig. 6.4 CAPTCHA characters recognition using ChatGPT

6.3 Reinforcement Learning for Visual Control

In 2025, Professor Andrew Barto and Professor Richard Sutton received ACM Turing Award 2024 for their contributions to Reinforcement Learning, especially for developing the conceptual and algorithmic foundations of reinforcement learning. Professor Barto and Professor Sutton have published the famous book [45] as the pioneers of Reinforcement Learning. Reinforcement learning is regarded as the cornerstone of contemporary AI such as OpenAI ChatGPT software, Qwen, and DeepSeek software [58].

In Fig. 6.5, a vacuum robot is moving on a table, and the robot can be facilitated with various sensors without falling down from the table. In this section, the explanation regarding how to control a robot to fulfill our tasks by using reinforcement learning will be elucidated [29, 45].

Reinforcement learning is a goal-directed computational approach where a computer learns to perform a task by interacting with an unknown dynamic environment [31, 45]. Reinforcement learning has been applied to AlphaGo. AlphaGo is a computer program that plays the game Go [29, 43].

The reinforcement learning approach [6, 15] enables computers to make a series of decisions and maximizes cumulative reward for the task without human intervention, without being explicitly programmed to achieve the tasks [23]. The aim of reinforcement learning [24] is to train an agent to complete a task. An agent is a robot or algorithm. Reinforcement learning [45] is working for an unknown dynamic environment [31].

Fig. 6.5 A robotic vision system

The agent receives a sequence of observations and corresponding rewards from the environment and sends actions to the environment. The reward is a measure of how successful an action is with respect to completing the task. The agent contains two components: a policy and a learning algorithm or state estimator. The policy is a mapping that selects actions based on observations from the environment. Typically, the policy is a function approximator with tunable parameters, such as the weights of a deep neural network. The algorithm continuously updates the policy parameters based on action, observations, and reward. The goal of reinforcement learning algorithm is to find an optimal policy that maximizes the cumulative reward received [24, 45]. The pseudocode of PPO algorithm in reinforcement learning is shown in Algorithm 17. In summary, reinforcement learning [45] refers to an agent learning the optimal behavior through repeated trial-and-error interactions with the environment without human involvement [24]. The general workflow for training an agent through reinforcement learning [45] is comprised of the following steps:

- **Formulate Problem**: Define the task for the agent to learn.
- **Create Environment**: Define the environment within which the agent operates.
- **Define Reward**: Specify the reward signal that the agent uses to measure its performance.
- **Create Agent**: Create the agent.
- **Train Agent**: Train the agent policy representation.
- **Validate Agent**: Evaluate the performance of the trained agent.
- **Deploy Policy**: Deploy the trained policy representation.

Reinforcement learning is to learn what to do—how to map situations to actions—so as to maximize a numerical reward [24]. Reinforcement learning receives reward, penalty, or trial error for its actions to resolve a problem. Reinforce-

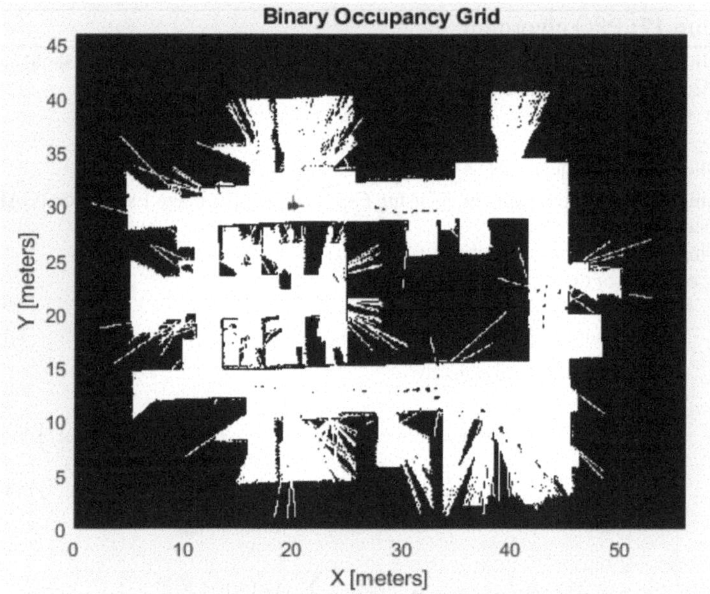

Fig. 6.6 A mobile robot to avoid obstacles in MATLAB

ment learning is able to learn the best policy and maximize the total reward [58]. The sequence of actions has the maximum cumulative reward. For each policy $\pi \in \Pi$, there is a reward $v^{\pi}(s_t) \in \mathscr{R}$ at state s_t, and the optimal policy is sought

$$v^*(s_t) = \max_{\pi}(v^{\pi}(s_t)), \forall s_t$$

Figure 6.6 shows a MATLAB example by using reinforcement learning to develop a strategy for a mobile robot to avoid obstacles. The objective of reinforcement learning is that the robot should avoid colliding into obstacles. This example shows an occupancy map of a known environment to detect obstacles and check collisions that the robot may make. The range sensor readings are observations, and linear and angular velocity controls are from the action [29].

6.4 Imitation Learning and Inverse Reinforcement Learning

In imitation learning, the agent aims to mimic human behaviors [29]. The agent learns from a dataset of demonstrations by an expert, typically a human. The goal is to replicate the expert's behavior in similar situations. When a human hand shows sign languages, the landmarks will lead the joint motion of machine hand [46]. Like reinforcement learning, imitation learning involves observing an expert performing

Algorithm 17: PPO algorithm

Input: Initial policy parameters θ, value function parameters ϕ, clipping threshold ε, learning rate η, number of iterations K

Output: Optimized policy π_θ

for $k \leftarrow 1$ **to** K **do**

  Collect a set of trajectories $\mathscr{D} = \{\tau_i\}$ by running policy π_θ;

  Compute advantage estimates $\hat{A}_t$ using Generalized Advantage Estimation (GAE) or other methods;

  Compute old policy probabilities $\pi_{\theta_{\text{old}}}(a_t|s_t)$ for each $(s_t, a_t) \in \mathscr{D}$;

  for *each epoch* **do**

    for *each minibatch* $\mathscr{B} \subset \mathscr{D}$ **do**

      Compute probability ratio: $r_t(\theta) = \frac{\pi_\theta(a_t|s_t)}{\pi_{\theta_{\text{old}}}(a_t|s_t)}$;

      Compute clipped objective:

$$L_t^{\text{CLIP}}(\theta) = \min\left(r_t(\theta)\hat{A}_t,\ \text{clip}(r_t(\theta), 1-\varepsilon, 1+\varepsilon)\hat{A}_t\right)$$

      Update policy parameters via gradient ascent: $\theta \leftarrow \theta + \eta \nabla_\theta \sum_{\mathscr{B}} L_t^{\text{CLIP}}(\theta)$;

      Update value function parameters ϕ by minimizing:

$$L^{\text{VF}}(\phi) = \sum_{\mathscr{B}} (V_\phi(s_t) - \hat{R}_t)^2$$

a task and learning to imitate those actions. The three steps of implementing this algorithm are:

- *Data Collection*: An expert demonstrates the task to be learned. The actions and decisions of the expert are recorded as data.
- *Learning*: The collected data is employed to train a deep learning model [1]. The model learns a policy—a mapping from observations of the environment to actions.
- *Evaluation*: The trained model is tested in the environment to assess how well it conducts compared to an expert. The goal is to minimize the differences between expert's performance and agent's performance.

Basically, there are two approaches in imitation learning:

- *Behavioral Cloning*: The model is trained in a supervised learning fashion by using state-action pairs from expert's demonstrations. The pseudocode of behavioral cloning is shown in Algorithm 18.
- *Inverse Reinforcement Learning (IRL)*: It aims to learn the underlying reward function that the expert seems to be maximizing. This approach can generalize better to unseen states. The pseudocode is shown in Algorithm 19.

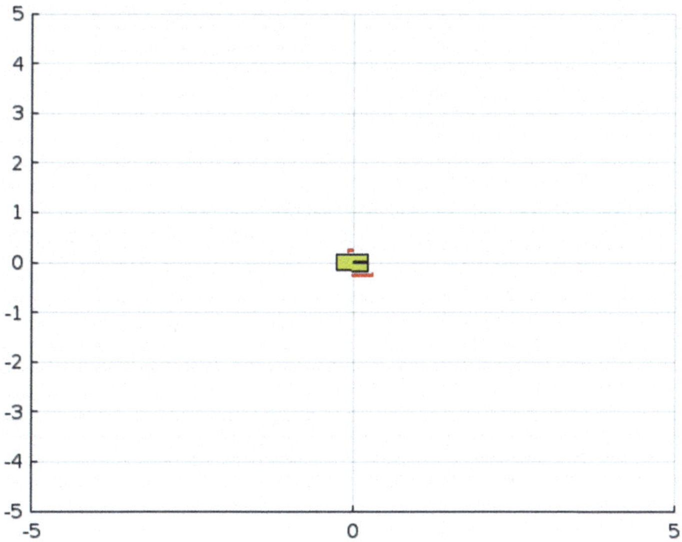

Fig. 6.7 Flying robot control using imitation learning

The challenges in imitation learning include:

- *Data Quality*: The quality of policy is highly dependent on the quality of demonstrations.
- *Distribution Shift Problem*: The agent may encounter states that were not covered in the demonstrations, leading to uncertain behavior.
- *Scalability*: Collecting expert demonstrations can be expensive and time-consuming, especially for complex tasks.
- *Generalization*: The ability for the agent to generalize the learned behaviors is a challenge, especially in dynamic and unpredictable environments [31].

MATLAB provides two examples for imitation learning. One is mobile vehicle lane keeping, and another is for flying robot control. In MATLAB, the deep neural network successfully imitates the behavior of Model Predictive Controller (MPC). The vehicle state and control trajectories for the controller and the deep neural network closely align. Figure 6.7 shows a MATLAB example of flying robot control.

6.5 Federated Learning and Distributed Models

Federated learning or collaborative learning [54] is a subfield of machine learning [18], and it collaborates with multiple entities or clients to train a model while ensuring that the data remains decentralized [1]. A server sends a distributed model to each client. Each individual client utilizes this distributed model to train a local

Algorithm 18: Behavior cloning algorithm in imitation learning

Input: Expert demonstration dataset $\mathscr{D} = \{(s_i, a_i)\}_{i=1}^{N}$
Output: Policy $\pi_\theta(a|s)$ parameterized by θ

Initialize policy network π_θ with random weights;
repeat
  Sample a mini-batch $\{(s_j, a_j)\}_{j=1}^{m}$ from $\mathscr{D}$;
  Compute loss: $\mathscr{L}(\theta) = \frac{1}{m}\sum_{j=1}^{m} \ell(\pi_\theta(s_j), a_j)$;
  `// ℓ is a suitable supervised loss function, e.g., cross-entropy or MSE`
  Update policy parameters: $\theta \leftarrow \theta - \eta \nabla_\theta \mathscr{L}(\theta)$;
  `// η is the learning rate`
until *convergence*;

Algorithm 19: Inverse reinforcement learning using maximum entropy

Input: Expert demonstrations $\mathscr{D} = \{\tau_i\}_{i=1}^{N}$, feature function $\phi(s)$, learning rate η, number of iterations K
Output: Reward function $R(s) = w^\top \phi(s)$

Initialize reward parameter vector w randomly;
for $k \leftarrow 1$ **to** K **do**
  Compute expert feature expectations: $\mu_E = \frac{1}{N}\sum_{i=1}^{N}\sum_{s\in\tau_i}\phi(s)$;
  Compute policy π_w using soft value iteration under current reward $R(s) = w^\top \phi(s)$;
  Generate trajectories $\{\hat{\tau}_j\}_{j=1}^{M}$ by rolling out policy π_w;
  Compute learner feature expectations: $\mu_\pi = \frac{1}{M}\sum_{j=1}^{M}\sum_{s\in\hat{\tau}_j}\phi(s)$;
  Compute gradient: $g = \mu_E - \mu_\pi$;
  Update reward parameters: $w \leftarrow w + \eta g$;

model with its own dataset. Updates to the model are sent back to the server, and the shared model is improved during the collaborative process. Due to the decentralized nature of clients' data, there is no guarantee that data samples held by each client are independently and identically distributed. Federated learning is generally concerned with and motivated by issues such as data privacy, data minimization, and data access rights [57]. The objective function for federated learning [19] is

$$f(x_1, x_2, \cdots, x_K) = \frac{1}{K}\sum_{i=1}^{K} f(x_i) \tag{6.3}$$

where $K \in \mathscr{N}$ is the number of nodes, $x_i \in \mathscr{R}$ are the weights of model as viewed by node $i \in \mathscr{N}$, and $f(\cdot)$ is node i 's local objective function; it describes how model weights x_i conform to node i's local dataset. The goal of federated learning is to train a model on all of the nodes, optimize the objective function, and achieve consensus on x_i.

The distributed learning aims at training a single model on multiple servers, and an underlying assumption is that the local datasets are independent and identically

Algorithm 20: Federated averaging algorithm

Input: Global model w_0, number of rounds T, number of clients K, local epochs E, learning rate η

Output: Trained global model w_T

for $t = 1$ **to** T **do**
- Server selects a subset of clients $\mathcal{S}_t \subseteq \{1, 2, ..., K\}$
- **foreach** *client* $k \in \mathcal{S}_t$ ***in parallel*** **do**
  - Client k receives global model w_{t-1}
  - Initialize $w_k^{(0)} \leftarrow w_{t-1}$
  - **for** $e = 1$ **to** E **do**
    - Client updates $w_k^{(e)} \leftarrow w_k^{(e-1)} - \eta \nabla \mathcal{L}_k(w_k^{(e-1)})$
  - **end**
  - Client sends $w_k^{(E)}$ to server
- **end**
- Server updates model:
  $w_t \leftarrow \sum_{k \in \mathcal{S}_t} \frac{n_k}{n} w_k^{(E)}$
  where n_k is the data size at client k, $n = \sum_{k \in \mathcal{S}_t} n_k$

end

distributed. The difference between federated learning and distributed learning lies in the properties of the local datasets. Federated learning originally aims at training on heterogeneous datasets.

In robotics, mobile robots learned navigation over diverse environments by using the federated learning-based method [25, 30, 61]. Federated learning is applied to improve multi-robot navigation under limited bandwidth, assisting better sim-to-real transfer. The pseudocode of federated learning algorithm is shown in Algorithm 20.

Ensemble methods [12, 51, 55, 59, 60] use multiple learning to obtain better predictive performance. Ensemble learning [2] typically refers to bagging (bootstrap aggregating), boosting [39], or stacking/blending methods to induce high variance among the base models [17]. Ensemble learning trains two or more machine learning algorithms [18] by using specific classification or regression [13, 39]. The algorithms are generally referred to as "base models," "base learners," or "weak learners." Empirically, the ensembles yield better results if there is a significant diversity among the models [38, 44].

Mixture of Experts (MoE) represents a form of ensemble learning. Each expert f_i, $i = 1, 2 \cdots, N$, takes the same input x and produces output $f_i(x)$. Each weighting function or gating function w takes input x and produces a vector of outputs $w(x)_i$, $i = 1, 2 \cdots, N$. Given an input x, the MoE produces a single output: $f(x) = \sum_i w(x)_i f_i(x), i = 1, 2 \cdots, N$. Both the experts and the weighting function are trained by minimizing loss function, generally via gradient descent. The model is trained by performing gradient descent on the mean-squared error loss $\mathcal{L} = \frac{1}{N} \sum_k \|y_k - f(x_k)\|^2, k = 1, 2 \cdots, N$.

In deep learning, the critical goal is to reduce the computing cost. In deep learning, the output of MoE for each query may involve a few experts' outputs.

Each expert i has an extra "expert bias" b_i, $i = 1, 2, \cdots, N$. If an expert is being neglected, then the bias increases and vice versa. During token assignment, each token picks the top-k experts, but with the bias added in. The expert bias matters for picking the experts, but not in adding up the responses from the experts.

6.6 Lab Session: Implementing Perception Algorithms with MATLAB

At the end of this chapter, we would like to recommend all readers complete the lab report. Please fill in the form shown in Table 6.1 after each lab session (2 hours).

An example of this lab report is:

- **Project title**: Avoid Obstacles Using Reinforcement Learning for Mobile Robots.
- **Project objectives**: The objective is to train a mobile robot using a reinforcement learning algorithm to avoid obstacles. By interpreting range sensor readings, the robot learns to control its linear and angular velocities to navigate without colliding in a known environment.
- **Configurations and settings**: MATLAB Online

Table 6.1 Lab report for robotic vision

Name	<First Name Last Name >
Email	<firstname.lastname@mailbox >
Lab date	<dd-mm-yy >
Submitted date	<dd-mm-yy >
Project title	Avoid Obstacles Using Reinforcement Learning for Mobile Robots
Lab objectives	The objective is to train a mobile robot by using reinforcement learning to avoid obstacles with a calibrated stereo camera
Configurations and settings	<The preferences, software, hardware, platforms, tools, etc. >
Methods	<The relevant scientific theories or concepts >
Workflow	<The step-by-step procedure for the experiment >
Datasets	<The data and materials for your experiments >
Input	<image filename, size, resolution >
Output	<image filename, size, resolution >
Testing steps	<Functional & non-functional testing methods step by step >
Bugs or problems	<The system error code, lines of the code >
Result analysis	<The tables, graphs, and figures, etc. >
Conclusion/reflection	<The strengths and weaknesses, or learned from this project >
References	https://au.mathworks.com/help/robotics/ug/avoid-obstacles-using-reinforcement-learning-for-mobile-robots.html

Appendix: <Source codes with comments and line numbers>

- **Methods**: An occupancy map of a known environment was employed to generate range sensor readings, detect obstacles, and check collisions the robot may make. The DDPG (Deep Deterministic Policy Gradient) agent observed range sensor readings, the linear and angular velocity controlled by using the DDPG-based reinforcement learning algorithm.
- **Implementation steps**:
  1. Load a map matrix representing the environment.
  2. Set up the range sensor and robot parameters.
  3. Visualize the map and robot positions.
  4. Create the environment model for actions, observations, and rewards.
  5. Define observation and action specifications.
  6. Build and configure the DDPG agent.
  7. Define the reward function.
  8. Train the agent.
  9. Simulate and visualize the agent's performance.
  10. Extend the model to simulate in new environments.
- **Testing steps**:
  1. Verify rigid body elements.
  2. Test joint connections.
  3. Validate robot assembly.
  4. Interact with the robot model.
  5. Simulation and performance testing.
- **Result analysis**: The result analysis of the trained DDPG-based mobile robot focuses on the robot's ability to navigate the environment efficiently, avoid obstacles, and adapt to new scenarios. Key metrics include success rate in avoiding collisions, path efficiency, and adaptability to varied environments. Visual representations such as trajectory plots are employed to assess performance. The overall goal is to ensure that the robot learns optimal control strategies to avoid obstacles.
- **Conclusion/reflection**: The DDPG-based reinforcement learning model successfully enables a mobile robot to avoid obstacles by learning optimal control actions based on sensor readings. Through model training, the robot improves its navigation efficiency and adaptability. The model's performance is validated through simulations, which showcase its ability to navigate while minimizing collisions; this makes it as a practical solution for autonomous navigation tasks in dynamic environments.
- **Readings**: https://au.mathworks.com/help/robotics/ug/avoid-obstacles-using-reinforcement-learning-formobile-robots.html

6.7 Exercises

Question 6.1 How to measure human IQ (Intelligence Quotient)?

Question 6.2 What are the characters of Reinforcement Learning? What is the relationship between Reinforcement Learning (RL) and Finite State Machine (FSM)?

Question 6.3 How to implement imitation learning? What is the relationship between Reinforcement Learning (RL) and Imitation Learning (IL)?

Question 6.4 How to implement inverse reinforcement learning?

Question 6.5 Why GA algorithm can always find the right solution of a given optimization problem?

Question 6.6 What are the differences between behavior cloning and behavior analogy?

Question 6.7 How to ensure the security of datasets during model training by using distributed models in deep learning?

References

1. Alpaydin E (2009) Introduction to machine learning. MIT Press, Cambridge
2. Andres O, Munilla J, Gorriz J et al (2016) Ensembles of deep learning architectures for the early diagnosis of the Alzheimer's disease. Int J Neural Syst 26(7):1650025
3. Ayer AJ (2001) Language, truth and logic. Nature 138(3498)
4. Browne J (2007) Darwin's origin of species: a biography. Grove Press
5. Bengio Y, Simard P, Frasconi P (1994) Learning long-term dependencies with gradient descent is difficult. IEEE Trans Neural Netw 5(2):157–166
6. Bengio Y, Lecun Y, Hinton G (2021) Deep learning for AI. Commun ACM 64(7):58–65
7. Biever C (2023) ChatGPT broke the Turing test—the race is on for new ways to assess AI. Nature 619(7971):686–689
8. Bird J, Kobylarz J, Faria D, Ekart A, Ribeiro E (2020) Cross-domain MLP and CNN transfer learning for biological signal processing: EEG and EMG. IEEE Access 8:54789–54801
9. Ertel W (2019) Introduction to artificial intelligence. Springer, Berlin
10. Fricke GM, Hecker JP, Griego AD, Tran LT, Moses ME (2016) A distributed deterministic spiral search algorithm for swarms. In: IEEE/RSJ international conference on intelligent robots and systems (IROS), pp 4430–4436
11. Gao X, Liu Y, Nguyen M, Yan W (2024) VICL-CLIP: enhancing face mask detection in context with multimodal foundation models. In: ICONIP'24
12. Gao X, Nguyen M, Yan W (2023) Enhancement of human face mask detection performance by using ensemble learning models. In:L PSIVT, pp 124–137
13. Gashler M, Giraud-Carrier C, Martinez T (2008) Decision tree ensemble: small heterogeneous is better than large homogeneous. In: International conference on machine learning and applications, pp 900–905
14. George D et al (2017) A generative vision model that trains with high data efficiency and breaks text-based CAPTCHAs. Science 358(6368)
15. Goodfellow I, Bengio Y, Courville A (2016) Deep learning. MIT Press, Cambridge

16. Hernandez-Orallo J (2000) Beyond the Turing test. J Logic Lang Inform 9(4):447–466
17. Polikar R (2006) Ensemble-based systems in decision making. IEEE Circuits Syst Mag 6(3):21–45
18. Jordan MI, Mitchell TM (2015) Machine learning: trends, perspectives, and prospects. Science 349(6245):255–260
19. Kairouz P et al (2021) Advances and open problems in federated learning. Found Trends Mach Learn 14 (1–2):1–210
20. Kontschieder P et al (2015) Deep neural decision forests. In: IEEE ICCV
21. Kriegeskorte N (2015) Deep neural networks: a new framework for modeling biological vision and brain information processing. In: Annual review of vision science, pp 417–446
22. Labbé M, Michaud F (2019) RTAB-Map as an open-source LiDAR and visual simultaneous localization and mapping library for large-scale and long-term online operation. J Field Robot 36(2):416–446
23. LeCun Y, Bengio Y, Hinton G (2015) Deep learning. Nature 521:436–444
24. Littman M (2015) Reinforcement learning improves behavior from evaluative feedback. Nature 521:445–451
25. Liu B, Wang L, Liu M (2019) Lifelong federated reinforcement learning: a learning architecture for navigation in cloud robotic systems. In: IEEE/RSJ international conference on intelligent robots and systems (IROS), pp 1688–1695
26. McCulloch WS, Pitts W (1943) A logical calculus of the ideas immanent in nervous activity. Bull Math Biophys 5(4):115–133
27. Mehtab S, Yan W, Narayanan A (2022) 3D vehicle detection using cheap LiDAR and camera sensors. In: International conference on image and vision computing. New Zealand
28. Ming Y, Li Y, Zhang Z, Yan W (2021) A survey of path planning algorithms for autonomous vehicles. Int J Commercial Veh 14:97–109
29. Mnih V et al (2015) Human-level control through deep reinforcement learning. Nature 518:529–533
30. Na S, Rouček T, Ulrich J, Pikman J, Krajník T, Lennox B, Arvin F (2023) Federated reinforcement learning for collective navigation of robotic swarms. IEEE Trans Cogn Developmental Syst 15(4):1
31. Narendra KS, Parthasarathy K (1990) Identification and control of dynamical systems using neural networks. IEEE Trans Neural Netw 1(1):4–27
32. Norvig P, Russell S (2016) Artificial intelligence: a modern approach, 3rd edn. Prentice Hall, Englewood Cliffs
33. Pan C, Yan W (2018) A learning-based positive feedback in salient object detection. In: International conference on image and vision computing. New Zealand
34. Pan C, Yan W (2020) Object detection based on saturation of visual perception. Multimedia Tools Appl 79(27–28):19925–19944
35. Pan C, Liu J, Yan W, Zhou Y (2021) Salient object detection based on visual perceptual saturation and two-stream hybrid networks. IEEE Trans Image Process 30:4773–4787
36. Peng D (2025) Vision perception optimization and adaptive control for resource-constrained platform: a Ping-Pong Ball Pickup & Place System. Master's thesis, Auckland University of Technology, New Zealand
37. Peng D, Yan W (2025) Test-time training with adaptive memory for traffic accident severity prediction. Computers 14(5):186
38. Opitz D, Maclin R (1999) Popular ensemble methods: an empirical study. J Artif Intell Res 11:169–198
39. Rriedman J, Hastie T, Tibshirani R (2000) Additive logistic regression: a statistical view of boosting. Ann Stat 38(2):337–374
40. Raven J, Raven JC, Court JH (2003) Manual for Raven's progressive matrices and vocabulary scales. San Antonio
41. Schmidhuber J (2015) Deep learning in neural networks: an overview. Neural Netw 61:85–117

42. Shah H, Warwick K (2009) Emotion in the Turing test: a downward trend for machines in recent Loebner prizes. In: Handbook of research on synthetic emotions and sociable robotics: new applications in affective computing and artificial intelligence. Information Science, IGI
43. Silver D et al (2018) A general reinforcement learning algorithm that masters chess, shogi, and Go through self-play. Science 362(6419):1140–1144.
44. Suk H, Lee S, Shen D (2017) Deep ensemble learning of sparse regression models for brain disease diagnosis. Med Image Anal 37:101–113
45. Sutton R, Barto A (2018) Reinforcement learning: an Introduction, 2nd edn. MIT Press, Cambridge
46. Tantiya R (2025) Design and implementation of a high DoF robot arm. Master's thesis, Auckland University of Technology, New Zealand
47. Turing A (1948) Machine intelligence. The essential Turing: the ideas that gave birth to the computer age. Oxford University Press, Oxford
48. Turing A (1950) Computing machinery and intelligence. Mind 59(236):433–460
49. Vaswani A et al (2017) Attention is all you need. In: The conference on neural information processing systems (NIPS), USA
50. Wang L, Li R, Sun J, Liu X, Zhao L, Seah HS, Quah CK, Tandianus B (2019) Multi-view fusion-based 3D object detection for robot indoor scene perception. Sensors 19(19):4092
51. Wang X, Yan W (2020) Cross-view gait recognition through ensemble learning. Neural Comput Appl 32(11):7275–7287
52. Webb S (2018) Deep learning for biology. Nature 554:555–557
53. Wechsler D (1939) The measurement of adult intelligence. Williams & Witkins, Baltimore
54. Wei J, He J, Chen K, Zhou Y, Tang Z (2017) Collaborative filtering and deep learning based recommendation system for cold start items. Expert Syst Appl 69:29–39
55. Xu G, Yan W (2023) Facial emotion recognition using ensemble learning. In: Deep learning, reinforcement learning, and the rise of intelligent systems, pp 146–158. IGI Global
56. Yan W, Kankanhalli M (2009) Cross-modal approach for Karaoke artefacts correction. In: Handbook of multimedia for digital entertainment and arts, pp 197–218
57. Yan WQ (2019) Introduction to intelligent surveillance: surveillance data capture, transmission, and analytics, 3rd edn. Springer, Berlin
58. Yan WQ (2023) Computational methods for deep learning: theory, algorithms, and implementations, 2nd edn. Springer, Berlin
59. Younas F, Usman M, Yan W (2023) A deep neural network ensemble framework for colorectal polyp classification. Multimedia Tools Appl 82:18925–18946
60. Younas F, Usman A, Yan W (2023) A deep ensemble learning method for colorectal polyp classification with optimized network parameters. Appl Intell 53:2410–2433
61. Yu X, Queralta J, Westerlund T (2022) Towards lifelong federated learning in autonomous mobile robots with continuous sim-to-real transfer. Procedia Comput Sci 210:86–93
62. Zhao H, Xu S, Yan W, Xu D (2025) Design and optimization of target detection and 3D localization models for intelligent muskmelon pollination robots. Horticulturae 11(8):905

Chapter 7
Vision-Based Robotic Control

Abstract Robot manipulators (i.e., robot arms) are extensively deployed in manufacturing, packaging, and processing factories. The robot arm is linked with end-effector Zhao et al (Horticulturae 11(8):905, 2025). In this chapter, visual servoing is brought into vision-based robot control, especially camera retreat will lead the robot to get the destination based on the acquired images. The significance of this chapter is to implement robot control via robotic vision.

7.1 Basics of Visual Servoing

Visual servoing [5, 10] is the method of controlling a robot's motion using real-time feedback [20] from vision sensors to execute tasks [15, 17]. The real-time information [8] from vision sensors like cameras [12] will control robots. Visual servoing is a model-free approach to actuate the robot based on high-level task to be executed. In visual servoing, the robot is instructed to move in order to align its current task progress with the desired task and gradually reduce the errors between the two. We have target matrix and current matrix, and visual servoing is implemented by using cameras [1, 5, 27] to control robots. Mathematically, visual servoing is to minimize the error [10]:

$$e(t) = f(m(t), \mathbf{a}) - f^*(m(t), a) \tag{7.1}$$

where $e(\cdot) \in \mathscr{R}$ is the error, $t \in \mathscr{R}$ is the time, $m(\cdot) \in \mathscr{R}$ is the collection of regions of interest in the image, and $\mathbf{a}$ is the collection of camera intrinsic parameters and extrinsic parameters. The function [14] $f^*(\cdot) \in \mathscr{R}$ represents the desired set of visual features, while $f(\cdot) \in \mathscr{R}$ reflects the actual features [12].

Visual features are computable vectors extracted from digital images [29], such as corner, edge, blob, contour [28], motif, etc. Depending on the positioning of cameras [12], visual servoing [4, 7] has two paradigms: eye-in-hand and eye-to-hand [18]. The eye-in-hand camera is the visual sensor mounted on a robot, and the eye-to-hand camera is applied to monitor our environment [25, 33, 34] as shown in Fig. 7.1. From the view angles of the two cameras, the visual objects and field

W. Q. Yan, *Robotic Vision*, Advances in Computer Vision and Pattern Recognition,
https://doi.org/10.1007/978-981-95-4360-1_7

Fig. 7.1 The eye-to-hand camera and eye-in-hand camera on a wheeled robot

of view (FoV) [26] are different. What we should know is that visual information is reliable for robot locating. However, GPS information is not reliable or weak because in a tunnel, GPS information will be lost.

Visual servoing [3] is to control the pose of robot's end-effector by using visual features extracted from the image which contains two approaches [24]: Position/Pose-Based Visual Servo (PBVS) and Image-Based Visual Servo (IBVS). PBVS takes use of observed visual features, a calibrated camera and a known geometric model of the target to determine the pose of target with respect to the cameras [1, 12, 27]. 3D cameras are employed to detect object depth [26]. LiDAR system is too expensive and may loss the details of visual information. IBVS omits the pose estimation step, and it adopts the image features directly. That means the system has data conversation from image to image. The desired camera pose with respect to the target is defined implicitly by using the image features at the goal pose [1, 27].

PBVS usually makes use of depth cameras to obtain 3D pose/position and orientation of the regions/objects of interest [26]. The error term is the Cartesian pose difference between the two. The servoing scheme [3, 22] is to minimize it by moving the robot around, ideally toward the final desired pose [11]. Based on the location of visual object [26] in the image, the scheme generates the ideal grasp pose for the end-effector and converges the robot to it [36]. PBVS works with real-world poses which needs at least a 6-DoF robot arm to successfully implement the solution without getting stuck in local minima. Six DoF is the minimum degrees of freedom with low risk to reach object without singularity; our human body has 7-DOF at least. PBVS makes use of robot inverse kinematics (IK) to convert Cartesian control instructions into joint angles of the robot [9]. The inverse kinematics means that the end-effector needs to be moved to a position first if the manipulator is required to be moved. Other joints will be moved near to the object. Controversially, the forward kinematics (FK) refers to that the foot of robots is required to move first, and then the joints will be followed to the end-effector. The difference between inverse kinematics and forward kinematics is the computing costs and time. The inverse kinematics needs to compute the joint chain; thus its computing is slow [29].

Since obtaining the information regards 3D pose comprehends of the conversion from camera frame to robot frame, camera calibration [11, 12] plays a critical role in PBVS process [12]. The intrinsic parameters and extrinsic parameters of the given cameras are related to camera calibration. Camera calibration bridges the gap between image space and 3D object space in the real world.

Compared to PBVS [24], IBVS is to omit the pose estimation. The camera in hand, joint controller [9], feedback, and feature extraction are the same. The information fusion step is also the same [1, 27]. IBVS extracts visual features and formulates the errors in image plane. The desired image and the current image are compared, and the differences will be calculated. The visual servoing converges visual feature to the desired coordinates and moves the robot accordingly in image space [22].

Visual feature extraction in IBVS is prone to camera performance, synchronization issues, and computational requirements [29]. Cameras [12] usually have high definition (HD) or high resolution and high speed (i.e., frames per second). Computational requirements refer to software and hardware. Hereinafter, the hardware refers to GPUs and FPGAs, and the software links to the algorithms for extracting visual features. The synchronization means that two or many cameras [1, 27] are working together within the same pace, and they will acquire and process the images from the same scene [21].

The first step of IBVS is the projection of 3D object on a 2D image plane. Mathematically, the mapping from 3D space to 2D space is based on transformation: $x = X/Z \in \mathscr{R}$ and $y = Y/Z \in \mathscr{R}$, where $Z \neq 0$, $(X, Y, Z) \in \mathscr{R}^3$ is a point location on a 3D object, and $(x, y) \in \mathscr{R}^2$ is a pixel location on an image. The depth has been disappeared on the image. IBVS differs fundamentally from PBVS by not estimating the relative pose of the target. The relative pose is implicit in the image features. The pose is hidden or stored in the 2D images. IBVS is an image-to-image approach, a kind of end-to-end approach. IBVS is remarkably robust to vision-based robot control [15]. IBVS is formulated to work with other image features such as corner, straight line, circle, rectangle, etc.

7.2 Advanced Visual Servoing

A number of autonomous robot operations [16] are employed to relieve the lack of labor problems [35]. Robots with sufficient electric power have no errors, and they can work without rests and save a vast of costs [16]. Hence, human labors could be employed to other business or work. Visual servoing [3] is one of the most important technologies. Industries often need robots to be running at lightning-fast speeds, and visual servoing is far from achieving speedy performances [35]. Currently, our hardware and software tools are still working slowly even with supercomputing.

Computational bottlenecks in image processing and inverse kinematics (IK) are on using GPUs and parallel programming [4, 29]. In visual servoing [37], camera retreat [6] refers to the cameras that need to be moved back (or "retreated") so as to capture an entire scene [21] or visual object [26] within the viewing frustum. The frustum is a visible area of visual scene [13, 30]. The problem of camera retreat (moving back) is happened in an IBVS system because the object is too large or too close. The pseudocode of camera retreat algorithm is shown in Algorithm 21.

Algorithm 21: Camera retreat algorithm

Input: Current position of camera C, target object position T, minimum safe distance $d_{\min}$, step size s

Output: Updated camera position C

while *distance*$(C, T) < d_{\min}$ **do**

  `// Compute direction vector from target to camera`

  $\vec{v} \leftarrow \frac{C-T}{\|C-T\|}$;

  `// Move camera backward by step size`

  $C \leftarrow C + s \cdot \vec{v}$;

return C;

The camera position in 3D space is adjusted through affine transformation such as rotation, scaling, and translation. Relatively, the object could be moved or scaled to match the clipping window of the image. The clipping operation refers to select regions of an image to display. A clipped image is shown in Fig. 7.2.

The scaling change is achieved by Z-axis translation. The XY/Z hybrid schemes take into account of X-axis and Y-axis as one group and Z-axis as another group.

Fig. 7.2 An example of camera retreat. (**a**) The full image and (**b**) the clipped image

(a) The full image

(b) The clipped image

Thus, if the movement of a robot is planned, we are able to fully utilize the two groups to reach the destination. XY/Z-partitioned methods eliminate camera retreat [6] by using IBVS to control the degrees of freedom (DoF) while taking a different controller for the remaining degrees of freedom [9]. It is advantageous to select the longest line segment of trajectory or path. The longest line segment in robot moving will save our time and energy.

For a rotated camera, the points will naturally be moved along circular arcs with the assigned radius. The edges and corners of an object will be rotated correspondingly. The desired rotational rate is obtained by using a simple proportional control law. The proportional control law has been harnessed in the control of a bicycle or a car with four wheels. The simplest example is a bicycle with two wheels. When a car or a bicycle is moving, all wheels should follow the proportional control law with different radii.

If a robot is armed with cameras, visual features are projected from one or more images [12] onto spherical image plane and compute the control law in terms of spherical coordinates. The spherical plane refers to the surface of 3D sphere.

In polar coordinates, image point is denoted as $(r, \phi) \in \mathscr{R}^2$, $r \in \mathscr{R}$ is the distance, $r = \sqrt{u^2 + v^2}$, $u, v \in \mathscr{R}$, and u-axis and v-axis are the image coordinates. The angle from u-axis to a line is $\phi = tan^{-1}(\frac{v}{u}) \in \mathscr{R}$, $u \neq 0$. The two coordinate representations are related to $u = r\cos(\phi) \in \mathscr{R}$ and $v = r\sin(\phi) \in \mathscr{R}$. The world point $(X, Y, Z)^\top, X, Y, Z \in \mathscr{R}$ in the camera frame is projected onto the surface of sphere at the point $(x, y, z)^\top, x, y, z \in \mathscr{R}$, $x = X/R$, $y = Y/R$, $z = Z/R$, $R \in \mathscr{R}$, $R \neq 0$ is the distance from the camera origin to the world point. A minimal spherical coordinate system comprises the angle of colatitude $\theta = \sin^{-1}(y/r) \in \mathscr{R}$, $\theta \in [0, \pi] \in \mathscr{R}$, $r = \sqrt{x^2 + y^2} \in \mathscr{R}$, $r \neq 0$. Thus, the feature vector is $\mathbf{p} = (\theta, \phi)$, $\phi = sin^{-1}(\frac{z}{r}) \in \mathscr{R}$. Hence, $X = R \cdot \cos(\theta)\cos(\phi)$, $Y = R \cdot \cos(\theta)\sin(\phi)$, $Z = R \cdot \sin(\theta)$, $R = \sqrt{X^2 + Y^2 + Z^2}$.

The space of spherical images and the space of 2D images can be transformed mutually. The spherical mapping projects our images onto the standard sphere as shown in Fig. 7.3. A spherical camera eliminates the need to explicitly keep visual features in the field of view (FoV) with both position-based visual servoing and hybrid schemes [37]. For a spherical camera, this ambiguity is reduced.

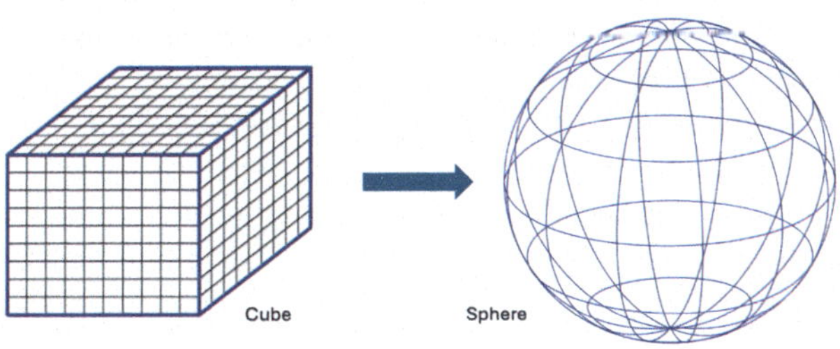

Fig. 7.3 From cube to sphere

The spherical cameras are independent on the FoV. In six-axis arm-type robot, a perspective camera with default parameters is mounted on the robot's end-effector, and its axes are aligned with the coordinate frame. This system drives the robot to the desired pose. In a mobile robot [2], a camera is mounted on a mobile robot that can be moved in a planar environment, and the visual servo controller will drive the robot until its view of landmarks matches the desired view [3, 37].

7.3 Vision-Based Navigation and Path Planning Algorithms

Robot navigation is defined as the combination of three fundamental competences: (1) self-localization, (2) path planning,[23] and (3) map building and map interpretation. Vision-based navigation or optical navigation makes use of computer vision algorithms and optical sensors, this includes laser-based range finder and photometric cameras, and it extracts the visual information required to the localization in the surrounding environment [33, 34].

Google and Apple have provided precise navigation and locating service in outdoor environment [32]. Image-based navigation methods attract much attention as a powerful alternative to traditional map-based navigation. The Google Street View is a method featured in Google Map that allows users to navigate through large-scale outdoor environment with 360 degree imagery. However, Google Street View cannot provide timely updates because it requires immense data; this method involving a panoramic camera has not been extended due to its data collection permission.

Our early prototype [32] was able to locate current position by matching query image in the database as shown in Fig. 7.4. If a match is found, the system roughly figures out the position of query image based on position by using SIFT feature detection. It can roughly locate a query image on the map by using IPM (Inverse Perspective Mapping). Thus, it enables interactive navigation and knowledge sharing among users [31]. By using QR codes with the navigation, the current location and the shortest path to the destination are available [19].

Robot localization denotes the robot's ability to establish its own position and orientation. Path planning [23] is effectively an extension of localization; it requires the determination of robot's current position and a position of a goal location, both within the same frame of reference or coordinates system.

Self-driving vehicles will firstly make use of global path planning [23] to decide which roads to be taken to arrive the destination. When these vehicles are on the road, they have to be constantly adaptive to the changing environment. This is where local path planning methods allow the vehicle to plan a safe and fast path to the target location.

Fig. 7.4 Precise indoor navigation without GPS information within a building

7.4 Lab Session: Visual Servoing with MATLAB

At the end of this chapter, we would like to recommend all readers complete the lab report. Please fill in the form shown in Table 7.1 after each lab session (2 hours). An example of this lab report is:

- **Project title**: Automated Parking Valet with ROS 2
- **Project objectives**: The goal of this experiment is to simulate an autonomous parking system by using ROS (Robot Operating System) to achieve automatic vehicle navigation, path planning, and parking operations.
- **Configurations and settings**:

  1. MATLAB Online
  2. ROS node configuration
  3. ROS message topics
  4. Callback function setup
  5. Simulated vehicle configuration
  6. Path planning and control strategy

- **Methods**: Initially, we upload a route plan and the specified cost map by using the behavior planner and path analyzer. The control node is responsible for longitudinal and lateral controllers. We initialize the simulation by sending the first velocity message and current pose message. This message causes the planner to start the planning loop. The main loop waits for the behavioral planner to say the vehicle reached the park position. The parking maneuver callbacks are slightly different from the normal driving maneuver.

Table 7.1 Lab report for robotic vision

Name	<First Name Last Name >
Email	<firstname.lastname@mailbox >
Lab date	<dd-mm-yy >
Submitted date	<dd-mm-yy >
Project title	Automated Parking Valet with ROS 2
Lab objectives	The objective is to simulate an autonomous parking system by using ROS
Configurations and settings	<The preferences, software, hardware, platforms, tools, etc. >
Methods	<The relevant scientific theories or concepts >
Workflow	<The step-by-step procedure for the experiment >
Datasets	<The data and materials for your experiments >
Input	<image filename, size, resolution >
Output	<image filename, size, resolution >
Testing steps	<Functional & non-functional testing methods step by step >
Bugs or problems	<The system error code, lines of the code >
Result analysis	<The tables, graphs, and figures, etc. >
Conclusion/reflection	<The strengths and weaknesses, or learned from this project >
References	https://au.mathworks.com/help/ros/ug/automated-valet-using-ros2-matlab.html

Appendix: <Source codes with comments and line numbers >

- **Implementation steps**:
  1. Load a route plan and a given cost map
  2. ROS initialization
  3. Publisher and subscriber creation
  4. Callback functions
  5. Vehicle status update
  6. Goal reach check
  7. Visualization and simulation shutdown
  8. ROS network shutdown
- **Testing steps**:
  1. Functional testing
  2. Simulation testing
  3. Edge case testing
  4. Parking maneuver
- **Result analysis**: Through visualization, the vehicle follows the planned path without deviating or colliding with any obstacles. The path planning successfully guided the vehicle from the starting point to the target spot.
- **Conclusion/reflection**: The autonomous parking system successfully achieved vehicle self-parking in the simulation, its effectiveness in path planning, vehicle

control, and real-time feedback is demonstrated. Through accurate path planning and precise control commands, the vehicle was able to smoothly travel from the starting point to the destination spot and safely stop upon arrival.

- **Readings**: https://au.mathworks.com/help/ros/ug/automated-valet-using-ros2-matlab.html.

7.5 Exercises

Question 7.1 What is visual servoing?

Question 7.2 What is advanced visual servoing?

Question 7.3 How to implement camera retreat?

Question 7.4 How do the current algorithms play their roles in robotic navigation, planning, and scene understanding?

References

1. Baek J, Lee, E, Park M, Seo D (2015) Mono-camera based side vehicle detection for blind spot detection systems. In: International conference on ubiquitous & future networks, pp 147–149
2. Bouzoualegh S, Guechi E-H, Kelaiaia R (2019) Model predictive control of a differential-drive mobile robot. Acta Universitatis Sapientiae, Electr Mech Eng 10(1):20–41
3. Cao C (2022) Research on a visual servoing control method based on perspective transformation under spatial constraint. Machines 10(11):1090
4. Colombo FT, de Carvalho Fontes JV, da Silva MM (2019) A visual servoing strategy under limited frame rates for planar parallel kinematic machines. J Intell Robot Syst 96(1):95–107
5. Cong VD, Hanh LD (2023) A review and performance comparison of visual servoing controls. Int J Intell Robot Appl 7(1):65–90
6. Corke P, Hutchinson SA (2001) A new partitioned approach to image-based visual servo control. IEEE Trans Robot Autom 17 (4):507–515
7. Corke P, Hutchinson S, Gans NR (2002) Partitioned image-based visual servo control: Some new results. In: Sensor based intelligent robots (LNCS 2238)
8. Cover T, Thomas J (1991) Elements of information theory. John Wiley & Sons, London
9. Cui M, Liu H, Wang X, Liu W (2023) Adaptive control for simultaneous tracking and stabilization of wheeled mobile robot with uncertainties. J Intell Robot Syst 108(3):46
10. Gans NR, Hu G, Shen J, Zhang Y, Dixon WE (2012) Adaptive visual servo control to simultaneously stabilize image and pose error. Mechatronics 22(4):410–422
11. Han T, Zhu H, Yu D (2024) Data-driven model predictive control for uncalibrated visual servoing. Symmetry 16(1):48
12. Hane C, Sattler T, Pollefeys M, Heng L, Lee GH, Fraundorfer F, Furgale P (2017) 3D visual perception for self-driving cars using a multi-camera system: calibration, mapping, localization, and obstacle detection. Image Vision Comput 68:14–27
13. Kim D, Choi J, Yoo H, Yang U, Sohn K (2015) Rear obstacle detection system with fisheye stereo camera using HCT. Expert Syst Appl 42:6295–6305
14. Kivinen J, Warmuth MK (1998) Relative loss bounds for multidimensional regression problems. In: Advances in neural information processing systems, pp 287–293

15. Klette R (2014) Concise computer vision: an introduction into theory and algorithms. Springer, London
16. Koch M (2018) Artificial intelligence is becoming natural. Cell 173(3):531–533
17. Kriegeskorte N (2015) Deep neural networks: a new framework for modelling biological vision and brain information processing. Ann Rev Vision Sci 1(1):417–446
18. Lalonde M, Byrns D, Gagnon L, Teasdale N, Laurendeau D (2007) Real-time eye blink detection with GPU-based SIFT tracking. In: Canadian conference on computer and robot vision, pp 481–487
19. Li J (2014) Tour navigation: a cloud based tourist navigation system. Master's thesis, Auckland University of Technology, New Zealand
20. Littman M (2015) Reinforcement learning improves behavior from evaluative feedback. Nature 521:445–451
21. Liu X (2023) Vehicle-related scene understanding using deep learning. PhD thesis, Auckland University of Technology, New Zealand
22. Machkour Z, Ortiz-Arroyo D, Durdevic P (2021) Classical and deep learning based visual servoing systems: a survey on state of the art. J Intell Robot Syst 104(1):11
23. Ming Y, Li Y, Zhang Z, Yan W (2021) A survey of path planning algorithms for autonomous vehicles. Int J Commer Veh 14:97–109
24. Peng Y-C, Jivani D, Radke RJ, Wen J (2020) Comparing position- and image-based visual servoing for robotic assembly of large structures. In: IEEE 16th international conference on automation science and engineering (CASE), pp 1608–1613
25. Petrushin VA (2005) Mining rare and frequent events in multi-camera surveillance video using self-organizing maps. In: ACM international conference on knowledge discovery in data mining, pp 794–800
26. Serre T, Wolf L, Bileschi S, Riesenhuber M, Poggio T (2007) Robust object recognition with cortex-like mechanisms. IEEE Trans PAMI 29(3):411–426
27. Shen Y, Yan W (2018) Blindspot monitoring using deep learning. In: IEEE IVCNZ'18
28. Shen W, Wang X, Wang Y, Bai X, Zhang Z (2015) DeepContour: a deep convolutional feature learned by positive-sharing loss for contour detection. In: IEEE conference on computer vision and pattern recognition, pp 3982–3991
29. Stoer J, Bulirsch R (1991) Introduction to numerical analysis, 2nd edn. Springer, Berlin
30. Sung K, Shirley P, Baer S (2008) Essentials of interactive computer graphics: concepts and implementation. CRC Press, Boca Raton
31. Wang L (2012) iNavigation: an image based indoor navigation system. Master's thesis, Auckland University of Technology, New Zealand
32. Wang L (2013) iNavigation: an image based indoor navigation system. Multimedia Tools Appl 73:1597–1615
33. Yan WQ (2019) Introduction to intelligent surveillance: surveillance data capture, transmission, and analytics, 3rd edn. Springer, Berlin
34. Yan WQ (2023) Computational methods for deep learning: theory, algorithms, and implementations, 2nd edn. Springer, Berlin
35. Ye Z, He Y, Pieters RS, Mesman B, Corporaal H, Jonker PP (2011) Bottlenecks and tradeoffs in high frame rate visual servoing: a case study. In: IAPR conference on machine vision applications, pp 55–58
36. Zhao H, Xu S, Yan W, Xu D (2025) Design and optimization of target detection and 3D localization models for intelligent muskmelon pollination robots. Horticulturae 11(8):905
37. Zhou Z, Guo J, Zhu Z, Guo H (2024) Uncalibrated visual servoing based on Kalman filter and mixed-kernel online sequential extreme learning machine for robot manipulator. Multimedia Tools Appl 83(7):18853–18879

Chapter 8
Computational Tools for Robotic Vision

Abstract In this chapter, we embark on Robot Operating System (ROS), and it was designed as middleware for robot instruction. The challenges of modern computing will be spelt out, and the multicore computing and multithread computing are expounded. GPUs are utilized to accelerate our computing for robotic vision and robotic control for autonomous systems. Python programming is taken into account as the example to specify the supercomputing. Another is mobile computing, and the sensor data is gained by using MATLAB. The significance of this chapter is to implement robotic vision through mobile computing and supercomputing.

8.1 Robot Operating System (ROS)

Robot Operating System (ROS) [3, 19] is a framework or a collection of software libraries, and it assists developers to create robotic applications. With our application development, our data will be exported to the ROS system, and ROS will be linked to hardware automatically. ROS was designed as middleware, and it provides services such as hardware abstraction, device control, message passing between processes, and package management.

Pertaining to modularity, ROS breaks down a complex robotic system into manageable components, called as nodes. Each node performs a specific task and communicates with other nodes. Moreover, ROS provides a layer of abstraction between hardware and software, and our developers have not to care about the underlying hardware specifics. In communications, ROS offers a flexible and efficient communication infrastructure within the same machine or across multiple machines on a network. Regarding tools, ROS comes with a suite of powerful tools for debugging, visualization, and simulation. With regard to package management, ROS organizes code into packages, and the code can be easily shared and reused, conveniently integrated into the third-party software.

ROS 2 [25] is the second generation of the Robot Operating System (ROS), and it was designed with real-time performance. It utilizes Data Distribution Service (DDS) as the communication framework that enables reliable, real-time, and scalable communications between distributed systems. ROS 2 puts forward the

W. Q. Yan, *Robotic Vision*, Advances in Computer Vision and Pattern Recognition,
https://doi.org/10.1007/978-981-95-4360-1_8

enhanced security features, including secure communications and data encryption. The feature avoids the risk of attacks such as man-in-the-middle, the attacks are possible to exist between ROS and robots, and it ensures information security [4]. ROS 2 is better suited for coordinating multiple robots working together (co-work). ROS accommodates better support for multiple operating systems, including Microsoft Windows and Apple macOS. The operating system supplies with the improved tools for testing, debugging, and monitoring robotic systems [20, 23, 24].

MATLAB released two versions each year, namely *a* and *b* versions. The ROS Toolbox showcases an interface connecting MATLAB and Simulink with the Robot Operating System (ROS and ROS 2). MATLAB has links and interface with ROS. With the toolbox, our users are able to design a network of ROS nodes; typically, we combine MATLAB or Simulink together to generate ROS nodes with the existing ROS network. The toolbox includes MATLAB functions to visualize and analyze ROS data by recording, importing, and playing back ROS files. ROS files have been employed to multiple purposes. The toolbox verifies ROS nodes via simulation by connecting to external robot simulators.

MATLAB accommodates an example of how to park a car by using ROS, and it is called car valet. The example consists of localization, perception, planning, and inference [5, 13, 14], and vehicles [1, 2]. The planning method encompasses behavior planning [16], decision-making [12, 13], goal check, path planner, path smoother, velocity profiler, etc. All robots [1, 15] are the same in operations no matter flying in sky, moving on ground, or swimming under water, and they need to be linked to ROS system.

8.2 Modern Computing for Robotics

8.2.1 Supercomputing

Supercomputing refers to historically vector computers, but now parallel vector. Vector computation is based on vectors in linear order. All elements of a vector could be calculated simultaneously. MATLAB computing is based on vector operations. A master computer can get all information from the distributed ones [18].

High-Performance Computing (HPC) is to resolve problems via supercomputers with fast networks and data visualization. Every year, the world top 500 computer list, namely TOP500 list, has been updated twice since 1993. In sequential computing or serial computing, the components of a program are executed step by step to produce correct results. For instance, arithmetic operations, such as addition, subtraction, multiplication, and division, will be executed in the same time, no matter which operation will be executed, and the final operations are all addition-based. Parallelism is a condition wherein multiple tasks or distributed parts of a task run independently and simultaneously on multiple processors. As we know, OpenAI needs a vast number of GPUs to train their GPT models.

```
import threading
import time

def calc_square(numbers):
    for n in numbers:
        print(f'\n{n} ^ 2 = {n*n}')
        time.sleep(0.1)

def calc_cube(numbers):
    for n in numbers:
        print(f'\n{n} ^ 3 = {n*n*n}')
        time.sleep(0.1)

numbers = [2, 3, 5, 8]

start = time.time()

square_thread = threading.Thread(target=calc_square, args=(numbers,))
cube_thread = threading.Thread(target=calc_cube, args=(numbers,))

square_thread.start()
cube_thread.start()

square_thread.join()
cube_thread.join()

end = time.time()

print('Execution Time: {}'.format(end-start))
```

Fig. 8.1 Multithreading in Python

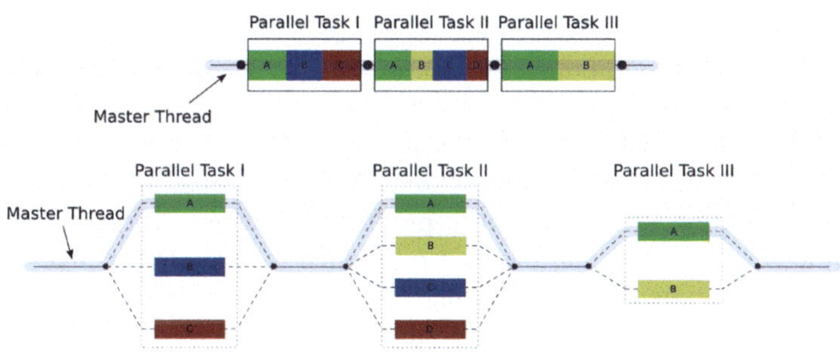

Fig. 8.2 Fork-join model

A process is a program in execution with its own address space, memory, data stack, etc. under one operating system. Multithread computing means there are a number of threads, while the threads are employed for various purposes such as matrix addition, subtraction, multiplication, etc. The multiple threads execute within the same process and share the same context.

The multithreading in Python is listed in Fig. 8.1. For example, Python programming is conducted to implement fork-join model for parallel programming. In this example, we load the libraries: threading and time, and we define the two threads: cube and rectangle; we join them together. The executive time is obtained after the two threads are working together. In Fig. 8.2, the fork model is needed, after completed each thread, the master thread will join them together. Previously, it was

```python
import numpy as np
from multiprocessing import Pool

# Define the matrix multiplication function
def matrix_multiply(args):
  A, B = args
  return np.dot(A, B)

# Create two random matrices of size 1000x1000
A = np.random.rand(1000, 1000)
B = np.random.rand(1000, 1000)

# Split the matrices into 4 parts
A_parts = np.array_split(A, 4, axis=1)
B_parts = np.array_split(B, 4)

# Create a multiprocessing pool with 4 workers
pool = Pool(4)

# Map the matrix multiplication function to the 4 parts of the matrices
C_parts = pool.map(matrix_multiply,
  [(A_part, B_part) for A_part, B_part in zip(A_parts, B_parts)])

# Concatenate the parts of the result matrix
C = np.concatenate(C_parts, axis=1)

print(C)
```

Fig. 8.3 Parallel computing for matrix multiplication in Python

manually assigned in programming time; now MATLAB system automatically finds GPU resources in run time.

In Fig. 8.3, multithreading for matrix multiplication is taken into account. In the beginning, Python libraries, NumPy and multiprocessing, are loaded, and two matrices are multiplied by using inner product of vectors. The given matrix is segmented to 4×4 blocks, and they are multiplied together, respectively. Finally, the results are generated as the output. The matrix multiplication is based on operation addition. No matter how complicated the multiplication of matrices is, all arithmetic multiplications are based on hardware adders. They are operating with binary numbers in circuits of a computer system. In 1 second, how many addition operations can be carried out for the binary digits is applied to measure the computing speed of the processor.

Regarding matrix multiplications, two matrices $\mathbf{A} = \{a_{ij}\} \in \mathscr{R}^{n\times n}$ and $\mathbf{B} = \{b_{ij}\} \in \mathscr{R}^{n\times n}$ are multiplied together, $\mathbf{C} = \mathbf{A} \times \mathbf{B} = \{c_{ij}\} \in \mathscr{R}^{n\times n}$, $a_{ij} \in \mathscr{R}$, $b_{ij} \in \mathscr{R}$, $c_{ij} \in \mathscr{R}$. The corresponding matrix will be shown as

$$c_{ij} = \sum_k a_{ik} \times b_{kj}, i, j, k = 1, 2, \cdots, n, n \in \mathscr{Z}^+ \tag{8.1}$$

In parallel computing, c_{ij} is independent of $i \in \mathscr{R}$ and $j \in \mathscr{R}$. If one element is calculated, all elements of the matrix will be computed to completion.

8.2.2 GPU Acceleration

In robotics, we have the challenges in computing acceleration from CPUs and GPUs. CPUs are slower, and GPUs are faster. Regarding CPUs, we have multicore computing or multithread computing. Graphics Processing Unit (GPU) is a rapid way for us to train Large Language Models (LLMs). Pertaining to the games like Minecraft, GPUs will accelerate the game play.

A GPU is a specialized electronic circuit to accelerate the creation of images in a frame buffer for output to a display device. Modern GPUs are efficient at manipulating computer graphics and image processing. In a personal computer, a GPU can be presented on a video card or embedded on the motherboard. Previously, a picture was drawn in scan line order of pixels, which needs long time. Now GPUs render the picture in the same time for all pixels. GPU computing is powerful for supercomputing. Regarding the architecture of GPUs, we have graphics memory control, graphics and computer array, unit, bus interface for communication, video processing unit, display interface, etc.

MATLAB supports for CUDA-empowered NVIDIA GPUs, and it has the ability to run workers locally on a desktop. CUDA (i.e., Compute Unified Device Architecture) was created by Nvidia in 2006; it is a parallel computing platform and application programming interface (API) that allows software to facilitate with GPUs. CUDA can accelerate general-purpose processing.

MATLAB offers computer cluster and grid support with MATLAB Distributed Computing Server. MATLAB provides the interactive and batch execution of parallel applications. The distributed arrays and Single Program Multiple Data (SPMD) are constructed for large dataset handling and data-parallel algorithms.

Google Colaboratory or Google Colab allows us to write and execute Python codes in a web browser. Google Colab is adopted extensively in the machine learning community with applications [10]. In deep learning and robotic intelligence [17], transfer learning and ensemble learning as well as federated learning and distributed learning are employed to enhance the classification ability of deep learning models. All the models need parallel computing and GPU computing.

8.2.3 Mobile Computing for Robotics

Mobile computing means we conduct programming for mobile devices, while robots are moving around from one place to another by using mobile communications based on robotic vision [26]. Cloud computing for robotics is associated with mobile computing. We archived data in the cloud. Multicore processors are multiple processors (cores) based on a single chip, such as CPUs. With regard to programming, we allocate one thread for each core. The comparisons of two laptops with and without GPUs are shown in Figs. 8.4 and 8.5. Parallel computing is simultaneous adoption of multiple processors. The cables are needed to link different computers together.

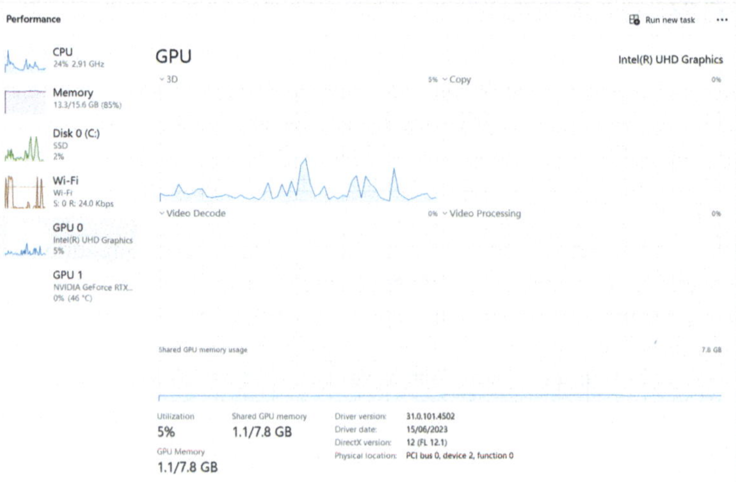

Fig. 8.4 A GPU computer

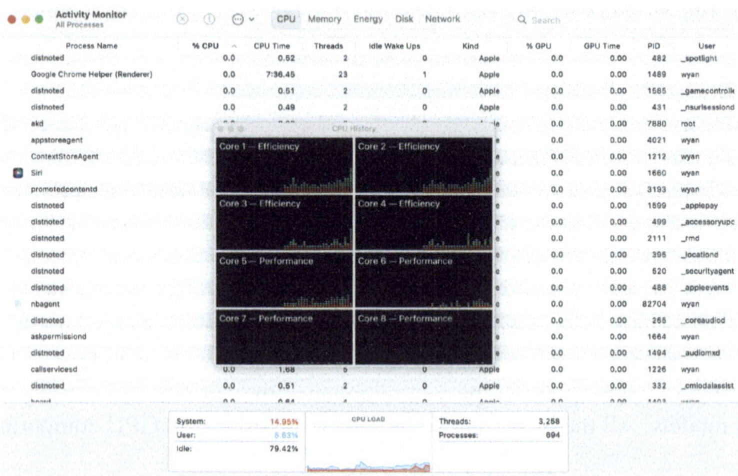

Fig. 8.5 A multicore computer

The CPU workstation cannot move around, but laptops can. Cluster computing is a hierarchical combination of commodity units to build parallel system within a tree structure.

Wireless communications like Wi-Fi are the must for moving robots. The cabled connections to mobile robots are not possible. Robots need cordless communications. MATLAB offers hardware infrastructure for parallel computing as shown in Figs. 8.6 and 8.7. Thus, the mobile computing has:

- **Connection**: Connect to a MATLAB session running on MathWorks Cloud. Cloud can save a huge amount of data.

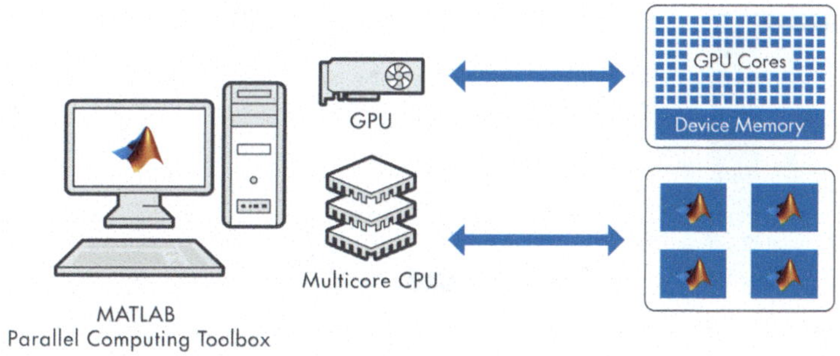

Fig. 8.6 MATLAB hardware configuration for GPUs

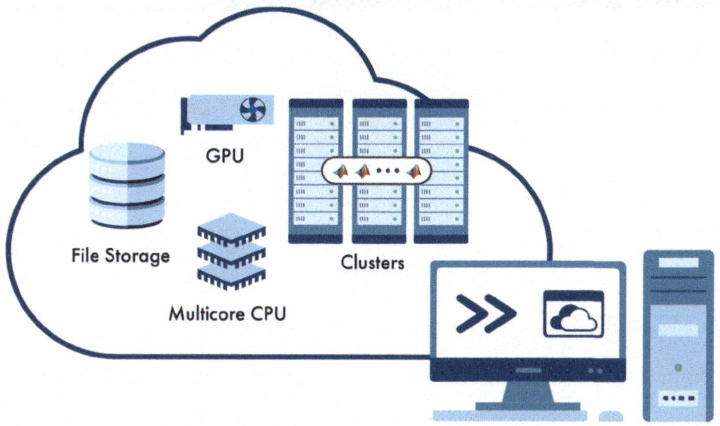

Fig. 8.7 MATLAB hardware configuration for clusters

- **Acquisition**: Acquire data from device sensors—like the accelerometer and GPS—and analyze the data in MATLAB. GPS can locate robots in real time.
- **Capturing**: Take pictures and record video/audio for further processing and analysis [22]. We upload multimodal data to the Internet [6].
- **Teaching and Learning**: Mobile device is powerful and flexible for teaching purposes [17].

MATLAB acquires data from built-in sensors [9] on mobile device and stream sensor data directly to the MathWorks Cloud. The data includes:

- Acceleration on three axes $(x, y, z \in \mathscr{R})$
- Angular velocity on three axes $(x, y, z \in \mathscr{R})$
- Magnetic field on three axes $(x, y, z \in \mathscr{R})$
- Orientation (azimuth, pitch, and roll) $(\alpha_x, \alpha_y, \alpha_z \in \mathscr{R})$
- Position (latitude, longitude, altitude, horizontal accuracy, speed, and course). The concept course refers to bearing angle.

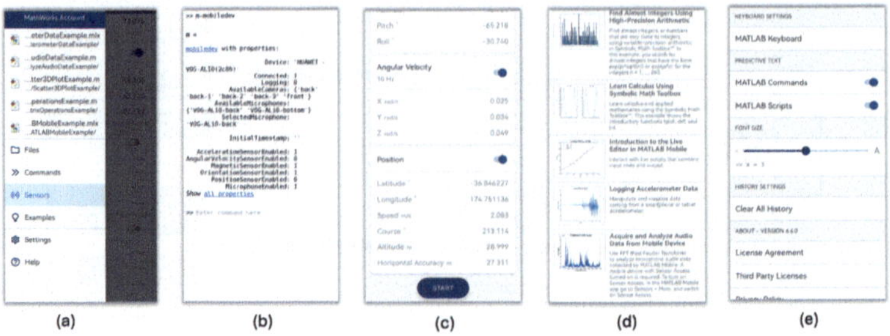

Fig. 8.8 MATLAB Mobile interface

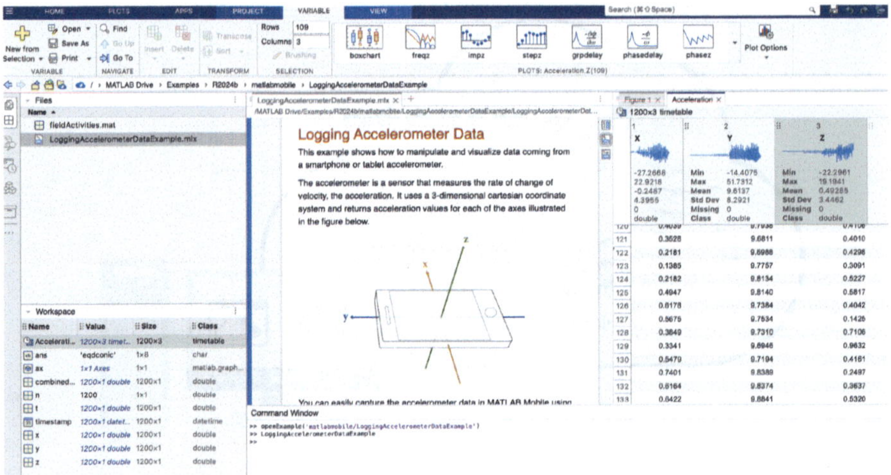

Fig. 8.9 MATLAB Mobile example

MATLAB Mobile sends all commands that were entered on the device to the cloud for evaluations. Autocomplete in MATLAB Mobile makes typing easier. MATLAB Mobile displays thumbnails and larger previews when figures are created or updated with MATLAB commands. MATLAB Mobile deletes unwanted commands to improve scrolling performance in history.

In Fig. 8.8, we list the functions of MATLAB Mobile as shown in Fig. 8.8a, the commands windows in Fig. 8.8b, the sensors in Fig. 8.8c, the examples in Fig. 8.8d, and the settings in Fig. 8.8e. The example in Fig. 8.9 shows Logging Accelerometer data from MATLAB Mobile by using MATLAB Online. It indicates how to manipulate and visualize data from a smartphone or tablet accelerometer.

8.3 Tools for Parallel Computing in Robotics

The key topics and concepts in parallel algebra [8] include:

Matrix Multiplication Parallelizing matrix operations often uses the methods like block decomposition, to distribute parts of the matrices across processors. The pseudocode is shown in Algorithm 22.

Algorithm 22: Parallel matrix multiplication

Input: Matrix $A \in \mathbb{R}^{m \times n}$, Matrix $B \in \mathbb{R}^{n \times p}$, Number of processors P
Output: Matrix $C = AB \in \mathbb{R}^{m \times p}$

Partition matrix A row-wise into P blocks: $A_1, A_2, \ldots, A_P$
Broadcast matrix B to all processors
foreach *processor* $i \in \{1, 2, \ldots, P\}$ ***in parallel*** **do**
    Compute $C_i = A_i \cdot B$
end
Gather all C_i blocks to form the final matrix C

LU Decomposition Parallel algorithms for matrix factorization methods in solving linear systems of equations. The LU decomposition algorithm in parallel is shown in Algorithm 23.

Algorithm 23: Parallel LU decomposition to solve linear systems

---

Input: Matrix $A \in \mathbb{R}^{n \times n}$, vector $b \in \mathbb{R}^n$
Output: Solution vector x

In parallel: Compute LU decomposition $A = LU$
In parallel: Solve the system $Ly = b$ using forward substitution
for $i = 1$ **to** n **do**
    $y_i = \frac{b_i - \sum_{j=1}^{i-1} l_{ij} y_j}{l_{ii}}$
end
In parallel: Solve the system $Ux = y$ using backward substitution
for $i = n$ **to** *1* **do**
    $x_i = \frac{y_i - \sum_{j=i+1}^{n} u_{ij} x_j}{u_{ii}}$
end
return x

Eigenvalue Computations The parallelizing computations of eigenvalues and eigenvectors are computationally intensive for large matrices. The pseudocode for QR iteration algorithm is shown in Algorithm 24.

Algorithm 24: Parallel QR iteration to compute eigenvalues

Input: Matrix $A \in \mathbb{R}^{n \times n}$, maximum iterations T, tolerance ϵ
Output: Approximate eigenvalues on the diagonal of A

for $k = 1$ **to** T **do**
  `// Step 1: Parallel QR Decomposition`
  In parallel: compute $A_{k-1} = Q_k R_k$
  `// Step 2: Parallel matrix multiplication`
  In parallel: compute $A_k = R_k Q_k$
  `// Step 3: Check for convergence`
  if $\|A_k - A_{k-1}\| < \epsilon$ **then**
    break
  end
end
return *Eigenvalues* $\lambda_i \approx A_T(i,i)$ *for* $i = 1, \ldots, n$

Data Distribution Efficiently distributing data (e.g., matrices, vectors) across multiple processors to minimize communication overhead and maximize parallel efficiency.

Sparse Matrix Operations Specialize parallel algorithms to handle sparse matrices, which have large dimensions but few nonzero elements.

Parallel Solvers Iterative methods such as conjugate gradient or generalized minimal residual (GMRES). A parallel GMRES (Generalized Minimal Residual) method is an approach for solving large linear systems by using a multicore CPU cluster.

- BLAS (i.e., CUDA Basic Linear Algebra Subprograms) supports operations like matrix-vector multiplication , matrix-matrix multiplication, vector addition, scalar products, and optimization [11, 21] for dense matrices.
- SOLVER provides high-performance solvers for linear systems, eigenvalue problems, and singular value decomposition (SVD) on GPUs.
- FFT (Fast Fourier Transform) offers routines for computing 1D, 2D, and 3D FFTs (Fast Fourier Transforms) on GPUs.
- GPU-accelerated RNG library
- DNN (i.e., deep neural network library) is applied to frameworks like TensorFlow and PyTorch to accelerate training and inference of neural networks.
- SPARSE (i.e., sparse matrix library) accommodates routines for sparse matrix computations, optimized for the efficient use of GPU memory and performance [11].
- Tensor is a library for efficient tensor algebra [7] computations, primarily in deep learning, physics simulations, and scientific computing.

8.4 Lab Session: Working with MATLAB for ROS and GPU-Accelerated Algorithms

At the end of this chapter, we would like to recommend all readers complete the lab report. Please fill in the form shown in Table 8.1 after each lab session (2 hours).

An example of this lab report is:

- **Project title**: Supercomputing and mobile computing for robotics
- **Project objectives**: The objective of this project is to utilize the parallel computing toolbox to enhance the performance of robots by leveraging multicore processors, GPUs, and computer clusters.
- **Configurations and settings**:

  1. Install Python and necessary libraries (e.g., OpenCV, NumPy, TensorFlow).
  2. Install MATLAB and configure MATLAB Mobile for data logging.
  3. Set up Google Colab for GPU access.

- **Methods**: Performance can be improved by processing data simultaneously. Machines can now comprehend and analyze visual data.
- **Implementation steps**:

  1. Use MATLAB Mobile to capture images with the mobile device camera.
  2. Save images in a predefined format (e.g., JPEG).

Table 8.1 Lab report for robotic vision

Name	<First Name Last Name >
Email	<firstname.lastname@mailbox >
Lab date	<dd-mm-yy >
Submitted date	<dd-mm-yy >
Project title	Supercomputing and mobile computing for robotics
Lab objectives	The objective is to enhance the performance of robotics by leveraging multicore processors and GPUs
Configurations and settings	<The preferences, software, hardware, platforms, tools, etc. >
Methods	<The relevant scientific theories or concepts >
Workflow	<The step-by-step procedure for the experiment >
Datasets	<The data and materials for your experiments >
Input	<image filename, size, resolution >
Output	<image filename, size, resolution >
Testing steps	<Functional & non-functional testing methods step by step >
Bugs or problems	<The system error code, lines of the code >
Result analysis	<The tables, graphs, and figures, etc. >
Conclusion/reflection	<The strengths and weaknesses, or learned from this project >
References	https://au.mathworks.com/help/matlabmobile/ug/logging-accelerometer-data.html

Appendix: <Source codes with comments and line numbers >

3. Use MATLAB Mobile to log accelerometer data.
4. Save data in .CSV format for further analysis.
5. Write a Python script by using OpenCV to process, and analyze captured images.
6. Utilize GPU acceleration to enhance processing speed.
7. Employ MATLAB Parallel Computing Toolbox to run multiple processes concurrently, improving efficiency.

- **Testing steps**:

  1. **Run GPU Code**: Measure execution time to assess GPU performance.
  2. **Benchmark GPU vs. CPU**: Run the same code on the CPU, and compare execution times.
  3. **Profile GPU Usage**: Monitor GPU resource usage during execution.
  4. **Test with Different Dataset Sizes**: Evaluate the system's performance by using small, medium, and large datasets.
  5. **Validate Output**: Ensure GPU-based outputs match expected results and refine code for efficiency.

- **Result analysis**: Parallel computing and GPU acceleration significantly improved real-time data processing and matrix operations; they enhance efficiency for robotic control.
- **Conclusion/reflection**: The integration of parallel computing, GPU acceleration, and mobile data acquisition proved effective for real-time robotics.
- **Readings**: https://au.mathworks.com/help/matlabmobile/ug/logging-accelerometer-data.html.

8.5 Exercises

Question 8.1. What are the differences between ROS 1 and ROS 2?
Question 8.2. What is multicore programming? How is it related to CPUs and GPUs?
Question 8.3. Why mobile computing is closely related to robotics?
Question 8.4. Why GPUs are important in modern computing?
Question 8.5. How are programming languages taking effects in supercomputing?
Question 8.6. What is the effective way to reduce the complexity of matrix multiplications?

References

1. Alonso JD, Vidal ER, Rotter A, Muhlenberg M (2008) Lane-change decision aid system based on motion-driven vehicle tracking. IEEE Trans Veh Technol 57(5):2736–2746

2. Chen CT, Chen YS (2009) Real-time approaching vehicle detection in blind-spot area. In: International IEEE conference on intelligence transport system, vol. 1
3. Bermudez G, Pedro GDG, Medeiros VS, Boaventura T (2024) Comparative analyses of ROS local planners for quadrupedal locomotion: a study in real and simulated environments. In: Walking robots into real world. Springer Nature Switzerland, pp 294–303
4. Cover T, Thomas J (1991) Elements of information theory. John Wiley & Sons, London
5. Ertel W (2017) Introduction to artificial intelligence. Springer, Berlin
6. Gao X, Liu Y, Nguyen M, Yan W (2024) VICL-CLIP: enhancing face mask detection in context with multimodal foundation models. In: ICONIP
7. Itskov M (2011) Tensor algebra and tensor analysis for engineers, 4th edn. Springer. Berlin
8. Jacobson N (2009) Abstract algebra, 2nd edn. Dover Publications, New York
9. Jia X, Hu Z, Guan H (2011) A new multi-sensor platform for adaptive driving assistance system (ADAS). In: World congress on intelligent control and automation, p 1224
10. Jordan MI, Mitchell TM (2015) Machine learning: trends, perspectives, and prospects. Science 349(6245):255–260
11. Ko YH, Kim KJ, Jun CH (2005) A new loss function-based method for multiresponse optimization. J Quality Technol 37(1):50–59
12. Koch M (2018) Artificial intelligence is becoming natural. Cell 173(3):531–533
13. Kontschieder P et al (2015) Deep neural decision forests. In: ICCV
14. Kriegeskorte N (2015) Deep neural networks: a new framework for modelling biological vision and brain information processing. Annu Rev Vision Sci 1(1):417–446
15. Lalonde M, Byrns D, Gagnon L, Teasdale N, Laurendeau D (2007) Real-time eye blink detection with GPU-based SIFT tracking. In: Canadian conference on computer and robot vision, pp 481–487
16. Littman M (2015) Reinforcement learning improves behavior from evaluative feedback. Nature 521:445–451
17. Lu H, Li Y, Chen M, Kim H, Serikawa S (2018) Brain intelligence: go beyond artificial intelligence. Mobile Netw Appl 23(2):368–375
18. Manning C, Raghavan P, Schutze H (2008) Introduction to information retrieval. Cambridge University Press, Cambridge
19. Peng D (2025) Vision perception optimization and adaptive control for resource-constrained platform: a Ping-Pong ball pickup & place system. Master's thesis, Auckland University of Technology, New Zealand
20. Petrushin VA (2005) Mining rare and frequent events in multi-camera surveillance video using self-organizing maps. In: ACM international conference on knowledge discovery in data mining, pp 794–800
21. Rao S (2009) Engineering optimization: theory and practice, 4th edn. ISBN: 978-0-470-18352-6
22. Stoer J, Bulirsch R (1991) Introduction to numerical analysis, 2nd edition. Springer, Berlin
23. Yan WQ (2019) Introduction to intelligent surveillance: surveillance data capture, transmission, and analytics, 3rd edn. Springer, Berlin
24. Yan WQ (2023) Computational methods for deep learning: theory, algorithms, and implementations, 2nd edn. Springer, Berlin
25. Ye Y, Nie Z, Liu X, Xie F, Li Z, Li P (2023) ROS2 real-time performance optimization and evaluation. Chinese J Mech Eng 36(1):144
26. Zhao H, Xu S, Yan W, Xu D (2025) Design and optimization of target detection and 3D localization models for intelligent muskmelon pollination robots. Horticulturae 11(8):905

Glossary

3D reconstruction In computer vision, the creation of three-dimensional models from a set of digital images

Activation function In artificial neural networks, the activation function of a node defines the output of that node given an input or a set of inputs.

Camera resectioning In camera calibration, the process of estimating the parameters of a pinhole camera model approximating the camera that produced a given photograph or video

Camera retreat Camera retreat is a phenomenon that occurs in visual servoing when a camera moves away from a target and then returns. It can cause problems with visual servoing control tasks, such as those involving multi-joint manipulators.

Dead reckoning In navigation, dead reckoning is the process of calculating the current position of a moving object by using a previously determined position, or fix, and incorporating estimates of speed, heading (or direction or course), and elapsed time.

Depth perception It is the ability to perceive distance to visual objects in the world by using the visual system and visual perception.

Distillation In machine learning, distillation is the process of transferring knowledge from a large model to a smaller one.

Emotional quotient It is the ability to perceive, use, understand, manage, and handle emotions.

Federated learning is a subfield of machine learning with multiple entities collaboratively to train a model while ensuring that the data remains decentralized.

Forward kinematics The use of kinematic equations of a robot to compute the position of end-effector from specified values for joint parameters

Image skeletonization A skeleton (or medial axis) representation of a shape or binary image, computed by means of morphological operators

Imitation learning A paradigm in reinforcement learning, where an agent learns to perform a task by supervised learning from expert demonstrations

W. Q. Yan, *Robotic Vision*, Advances in Computer Vision and Pattern Recognition,
https://doi.org/10.1007/978-981-95-4360-1

Intelligence quotient A total score derived from a set of standardized tests or subtests designed to assess human intelligence

Inverse reinforcement learning is to learn the underlying reward function that the expert seems to be maximizing.

Inverse kinematics The mathematical process of calculating variable joint parameters needed to place the end of a kinematic chain

Mobile computing In human-computer interaction, a computer is expected to be transported during normal usage and allow for transmission of data, which can include voice and video transmissions.

Path planning A computational problem to find a sequence of valid configurations that moves the object from source to destination

Reinforcement learning An interdisciplinary area of machine learning and optimal control concerned with how an intelligent agent should take actions in a dynamic environment in order to maximize a reward signal

Robotic control The system contributes to movement of robots.

Robot end-effector The device at the end of a robotic arm, designed to interact with the environment

Robot operating systems ROS is an open-source robotics middleware suite.

Robot manipulator A device used to manipulate materials without direct physical contact by the operator

Robotic olfaction The automated simulation of the sense of smell

Spline curve In mathematics, a spline is a function defined piecewise by polynomials.

Stereo imaging A technique for creating or enhancing the illusion of depth in an image by means of stereopsis for binocular vision

Third-eye method Third-eye method maps a reference image of a pair of stereo camera into the pose of a third camera, measuring the similarity between created virtual image and the actually recorded third image.

Triangulation In trigonometry and geometry, triangulation is the process of determining the location of a point by forming triangles to the point from known points.

Turing test A test of a machine's ability to exhibit intelligent behavior equivalent to, or indistinguishable from, that of a human

Visual servoing A method that makes use of feedback information extracted from a vision sensor to control the motion of a robot

Names in This Book

Reverend Thomas **Bayes** (1701–1761)
Andrew **Barto** (1948/1949–)
John F. **Canny** (1958–)
Richard Ernest **Bellman** (1920–1984)
Yoshua **Bengio** (1964–)
Sergei Natanovich **Bernstein** (1880–1968)
Pierre **Bézier** (1910–1999)
Valentino **Braitenberg** (1926–2011)
Paul **de Casteljau** (1930–2022)
Maurice **Fréchet** (1878–1973)
Carl Friedrich **Gauss** (1777–1855)
David **Hilbert** (1862–1943)
Geoffrey **Hinton** (1947 –)
John **Hopfield** (1933 –)
Rudolf Emil **Kálmán** (1930–2016)
Carl Gustav Jacob **Jacobi** (1804–1851)
Reinhard **Klette** (1950–2020)
Johann Heinrich **Lambert** (1728–1777)
Yann Andre **LeCun** (1960–)
David Courtenay **Marr** (1945–1980)
August Ferdinand **Möbius** (1960–)
John Carlyle **Raven** (1902–1970)
Irwin **Sobel** (1940–)
Isaac Jacob **Schoenberg** (1880–1968)
Richard **Sutton** (1957/1958–)
Alan **Turing** (1912–1954)
Georgy Feodosevich **Voronyi** (1868–1908)
David **Wechsler** (1896–1981)

W. Q. Yan, *Robotic Vision*, Advances in Computer Vision and Pattern Recognition,
https://doi.org/10.1007/978-981-95-4360-1

Key Points of This Book

This book symmetrically delivers the content of robotic vision associated with deep learning and robotic intelligence, in the core area of contemporary AI knowledge. The research scientists and computer engineers will benefit from this book.

This book exactly matches with the postgraduate students' needs in universities. The book provides the first-hand experience of higher education teaching with the content selected from the student's reactions in the classes. The PG students will benefit from the textbook without difficulties.

The peer colleagues and teachers in universities and research institutions will benefit from the textbook, and they will find the suitable teaching materials and pedagogies in the knowledge delivery and example lab reports of lab sessions from this book.

W. Q. Yan, *Robotic Vision*, Advances in Computer Vision and Pattern Recognition,
https://doi.org/10.1007/978-981-95-4360-1

Index

W. Q. Yan, *Robotic Vision*, Advances in Computer Vision and Pattern Recognition,
https://doi.org/10.1007/978-981-95-4360-1

The manufacturer's authorised representative in the EU is Springer Nature Customer Service Centre GmbH, Europaplatz 3, 69115 Heidelberg, Germany. If you have any concerns regarding our products, please contact ProductSafety@springernature.com

Printed and bound by CPI Group (UK) Ltd, Croydon, CR0 4YY
21/09/2026
02219988-0001

The manufacturer's authorised representative in the EU is Springer Nature Customer Service Centre GmbH, Europaplatz 3, 69115 Heidelberg, Germany. If you have any concerns regarding our products, please contact ProductSafety@springernature.com

Printed and bound by CPI Group (UK) Ltd, Croydon, CR0 4YY

16/09/2026

02217783-0003